Perón and Perónism
The Life & Thoughts of Juan Domingo Perón

by

Kerry R. Bolton

Perón and Perónism
The Life & Thoughts of
Juan Domingo Perón
by
Kerry R. Bolton

ISBN-13: 978-0-9927365-4-5

Black House Publishing Ltd

Kemp House

152 City Road

London

UNITED KINGDOM

EC1V 2NX

www.blackhousepublishing.com

Email: info@blackhousepublishing.com

Contents

Contents

Introduction

The name Perón is now relatively well-known across much of the English-speaking world, thanks to the long-playing Andrew Lloyd Webber and Tim Rice stage musical *Evita* (1978-) and the film of the same name (1996). These also spawned the publication or republication of books, again for the most part about Evita Perón, ranging from the relatively useful, such as Alicia Dujovne Ortiz's *Eva Perón: A Biography* (1997), and *Evita: An Intimate Portrait of Eva Perón* by Tomas de Elia and Juan Pablo Quieroz (1997), to the thoroughly scabrous Mary Main biography *Evita: The Woman with the Whip* (first published in 1952, and vomited forth again in 1996). As Francisco M. Rocha states in his introduction to *Evita: An Intimate Portrait*, 'the popular cult of Evita has over the years persisted, reached immense proportions, and remained intact despite attacks and efforts to demythologize her'. (p. 190).

However, General Juan Domingo Perón, the man responsible for the Evita of world fame, is not so well known other than as Eva's husband. Even those who write of Perón in a more substantial manner, do so inadequately. They do so with hints, at most, that he was not 'just another Latin American dictator'.

In particular, little is written of Perón as a philosopher, who drew readily from Aristotle, Thomas Aquinas, Plato, and a range of others across time, nation, and culture. Even less is the English reader given the opportunity to know that Perón formulated a philosophy, Justicialism that has an impressive corpus of literature rivalling the accumulated tomes of liberalism, capitalism and Marxism.

In this book I hope to have presented the reader, and in particular the English reader, probably for the first time, with an adequate overview of Perónism in theory and practice, as part of a national-social synthesis that remains relevant to the present age of globalisation and super-power hegemony. I hope to have shown that Perón was in many ways far ahead of his time. He addressed issues that are only now being discussed at world forums, but in Perón's case, with the insistence that problems must be solved within a national and more broadly continental context rather than imposing upon humanity a 'new world order' in which we are reduced to being a nebulous mass of economic cogs or, as Perón would say, 'insectified' for the sake of economics.

Kerry R. Bolton

Kapiti Coast, New Zealand

Juan Domingo Perón: A Biographical Sketch

This book is not primarily intended as a biography of Juan Domingo Perón, but as an examination of the doctrine of Perónism, or Justicialism, of which there are few in the English language. However, given that Perón lends his name to the doctrine his personality, thoughts and experiences are important for understanding the movement and the doctrine he formed. This chapter will provide a broad outline of Perón's life, although other biographic details are infused throughout the book.

Perón, the military strategist and professor, an officer of the armed forces in a part of the world where the military is too often synonymous with 'oligarchic' interests, achieved a rare synthesis for Latin America, and indeed for most of the rest of the post-1945 world: Perón united the interests of all productive Argentine sectors into an organic national totality on the basis that the nation is a social unit. The 'nation' is not an area of contending economic forces – as per Marxism and capitalism – but a territorial expression of a shared heritage and destiny that goes to form a 'people'. 'Social justice', the meaning of Justicialism, is the foundation upon which to build a 'nation'.

What then of Juan Domingo Perón, the man, and the forces that shaped his life and work? He was born on 8 October 1895, in the provincial town of Lobos in the province of Buenos Aires, the second son of Mario and Juana Perón. His father was an employee of the local court, who was also involved in agriculture. Mario abandoned his family when Juan was five year old. Juana married a farm hand on the family *estancia*. When Juan was ten he went to live with his uncle in Buenos Aires and there began his formal education.

At sixteen Juan entered the national military academy, Colegio Militar, from 1911 to 1913, to continue his education. He then went to the Escuela Superior de Guerra from 1926 to 1929. The Argentine military academies, as elsewhere in Latin America,

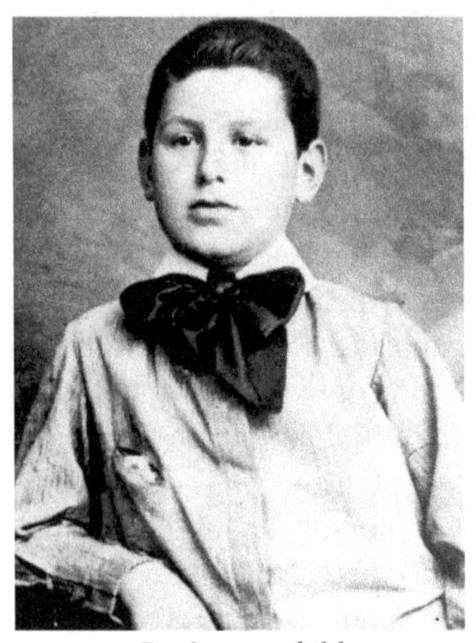

Perón as a child

had a significant German influence, the academy having been established by a German military mission. The faculty included Germans when Perón studied there. As such the Argentine military was imbued with a strong pro-German sentiment. This encouraged a more sympathetic outlook towards the Third Reich than Anglo-American and other interests would have wished.

Perón graduated in 1915 with the rank of sublieutenant, lieutenant in 1919, and captain in 1924.[1] His early career was militarily uneventful, other than having peacefully defused a strike in 1917,[2] and commanding a unit that suppressed rioting in Buenos Aires during *Semana Trágica* (Tragic Week) in 1919, an abortive revolt that had been fomented by Jewish Communists.[3] The decade was eventful however in establishing Perón as a military scholar, during which he wrote *Military Morale*, *Military Hygiene*, *Campaigns of Upper Peru*, and *The Eastern Front in World War I: Strategic Considerations*, which were used as textbooks. He served as a Professor of Military History at the War College from 1930. He continued to publish military texts and wrote a study on the language of the Araucanian Indians of the Patagonian region,

1 Alicia Dujovne Ortiz, *Eva Perón: A Biography* (London: Warner Books, 1997), 84.

2 Ibid.

3 Of the forty leaders of the Communist cell that organised the revolt, all were Jewish. Until the 'Nazi' era, which has made such discussions taboo, the Jewish involvement in subversion was readily discussed by diplomatic and military intelligence throughout the world, Argentina included. See: Ariel Svarch, 'Jewish Communist Culture and Identity in Buenos Aires', 12 October 2008, Perush: An Online Journal of Jewish Scholarship and Interpretation, http://perush.cjs.ucla.edu/index.php/volume-2/jewish-urban-history-in-comparative-perspective-jewish-buenos-aires-and-jewish-los-angeles/-5-ariel-svarch-jewish-communist-culture-and-identity-in-buenos-aires-ideas-on-comparative-approaches

Place Names Etymology Patagonian Araucana, in 1935; and in 1937 the study, *The Strategic Thought and Operational Idea of San Martin in the Campaign of the Andes.*

While Perón had established himself as a notable scholar while serving on the Army staff, he also spent much time on sports, building up a formidable physique, and honing his skills in boxing, archery, horseback riding, and as a notable skier and fencer. A biographer points out that, 'in a military where physical appearance contributed to power, Perón was six feet tall, dark haired and very muscular'.[4]

In 1928 Perón married a schoolteacher named Aurelia Tizón and adopted a daughter. Aurelia was an accomplished drawer and painter, and her knowledge of English allowed her to translate several military texts for Perón. She died of cancer in 1938.

In 1930 a coup led by General Jose F. Uriburu overthrew the Government of Hipólito Irigoyen. Perón's role in the coup saw him take the presidential palace and environs on 6 September, actions that drew him to the attention of his military superiors.

In 1931 he was promoted to major, and was a member of the committee that defined the borders between Bolivia and Argentina.[5] During 1930-1935 he served as private secretary to the Minister of War.

By 1936 he had reached the rank of Lieutenant Colonel and was teaching at the Escuela Superior de Guerra. During 1936-38 he served as Argentine military attaché to Chile, but amid accusations of espionage, which he always denied, Perón was recalled and embarked on a significant episode in the shaping of his thinking:

4 Lindon Ratliff,. 'Juan Domingo Perón: *"Fenómeno"*', *http://historicaltextarchive.com/sections.php?action=read&artid=65*

5 Ortiz, op. cit., 87.

He was a member of a military mission sent to study in Europe, residing first in Italy in 1939, where he specialised in Mountain Infantry. In 1940 he toured Spain, Germany, Hungary, France, Yugoslavia and Albania. He also saw the Soviet Union, then in alliance with Germany.

In 1941 he was promoted to the rank of Colonel. His study of Italy and Germany, and in particular his time in the former sate, made an enduring impact upon his political and philosophical thinking. He saw the success of Fascism in overcoming class divisions, mobilising the masses for national construction, and achieving national unity through social justice.

Perón, of Sardinian descent, 'spoke perfect Italian'. He closely studied Italian Fascism, and joined the mass rallies where Mussolini spoke to the crowds from the balcony of the Palazzo Venezia, a technique he was to master as a feature of his own regime. He regarded Italians and Argentines as similar, and saw how a variant of this national-social synthesis could be applied to his country.[6] It is here that he formulated his 'third position', recalling to the historian Felix Luna in 1968: 'When faced with a world divided by two imperialisms, the Italians responded: we are with neither side, we represent a third position between Soviet socialism and Yankee imperialism'. [7] Perón never repudiated this premise. When journalist Valentin Thiebault told Perón of Mussolini's death and said, 'We will have to erect a monument for him one day', Perón replied, 'One monument? Only one? Please say you mean one on every street corner!'[8]

Group of United Officers

Perón, returning to Argentina from Italy in 1941, joined the Group of United Officers (GOU), a brotherhood up to the rank of Colonel, who shared political ideas.

6 Ibid., 88.

7 Cited by Ortiz, ibid., 89.

8 Quoted by Ortiz, ibid.

With the resignation of Minister of War General Pedro Ramírez, at the insistence of President Ramón S. Castillo, and the impending appointment of Patron Costas, a large landowner with a pro-British sentiment, this prompted the GOU and other pro-German elements in the military, to act against the civilian government of Castillo. On 2 June 1943 the GOU met to plan a march on the presidential palace. Although Perón was not at the meeting, the plan of action he sent was approved. The next day the GOU and others marched on Buenos Aires. On 4 June Castillo resigned. The army took control of the nation, and gave due recognition to the role of the GOU. Ratliff writes: 'The three year long military regime saw many opportunities for officers to be promoted, however, it was Perón who gained the most. The key Minister of War post went to General Edelmiro Farrell, who before the coup had been Perón's immediate superior'.[9] Perón assumed the post of Secretary in the War Ministry.

The next pivotal event was in early 1944 when President Ramírez bowed to Allied pressure and broke off diplomatic relations with the Axis. In August 1943 the Ramirez government had asked the USA for arms. The USA responded that arms could not be sold to Argentina because of its neutrality. Ramirez then sent a mission to Germany to buy arms. The ship carrying the Argentine consul leading the mission was seized *en route* to Barcelona by the English. The English sent the documents of the mission to the USA. The American response was one of 'gunboat diplomacy', and ships moved menacingly towards Rio de la Plata (The River Plate), while American banks stopped the Argentine funds being transferred to Germany.[10] Although Argentina 'severed all relations with the Axis powers on 25 January 1944', 'this was not enough' for U.S. Secretary of State Cordell Hull who demanded total compliance with his wishes'. A ban on U.S. shipping to Argentina was imposed. Despite the pressures, and the impending defeat of the Axis, Argentina did not declare war on the Axis until 28 March 1945; too late to be of any real meaning.[11]

9 *Ibid.*

10 Ortiz, ibid., 93.

11 René De La Pedraja, *Oil and Coffee: Latin American Merchant Shipping from the*

A struggle between pro-Axis and pro-Allied factions in government ensued. The position of the GOU had been unequivocally pro-Axis, with an internal manifesto stating in 1943 that 'Germany is making a titanic effort to unify the European continent… Today, Germany is giving life a historic direction. We must follow this example. Hitler's fight, in times of peace and in times of war, will have to guide us from now on'. [12]Perón's opposition to U.S. pressure on Argentina to join the Allies in the war contributed to the personal animosity from U.S. Ambassador Spruille Braden. Lindon Ratliff writes:

> The result of the crisis was an almost total reorganisation of the military government. General Farrell became President and Perón was Vice President, Minister of War, Secretary of Labor and Social Reform, as well as Head of the Post-War Council. The USA refused to recognise the Farrell-Perón regime. In other words, even though [Perón] was not president he was the most powerful man in the government'.[13]

It was Perón's position as Secretary of Labor and Social Reform that was the basis of his influence. The military regime had alienated the masses, although Perón and the GOU sought an alliance with the labour unions. Perón had already established himself as the people's champion by enacting laws on social security and paid vacations, but most of all, because of his support for the unionisation of workers. His role in coordinating relief aid for San Juan after an earthquake on 15 January 1944, which took over 10,000 lives, had also gained him many supporters. It was through this involvement that he met his future wife Eva Duarte, a movie and radio actress, who was one of the celebrities helping with the work.

Eva Duarte was no vacuous First Lady there for the glitz and

Imperial Era to the 1950s (Westport, CT: Greenwood Publishing Group, 1998), 102.

12 GOU manifesto, 13 March 1943, quoted by Otiz, op. cit., 91.

13 Ratliff, op. cit.

General Edelmiro Julian Farrell June 1944

glamour. She had been a co-founder of the Radio Association of Argentina in 1943, the aim being to 'defend the interests of Argentinean radio's workers'. She had already been a forceful personality in defending her dignity as an actress, and was described as having an 'indomitable personality'.[14] When the earthquake struck San Juan, the Radio Association was one of the aid committees that helped organise a benefit concert to assist the homeless. It was as part of a delegation that Eva Duarte met Perón in the office of the secretary of labour and social affairs on 22 January.[15]

With Perón as the recognised leader of a major element in politics, not only among the military but among the masses of people, General Eduardo Avalos moved to pre-empt Perón's rise. A coup was staged which forced Perón to resign all posts on 10 October 1945. After being permitted to deliver a radio address to his supporters, on 13 October he was sent to the prison island of Martin Garcia, where Argentina's most important political prisoners were traditionally consigned.

14 Ortiz, op. cit., 65.

15 Ibid., 67.

October Revolution

After Perón had been forced to resign his posts in October 1945, the new regime began to annul the social reforms that had been achieved by Perón. This confirmed the growing belief that only Perón could advance the welfare of the people. At this time Eva Duarte lobbied for Perón's release, speaking before labour rallies, and keeping Perón informed of developments in her letters to him. The labour confederation (CGT) called a general strike for 18 October 1945. The day before, however, masses of workers marched on Buenos Aires and gathered at Plaza de Mayo. Protesting workers assembled outside the labour department demanding that they be paid the 'Aguinaldo' or share of company profits that Perón had legislated into effect. The only answer of the Government was to quip: 'go ask Perón to pay that to you'.[16] Workers from the industrial areas and suburbs converged on the city centre. When police blocked the bridges, workers commandeered boats to get to the Plaza in front of the presidential palace, the Casa Rosada.

Such was the wave of popular support that Perón was released. That night Perón spoke from the balcony of the Casa Rosada to workers crowding the square, declaring his candidacy for the presidency:

> Workers: Almost two years ago I had three honours in my life: to be a soldier, that of being a patriot and being the first Argentine worker. This afternoon, the Executive has signed my application for retirement from active Army duty. With that, I've given up voluntarily the most distinguished honour to which a soldier can aspire: to gain the palms and laurels of the General's Office. This I have done because I want to remain Colonel Perón, and put that name to the integral service of authentic Argentine people. I leave the holy and honourable uniform handed to me: to wear a jacket of the civil Patria, and mingle in that mass of suffering that produces the work and greatness of the country.

16 Adrian Salbuchi, 'Argentina's Perón and the "Third Position"', unpublished article.

> With that I give my final embrace of that institution, which is the mainstay of the country: the military. And also I give the first embrace to that great mass, which represents the synthesis of a feeling that had died in the Republic: the true civility of the Argentine people.
>
> From this time, it will be historic for the Republic, that Colonel Perón who makes the bond of union, that indestructible brotherhood among the people, the army and politics. An eternal and infinite union, that this people may grow in that spiritual unity of the true and genuine forces of nationality and order.
>
> On the brotherhood of working people we will build our beautiful homeland, in the unity of all Argentines. We will be incorporating from this beautiful day a movement not at all fractious and discontented, that will be together with us, as a patriotic mass.[17]

Perón then exhorted the crowd to return to their homes while he considered how to proceed. He did not want the regime to be given a pretext for violence:

> I know what labour movements have announced. Sorry, there is no cause for it. So I ask, as an older brother, who will return quietly to work and think: today I ask you to return calmly to your homes…[18]

The day, 17 October, has endured ever since in celebrations as 'Loyalty Day'. It was the day that not only were workers loyal to Perón, risking their lives to save their champion, but when, for the first time, the workers showed that they had the power to decide a nation's destiny.

---

17 Juan Perón's address to the people, from the balcony of Government House, 17 October 1945.

18 Ibid.

Perón married Eva Duarte that month. He prepared for the presidential election that had been called for 24 February 1946, after the military had been put on notice by the masses of people on 17 October. On 26 December 1945 Perón and Eva embarked on a train that he called *El Descamisado* (The Shirtless) in honour of the iconic masses of workers who were the backbone of Perónism. His opponents embarked on their campaign in a train dubbed 'Victory'. Both were subjected to attacks. The presence of Eva was the first time a woman had participated in a presidential campaign.[19]

> The military government weakened by events called presidential elections for February 24, 1946. Perón, in just four months, organized the political bases of support among workers, independent sectors and progressives who had detached from the Radical Civic Union, Conservative Party and Socialist Party. His opposition was a political front called 'Democratic Union' formed by the most conservative sectors of society in partnership with the internationalist Left and the Communist Party and openly supported by the Ambassador of the United States of America, Mr. Spruille Braden. The dilemma was 'Braden or Perón'.[20]

19 Ortiz, op cit., 169-170.

20 Juan Perón biography, Partido Justicialista, http://www.pj.org.ar/recursos/2011-12-05-04-38-40/biografias/

'Braden or Perón'

From this earliest period of Perón's political life, U.S. interests opposed him. At the time the U.S. Ambassador was Spruille Braden, whose opposition would continue when he was recalled to Washington to become Under-Secretary of State for the Western Hemisphere. Braden was a member of the Council on Foreign Relations (CFR), a globalist think tank founded in 1919 by international bankers, academics and industrialists, to promote a world state. The CFR has been referred to as the 'secret government of the USA' insofar as it has provided key advisers to every Democratic and Republican administration since the time of Woodrow Wilson. Rockefeller interests have long been dominant.[21] Braden had been a lobbyist for the United Fruit Company (UFC).[22] In 1954 he was a coordinator in the CIA-planned overthrow of Jacabo Arbenz, elected president of Guatemala.[23] Braden was a well-connected plutocrat, representing W. Averell Harriman Securities Corporation,[24] and was an agent for Standard Oil, a flagship corporation of the Rockefeller banking and oil dynasty. He was noted for his animosity towards trades unions.[25] On his own account, Braden was both an advisor and a close friend of Paul Warburg, the architect of the U.S. Federal Reserve Bank and a scion of the Warburg international banking dynasty.[26] Braden had a similar relationship with Nelson Rockefeller, who was Braden's predecessor as U.S. Under-Secretary of State.[27]

---

21 On the CFR see: K. R. Bolton, *Revolution from Above* (London: Arktos Media Ltd.) 2011, 30-47.

22 The UFC was a power in Central and South America and the political and economic authority it exercised inspired the term 'banana republic'. UFC controlled transport networks, managed Guatemala's postal service in 1901, and established the Tropical Radio and Telegraph Company. UFC was notorious for bribery, exploitation, and paid few taxes.

23 Adrian Salbuchi, 'Argentina's Perón and the "Third Position"', unpublished article.

24 *Who's Who in America 1976-1977*, Vol. 26, 295.

25 Jorrge Schvarzer, La industria que supimos conseguir. Una historia político-social de la industria Argentina (Buenos Aires: Planeta, 1996), 194.

26 Spruille Braden, *Diplomats and Demagogues: The Memoirs of Spruille Braden* (Arlington House, 1971), 94.

27 Ibid., 264.

Alicia Ortiz, whose father had been a member of the central committee of the Argentine Communist party who, along with his comrades, 'lived in a dismal prison' during 1943 to 1945, writes of Braden:

> He arrived in Buenos Aires as fresh as a rose and ready to intervene without any restraint. He was welcomed by the entire democratic coalition – oligarchs, radicals, Socialists, and confused Communists. In the face of the dangers of Nazism, this ruddy Mr. Clean played the part of the Messiah.[28]

According to Ortiz, Braden regarded himself as the 'messenger' of the USA's Jews to their Argentine brethren who were in danger, and that this was 'a profitable example that he could use to his advantage'.[29] That is to say, apparently, Braden hoped to mobilize Jewry against Perón if he did not tow the U.S. line. Ortiz writes that 'the rosy cheeked American' paid Perón a visit:

> Faced with Perón who displayed a choirboy's candour, Braden evoked 'the German and Japanese assets' that the Argentinean government could seize. He added, with raised eyebrows inspired by Groucho Marx, 'But, Colonel Perón, you know that if we work these affairs out, the U.S. will not get in the way of your future presidential candidacy'. 'Alas!' Perón cried, opening his arms, 'there is still a small problem'. 'What problem?' 'In this country, he who enters into this type of scheme with a foreign power is a son of a bitch'.
>
> Braden turned livid with rage and left without even a good-bye, in his haste forgetting his hat. Perón burst out laughing and threw the hat to 'his boys' for a little game of soccer...[30]

28 Ortiz, op. cit., 130.

29 Ibid. Ortiz citing Ignacio Klinch, a professor at the University of Buenos Aires who specialises in Arab and Jewish issues in Latin America.

30 Ibid., 131.

General Juan Perón in 1946

On 23 May 1946 the separate parties that had supported Perón, including the Labour Party, were merged into a single party, originally called the Sole Party of the Revolution and, shortly after, the Perónist Party, formally known as the Partido Justicialista,[31] which remains the 'official' Perónist party.

When Perón based his 1946 presidential campaign on the slogan 'Braden or Perón' this expressed a significant factor at work in the fight for Argentina and the doctrine of Perónism. Braden as a representative of U.S. plutocracy was connected with the highest echelons of international finance: Harriman, Rockefeller, Warburg. This international banking coterie, which has a firmer grip over the world than ever,[32] was challenged by Perónism. Perónism arose, moreover, in the aftermath of a world war that had been fought by those same plutocratic interests against the Axis states, whose doctrine, generically called 'national socialism', and 'fascism', had also attempted to overthrow

31 Jill Hedges, *Argentina: A Modern History* (London: I. B. Tauris Publishers, 2011), 114.

32 K. R. Bolton, *Revolution from Above*, op. cit.; *The Banking Swindle* (London: Black House Publishing, 2013).

parasitic finance-capitalism. It was little wonder that Braden and his colleagues hated Perón with such vehemence.

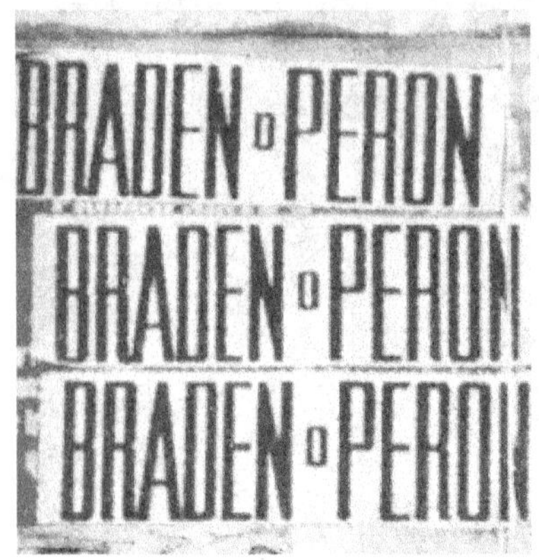

Perón election posters

At a farewell lunch before his return to the USA, Braden said in a speech that he would continue his fight against Perón from Washington', which received 'a standing ovation from the well-heeled audience', wrote Latin American specialist Dr. Jill Hedges.[33]

In February 1946, at a meeting of diplomats from Latin America called in Washington by the U.S. State Department, Secretary of State Dean Acheson, and his Under-Secretary, Braden, gave each delegate a copy of a book. The *New York Times* commented:

> Only one nation was absent —Argentina. A few minutes later that absent neighbor stood accused of virtually every crime in the book against democracy. The stern indictment was a 130-page booklet written in language no nation ordinarily uses unless it is prepared to go to war. [34]

The USA attempted to demonize Perón and isolate Argentina in a manner similar to the tactics pursued up to the present against resistant states such as the Afrikaner Republic, Saddam Hussein's Iraq, Assad's Syria, Milosevic's Serbia, Hugo Chavez's Venezuela, and Putin's Russia. What Braden had prepared was a 'Blue Book'[35] vilifying Perón. Although their were allusions

33 Jill Hedges, op. cit., 118

34 'Foreign Relations: Neighbor Accused', *New York Times*, 18 February 1946.

35 Consultation Among the American Republics with Respect to the Argentine Situation; Memorandum of the United States Government, U.S. Department of State, 11 February 1946, Publication 2473, Inter-American Series 29. Washington D.C., Government Printing Office, 1946.

to 'consultation' among American Republics, this was not the case. The document was an ultimatum to Latin American states. The State Department released the *Blue Book* two weeks before the February 1946 Argentine presidential elections in a flagrant effort to thwart a Perón victory. It purports to prove collusion between Perón and Germany and Italy during the Second World War. The salient points are:

1. Members of the military government collaborated with enemy agents for important espionage and other purposes damaging to the war effort of the United Nations.

2. Nazi leaders, groups and organizations have combined with Argentine totalitarian groups to create a Nazi-Fascist state.

3. Members of the military regime who have controlled the government since June 1943 conspired with the enemy to undermine governments in neighboring countries in order to destroy their collaboration with the Allies and in an effort to align them in a pro-Axis bloc.

4. Successive Argentine governments protected the enemy in economic matters in order to preserve Axis industrial and commercial power in Argentina.

5. Successive Argentine governments conspired with the enemy to obtain arms from Germany. This information warrants the following conclusions:

    1. The Castillo Government and still more the present military regime pursued a policy of positive aid to the enemy.
    2. Solemn pledges to cooperate with the other American republics were completely breached and are proved to have been designed to protect and maintain Axis

interests in Argentina.

3. The policies and actions of the recent regimes in Argentina were aimed at undermining the Inter-American System.
4. The totalitarian individuals and groups, both military and civilian, who control the present government in Argentina, have, with their Nazi collaborators, pursued a common aim: The creation in this Hemisphere of a totalitarian state. This aim has already been partly accomplished.
5. Increasingly since the invasion of Normandy, and most obviously since the failure of the last German counteroffensive in January 1945, the military regime has had to resort to a defensive strategy of camouflage. The assumption of the obligations of the Inter-American Conference on Problems of War and Peace to wipe out Nazi influence and the repeated avowals of pro-democratic intentions proceeded from this strategy of deception.
6. By its brutal use of force and terrorist methods to strike down all opposition from the Argentine people the military regime has made a mockery of its pledge to the United Nations to 'reaffirm faith in human rights, in the dignity and worth of the human person.' The information in support of these charges is respectfully submitted to the Governments of the American republics for their consideration in relation to the Treaty of Mutual Assistance to be negotiated at the forthcoming conference at Rio de Janeiro. By its terms the Act of Chapultepec lays the basis for a mutual assistance pact which will obligate the member governments to assist one another to meet an attack or a threat of aggression from any source whatsoever. This implementation would require a close cooperation in the development of security plans of vital importance to every American republic. It would also require cooperation in the

> maintenance of adequate military establishments for the defense of the continent. Such a defense structure can be built only on a foundation of absolute trust and confidence. Because the Government of the United States did not have such trust and confidence in the present Argentine regime, it took the position in October 1945 that it could not properly sign a military assistance treaty with that regime. It is submitted that the information transmitted to the Governments of the American republics in this memorandum makes abundantly clear a pattern which includes aid to the enemy, deliberate misrepresentation and deception in promises of Hemisphere cooperation, subversive activity against neighboring republics, and a vicious partnership of Nazi and native totalitarian forces. This pattern raises a deeper and more fundamental question than that of the adequacy of decrees and administrative measures allegedly enacted in compliance with Argentina's obligations under Resolution LIX of the Mexico Conference [at Chapultepec]. The question is whether the military regime, or any Argentine government controlled by the same elements, can merit the confidence and trust which is expressed in a treaty of mutual military assistance among the American republics.

The *Blue Book* was adopted by the Unión Democrática in the electoral fight against Perón, and it was widely cited by the Argentine press.

It is clear, particularly in the final paragraph above, that the USA was using the defeated 'Nazi' bogeyman to scare the American Republics into an alliance that would ensure U.S. control over the entire region. The tactic is familiar. The USA was soon using the USSR, when it fell out with its wartime ally over the issue of a United Nations world government and American control of nuclear technology,[36] to scare states into its fatal embrace during the 'Cold War'. Today it is the 'Islamist' bogeyman and the 'war on terrorism' being used for the same purpose in what President George W. Bush called the creation of a United Nations-based 'new world order'. Perón and Argentina stood as the obstacle in the way of U.S. hegemony over Latin America. However, the U.S. campaign, led by Braden, in alliance with oligarchs, communists and socialists in the Unión Democrática, only strengthened the resolve of the Argentines. Perón was victorious.

36 K R Bolton, *Stalin: The Enduring Legacy* (London: Black House Publishing, 2013), 125-139.

The Emergence of Justicialism

Justicialism translates as 'social justice'. Perón often referred to Justicialism as the 'National Doctrine', and to the 'National Justicialist movement'. Hence, there is an implicit character to Justicialism that is both national and social. Justicialism did not arrive out of an ideological void. The national and social synthesis had been fermenting among both Rightist and Leftist forces in Europe as a revolt against the Enlightenment doctrines of the 18th century, against French Jacobinism, whose 1789 Revolution had given rise to both liberal-capitalism and Marxism. The Right – in its traditional sense - as distinct from the way the term is now inaccurately used by political scientists and journalists - was never motivated solely by economic doctrines, while sections of the Left began to see economic explanations for history as inadequate.

In 1949 Perón delivered a series of lectures to the 'First Congress of Philosophy'. The lectures show that Perón was not only a man of action, but also a profoundly philosophical character, tracing his outlook from Hellenic philosophy. Perón considered that social justice was one aspect of a higher aim: that of the re-formation of humanity on principles of virtue and morality. He stated:

> it is necessary that moral values create an atmosphere of human virtue capable of compensating at any time, what is due and what has been achieved. In this aspect virtue reaffirms its efficient influence. It will not only be the unflagging heroism of liturgical precept; it is a mode of life which enables us to say that a man has courageously fulfilled his personal and public obligations; the man who was obliged to do and could do so, gave; the man who was obliged to perform, did so. That virtue does not close the roads of struggle, does not hamper the march onwards of progress, endows, not condemns, sacred revolt, but raises an impassable barrier to disorder.[37]

37 Juan Perón, 'Inaugural Message to the National Congress of Philosophy', 1 May 1949,

Returning to the Greek philosophers, Perón cites Aristotle that 'Man is a being meant for social relationship; therefore, supreme good is not obtained in individual human life but in the super-individual organisation of the State: ethics culminate in politics'.[38] This is the meaning of a greater purpose than one's ego, by the fulfilment of one's potential in service to others. Under Justicialism, and other similar ideologies, the individual actualises his life and realises his sense of purpose in service to his fellows, who in aggregate form a people and politically, a nation. The liberty with which one is born is justified insofar as it gives one the freedom to act according to 'ethical principles'. The life of the individual thereby transcends individual egoism and enables a life to be led that is higher than the mere pursuit of one's self-interest. It is egoism that 'gave birth to class struggles and inspired the most ardent anathemas of materialism', due to 'an overestimation of personal interests'.[39]

The class divisions of the prior century could now be superseded by 'social collaboration'.[40] Individualities are instead reaffirmed in their 'collective function'. This was not however to condone the 'omnipotence of the State over an infinite total of zeroes';[41] where the individual accounts for zero, which is precisely what the Marxists propounded.

That year, 1949, Perón stated that the Perónist concept of the state was an organic or corporative one, which he called the 'organised community'. In a book by that name, *La communidad organizada*, he wrote in the 'foreword' that the aim of the Justicialist state is 'the overcoming of class struggle by social collaboration and the dignifying of man. Society will have to be a harmony in which there is no dissonance'. The aim was an ascending humanity, 'an ideal of better humanity, the sum of individualities tending to continuous improvement'.

28.

38 Ibid, 31.

39 Ibid., 33.

40 Ibid., 38.

41 Ibid., 39.

Fundamentals of National Doctrine

Perón was continually developing, refining and explaining Justicialist doctrine. In 1966 he laid down some broad fundamentals. He returned to the Aristotelian premise that 'man is a social animal'.

I: Man: The basis of the 'broader community', which is the total of an accumulated historical and cultural legacy, is the family. The obligation of the individual is to contribute to the community, and even to sacrifice for it, in return for which the individual and the family receive protection. The 'social framework' provides for the development of the 'fully realised human being'. 'Heroism and to live heroically' gives a transcendent meaning to life. Only 'strong people make history'.[42]

II: Community: The concept of the 'organised community', which will be considered further, is hierarchical, with a multiplicity of federations (or syndicates), representing each sector of society, playing a 'particular role within the social organism'. A national community cannot develop and progress when one sectional element rules over the others, but all must work for the common good. There cannot be a national community without the three fundamentals of Justicialism:

- political sovereignty,
- economic independence and
- social justice.[43]

Defining the organic state, Perón wrote:

III: State: Federated Community groups are not only intended to coexist, but also to cooperate, in the precise sense of the word, such as family members. Each must play their particular role within the social organism. Their respective roles are

42 Juan Perón, Fundamentals of Partido Justicialism National Doctrine, I: Man, (Madrid: School of Policy, 1966).

43 Ibid., II: Community.

complementary. You cannot conceive of a harmonisation of many diverse and interdependent activities without a hierarchical order, which involves control. This is the primary reason why the whole community has a specialised organ in political leadership: the state.[44]

Perón is here describing the organic or corporative state, in which all Argentines would be represented by professional and occupational syndicates and federations. This syndicalist state was enacted in the provinces of Chaco from 1951 and La Pampa, until Perón's ouster in 1955.

IV: Bourgeois Subversion: Perón recognised the role of the bourgeoisie class as an agent for subversion. He ascribed the modern origins of this to the French Revolution, when the merchant class overthrow the traditional order, and inaugurated free trade. Perón here repudiates the doctrine of Jacobinism that was also the ideological basis for the USA, and for the current liberal-democracies, as well as its mirror image: Marxism.

> In the late eighteenth century the natural social order was broken by a pathological phenomenon whose consequences we continue to suffer. Marginalised groups in society, who were engaged in overseas trade and, clandestinely, loan interest, became rich without thereby achieving more material comforts. They aspired to power and, after a long process of ideological subversion, managed to seize the French State and then by force or propaganda, other states in the Western world.[45]

The Bourgeois regimes that replaced the monarchies, created commercial states, for the purpose of serving moneyed interests. Society was divided into economic classes, each with their own political parties, in a voting process that was designed to perpetuate the system. The craft guilds that had provided real representation under the old regimes, self-governing and imposing not only

44 Ibid., III: The State.

45 Ibid., IV: Bourgeois Subversion.

rights but social duties, were disbanded. Such federations were a hindrance to unbridled profit, and had maintained high ethical standards in craft and trade. The aim was to create a mass of individuals without any organic bonds, but as mere economic units in an 'undifferentiated herd'. 'On behalf of a mythical and unreal Freedom, the bourgeoisie effort was to remove from man the privileges and freedoms previously enjoyed by virtue of their function. And the Bourgeois succeeded greatly', Perón wrote That is to say, the guilds, which had functioned since ancient Rome (where they were called corporations), and remained the foundation of social community through the Medieval era, right through until the 1789 French Revolution, were eliminated. Workers and artisans were denied the sense of meaning, purpose and community that they had lived by since ancient times. This was done in the name of progress and freedom; which was just progress and freedom for commercial interests.

Ever since Perón had been the Secretary of Labour and Social Welfare, he had sought to integrate the trades unions into the national and social polity, and return to them something of the traditional guild character, rather than merely as instruments of class warfare serving only to eke out some extra remuneration for their members. Elevating the trades unions to organs of the national community is anathema to Marxists who see this as undermining the role of unions as nothing other than instruments of class war (albeit ruthlessly suppressed when communism triumphs).

V: Capitalism: Perón held that the democratic-liberal (or 'demoliberal') regimes were a facade for plutocracy. With the dissolution of the guilds and the legalisation of usury,[46] which had been anathema to the Catholic Church, the modern bourgeois liberal state came into being which promised 'freedom', but practised only freedom for plutocracy and oligarchy. Hence, the

46 Usury, interest on loans, despised as a sin against God since ancient times, and by Catholicism and Islam, is today regarded as essential business practice, and usurers are respectable businessmen, rather than being dragged through the streets and flogged as the lowest vermin. See K. R. Bolton, *The Banking Swindle* (London: Black House Publishing, 2013).

'free craftsman of yesteryear' became an employee; a wage-slave. He must sell his labour to capitalists, who set the price through the fraud called 'supply and demand'. Hitherto, the market had been regulated by the guilds, and ethics, morality and craftsmanship were the foundations of economy. The 'Estates' of the traditional regimes, became economic classes.[47]

All of the dogmatic Enlightenment ideas of the 18th century bourgeoisie and drawing-room intelligentsia had a negative impact on a traditional social order that had for centuries regarded work as a social function and not simply as the drudgery of some and the profit of others. While Perón regarded the overthrow of the traditional order as a negative development, Karl Marx regarded capitalism and the bourgeois revolutions as a necessary part of the dialectical cycle that would result in communism, and opposed the traditional ethos of the artisan, and his guild organisations, as 'reactionary'. The traditional social order of the Medieval era, which was corporatist, was one where 'every medieval man thought of himself not as an independent unit, but as a dependent, although component, part of a larger organism, church or empire or city or guild. This was the very essence of medieval life...' [48] Marx viewed the movement among artisans during the 19th century to restore a corporatist social order with 'the greatest chagrin' and condemned it with particular vehemence as 'reactionist'.[49] A return to a corporatist social order would, according to Marx, disrupt the process of capitalism, which was a necessary step towards communism. Under Perónism the guild-syndicate would be extended to all productive elements of the nation, and would manage the economic unit as part of a State national plan.

VI: State Capitalism: Perón alluded to Marx, where he states in

---

47 Juan Perón, Fundamentals of Partido Justicialism National Doctrine,op. cit., V: Capitalism.

48 W. D. P. Bliss, *New Encyclopaedia of Social Reform*, (New York: Funk and Wagnalls, 1908), 546.

49 Karl Marx, *The Communist Manifesto*, (Moscow: Progress Publishers, 1975), 46.

The Communist Manifesto that the means of production would become concentrated in fewer hands and that the bourgeois would become increasingly dispossessed in the struggle for competitive survival, and large elements of the bourgeoisie would become part of the proletariat. This was part of Marx's dialectical interpretation of history that would lead to communism, as the ranks of the working class would swell. Perón contended that the reverse was taking place: that the working class was becoming increasingly bourgeois. The USSR had become a technocratic form of state capitalism, and the Soviet bloc and capitalist states were becoming increasingly similar.[50]

Perón warned that by the year 2000 there would either be free nations or subject peoples.

VII: Labour: Perón described labour revolt in heroic terms, as Homeric in spirit. This is classic syndicalist doctrine as expounded by the French syndicalist philosopher Georges Sorel, who saw the General Strike as creating a new revolutionary myth and ethos superior to Marxism. The strike was the only weapon at the workers' disposal. While the general strike did not succeed against the army, the bourgeoisie did start to make concessions to union demands for the sake of social peace. However, the pacified unions became appendages to the 'democapitalist system', as Perón called it. The working class has become increasingly bourgeois, in outlook and aspirations if not in material comfort, rather than Marx's prediction of the bourgeois becoming increasingly proletarian.[51]

VIII: Supranational Power: 'The most serious mistake you can commit in studying the world today is to believe that liberal capitalism and state capitalism are irreconcilable enemies'.[52] Perón contended that an 'international synarchy' was in operation

50 Juan Perón, *Fundamentals of Partido Justicialism National Doctrine*,op. cit., VI: State Capitalism.

51 Juan Perón, *Fundamentals*, op. cit., VII: Labour.

52 Ibid., VIII: Supranational Power.

that includes both capitalism and communism, the latter being termed by Perón 'state capitalism'. While the capitalist and Soviet blocs vied for control of markets and territories, if a 'third position' arose, they would unite to defeat it. Perón alludes to the Second World War against the Axis, when the USSR combined with the plutocracies to defeat the autarchic trading and economic systems of Germany, Italy and Japan; the same alliance of liberal, capitalist and communist forces that combined against him: 'This was demonstrated clearly in the Second World War as well, in our country, as the conspiracy of liberals and communists in 1945 and 1955'. Furthermore, Perón suspected that above the Western and Soviet blocs there was a 'supranational power' that managed them both. Perón showed that he was thoroughly versed in the covert aspects of history and politics. He stated that:

> It is proven that an international banking consortium abundantly subsidised Trotsky in 1917. Big finance has no country, but only interests. The Cold War and localised conflicts are but episodes of mutual convenience, allowing the United States to keep its faltering economy afloat and the Soviet Union to strengthen the internal stress without which its empire runs in serious danger of disintegrating. Chances are that those who serve in Washington and Moscow, the phone that joins the White House to the Kremlin speaks the same language, and this language is neither Russian nor English.[53]

Many astute analysts regarded the rivalry between the USSR and the capitalist West as a ruse. While I contend that there was a genuine fall-out between these two wartime allies, the USSR and the USA, after Stalin declined to become the USA's junior partner in a 'new world order', the 'Cold War',[54] (like today's 'war on terrorism'), served as a means of corralling nations behind one antagonist or another. What is today disparagingly called the 'Third World', arose as a 'non-aligned bloc'. Perón

53 Juan Perón, *Fundamentals*, op. cit.

54 See K. R. Bolton, *Stalin: the Enduring Legacy*, op. cit., 125-139.

considered this to be a manifestation of the 'third position', and he was one of the founders of that bloc.[55]

The contention that the USSR and the USA were in collusion was a theme of the once best-selling author and widely experienced journalist, Douglas Reed, who had served as Chief European Correspondent for the *London Times* during the years leading up to the Second World War. He wrote:

> Today the scene is set for the third act, intended to complete the process. The money-power and the revolutionary-power have been set up and given sham but symbolic shapes ('Capitalism' or 'Communism') and sharply defined citadels ('America' or 'Russia'). Suitably to alarm the mass mind, the picture offered is that of bleak and hopeless enmity and confrontation… Such is the spectacle publicly staged for the masses. But what if similar men, with a common aim secretly rule in both camps and propose to achieve their ambition through the clash between those masses? I believe any diligent student of our times will discover that this is the case.[56]

When Perón remarked that 'the phone that joins the White House to the Kremlin speaks the same language, and this language is neither Russian nor English', there is little doubt that he was referring to a Jewish cabal, an opinion that was also expressed by Reed, for example.

As for Trotsky, who hurriedly returned from New York to Russia[57] to assume a leading role of the Bolshevik revolt and

55 We will consider this further.

56 Douglas Reed, *Behind the Scene* (Pinetown, Natal: Dolphin Press, 1976), ii.

57 The journey of Trotsky from New York to Russia was facilitated courtesy of William Wiseman, British intelligence operative in the USA during the First World War. After the war Wiseman assumed a prominent role with the New York bank, Kuhn, Loeb & Co., whose principal partner was Jacob Schiff. For a scholarly examination of Trotsky's journey from New York to Russia see: Dr. Richard Spence, Idaho State University, 'Hidden Agendas: Spies, Lies and Intrigue Surrounding Trotsky's American Visit January-April 1917', Revolution Russia, vol. 21, No. 1, June 2008, 33-55; also on Trotsky's high-level connections see K. R. Bolton, *Stalin: the Enduring*

subsequently as Commissar for Foreign Affairs and head of the Red Army, he and other Bolsheviks, including Lenin, had been funded by bankers in Germany, Sweden and the USA. While that was well-known from the start, in recent years it has been definitively documented by Stanford University research specialist Dr. Antony C. Sutton.[58] Henry Wickham Steed, editor of the *London Times*, had observed first-hand at the Paris Peace Conference of 1919 how it was international bankers who lobbied for the recognition of the Bolshevik regime, recalling that 'the prime movers were Jacob Schiff, Warburg and other international financiers who wished above all to bolster up the Jewish Bolsheviks in order to secure a field for the German and Jewish[59] exploitation of Russia'.[60] Samuel Gompers, president of the American Federation of Labor at the time of the international economic conference in Genoa in 1922, remarked on the same 'predatory international financiers', whom he called 'an Anglo-American-German banking group', who were promoting the Bolshevik regime.[61]

IX: Revolutionary Movement: The 19th century revolutions were directed by the bourgeoisie. Some fought for the concept of the nation-state, against the petty principalities or the imperial edifices, both of which prevented the development of nationhood. In this connection we might refer to the German Idealists such as Fichte whose *Addresses to the German Nation* (1807-1808) constitute a foundation for post-feudal nationalism. Nationalism was hence a revolutionary ideal. Others sought to uplift the working-class, and regarded nationalism as an enemy. Different interests were at work in the national revolts against the monarchical regimes; some national, others anti-national.

Legacy (Black House Publishing, 2012), 'Trotsky's Banking Connections', 95-109.

58 Antony C. Sutton, *Wall Street and the Bolshevik Revolution* (New York: Arlington House Publishers, 1974).

59 The predominance of international bankers not only in Germany but also in New York, were German-Jews, including Schiff, the Warburg brothers, Otto Kahn, et al.

60 Henry Wickham Steed, *Through Thirty Years, 1892-1922: A Personal Narrative* (New York: Doubleday Page & Co., 1924), Vol. II, 301.

61 Samuel Gompers, ' Charges Strong Group of Bankers with Readiness to accept Lenin's Betrayal of Russia', *New York Times*, 1 May 1922.

These revolts later diverged into nationalism and democratic-liberalism.

Perón wrote of this dialectic: 'Often, by mutual incomprehension, nationalists and socialists faced each other, neutralizing each other, duly incited by paid agitators'. Hence, the ideals of nationhood and of socialism came to be in conflict, thanks in particular, to the rise of Marxism within the labour movement. Perón explained that the two ideas, the national and the social, far from being antagonistic, are intrinsically bound, but that it is capitalism and Marxism that have kept them as antagonists, as neither recognise a higher purpose for man than the economic:

> For the revolution to be made possible, it was necessary that the nationalist groups become aware of the capitalist oppression they suffered just as the proletariat, and labour groups become aware of the historical subjugation of the Community by the bourgeois oligarchy. Then came other national revolutionary movements who knew the synthesis of nationalism and socialism, the spirit of tradition and the spirit of revolution. Denying outmoded antagonisms, these movements constituted supplementary States as real instruments guiding the purpose of their communities.[62]

Perón in the above passage is explicit in stating that the new 'national revolutionary movements' were a combination of nationalism and socialism. This cannot mean anything other than what is generically called 'fascism'. Perón was writing this is 1966 when it would have been politically opportune to repudiate such ideas. That he never did so shows that the often remarked quips about him being an 'opportunist' who ideologically shifted ground, are baseless. As I believe this book shows, Perón always maintained his principles regardless of the personal cost.

In proclaiming that the 'working class has no country and no

62 Juan Perón, *Fundamentals*, op. cit., IX: Revolutionary Movement.

nationality', Karl Marx had surrendered the working class to internationalism, while stating that capitalism would also become increasingly international. Marx had written of the internationalising tendency of capitalism as a necessary dialectical phase towards communism:

CGT poster in support of Perón

> National differences and antagonisms between peoples are daily more and more vanishing, owing to the development of the bourgeoisie, to freedom of commerce, to the world market, to uniformity in the mode of production and in the conditions of life corresponding thereto. The supremacy of the proletariat will cause them to vanish still faster.[63]

Not all socialists however, saw Marxism as the answer to capitalism, and a tendency emerged especially among the syndicalists, who regarded the economic interpretation of history and the detachment of the workers from the homeland in favour of a new loyalty to a nebulous thing called the 'international proletariat', as inadequate. Perón proceeds:

> National revolutions of our century were conducted in two stages. The first was the release of the State from bourgeois occupation, implying functional restructuring. The second, in the release of the Community and, in particular, of the proletariat, of their suffering from economic and social

63 Karl Marx, *The Communist Manifesto* (Moscow: Progress Publishers, 1975), 71-72

> exploitation, which meant the total transformation of the capitalist system of production and distribution. The second was more difficult than the first: recent history proves it.[64]

'Recent history' shows that those states that sought to break the international system of capitalism were faced with a world war, while Perónist Argentina faced economic sabotage from the plutocratic powers. The 'national revolutions of our century', described by Perón as being undertaken in two stages: the national and the social, again shows that Perón was referring to the 'national socialist' states.

X: Justicialist National Revolution: In Argentina the national revolution developed differently from those of Italy and Germany, although similar to those of Franco's Spain and Salazar's Portugal, where the military had intervened. It was revolutionary elements in the military that were able to pave the way for a new polity.

> In our country, the revolutionary process was developed in a somewhat different way. With the military coup of June 4, 1943 the State had already been released with a purely political approach when Perónism emerged, composed of civilian nationalist groups and the great mass of workers. The revolutionary movement had not been established, or refined and seasoned in the fight. It lacked doctrine and was even divided between parties and unions, rather than being an organic unit. It could not harden or become unified in power. Rather, we made the mistake of allowing and sometimes imposing indiscriminate party membership and thereby weakening our foundations further. Only unions constituted a coherent force, but by their very comprehensive class character.[65]

Although there had been the 'Nacionalistas', this was a term for

64 Juan Perón, *Fundamentals*, op. cit., X: Revolutionary Movement.

65 Ibid..

a disparate collection of ideas and groups, including the GOU. Hence, the origins of the Perónist revolution in the 1943 coup had only vague ideological concepts, and many of the Nacionalistas opposed Perón's national-socialist ideas, leading to his removal from government in 1945. Only Perón and a few ideologues such as those of FORJA, Dr. Manuel Fresco's UNA and the ALN had a clear conception of national revolution. Perón's position as champion of the workers within the military regime had made him the centre of what became a spontaneous workers' uprising with the support of elements in the Army. The strength of the Perónist movement continued to reside in the labour movement. Perón stated in the above passage that the Justicialist party had become too open, and incorporated elements that were negative, thereby weakening the movement rather than strengthening it.

Perón next considered the difficult circumstances under which the revolutionary military regime and the Perónist State tried to govern during 1943-1955. Perón wrote that not even the Justicialist State was able to effect the revolutionary changes that were required:

> On the other hand, when the national revolution erupted it developed in the most difficult international situation. Defeated in the country, the Democratic Union dominated the rest of the world with the name of the United Nations. The political and military pressure from the Allies had been very serious at times, irresistible in previous years and permanently latent. To completely change the political and economic structures would have been considered a real challenge, with potentially very dangerous consequences for our own sovereignty.[66]

Perón here stated that although the Democratic Union had been defeated by the Justicialists, their ideology was represented on a world scale through the United Nations. Although the question of Argentina's neutrality during the Second World War had been

66 Ibid.

a major issue, with most of the Army opposing entry, Argentina relented to intense U.S. pressure and declared war on the Axis, albeit – like Vargas' Brazil – at the last moment. When Perón alluded to a total change in Argentina's political and economic structures, despite the enormous changes he did render, he is relating the 'potentially very dangerous consequences' that would have been brought down on Argentina to the way the Axis states had been obliterated for having changed their political and economic structures. Perón recognised the real causes of the war against the Axis, and was stating here that the powers the Axis fought were the same as those which he confronted, which he called an 'international synarchy'. Cognisant of the way Italy and Germany had been destroyed, Perón had to tread a more cautious path, but one that was obviously not cautious enough to prevent his ouster in 1955:

> The Perónist state had, therefore, to act within the institutional framework created by the oligarchy, or with inadequate instruments. We just gave new meaning to outdated forms. In the political arena, the electoral majority that backed me allowed me to govern without deleting the party system. In the economic field, the solid support of the unions allowed for the establishing of social justice without destroying capitalism. Only in recent times our government for the first time, in somewhat relaxed international tensions, could begin to take away the mask. The constitutions of La Pampa and Chaco provided instead of political parties, union representation and some companies were socialised. But apart from these few exceptions, otherwise incomplete, the national revolution of justicialista simply removed effects while structural causes remained, constitutionally and legally effective.[67]

Perón regretted that Justicialism could not achieve a far-reaching national revolution due to the constraints he was obliged to work

67 Ibid., X.

within. These were of an international character of the type that controls, with ever more intrusiveness, the affairs of most nations, and bombs those nations that are reticent, as we have seen in recent years with Serbia and Iraq. Perón was only able to reform old political and economic institutions, rather than replace them. Of these old forms, Perón alluded to the retention of the political party system. He was a national-syndicalist, meaning that he ultimately aimed to create a Syndicalist state, which he also called the 'Corporate Nation', and more commonly, 'the organised community'. He had established Chaco and La Pampa as Syndicalist provinces.

XI: Today: Doctrine and Movement: During the years of exile, Perón had sought to refine and detail the Justicialist doctrine. This he said was the prerequisite for a real national revolution.

> You cannot organise revolutionary forces without first giving the doctrinal formation without which there is no discipline or awareness of the objectives to be achieved. Much has been done in recent years to clarify the great Justicialist ideological lines. Our revisionist historians have already won the battle, in their field, and the liberal mythology no longer fools anyone among us. Our sociologists and economists have deepened our doctrine, especially in its structural aspects. Today, the Movement's Higher Driving School policy is giving this task organic regulations and guidance from which our members can start.[68]

XII: Tomorrow: The Community State: As Perón had stated, the Justicialist revolution had been incomplete because its new conception of the State had not been implemented, but had merely worked within the concept of the bourgeoisie parliamentary system:

> We will return very soon to create the state. There must, then, remain no institutional remnant of bourgeois occupation.

68 Ibid., XI: Today: Doctrine and Movement.

> The State must respond to our reality and our needs, not only in its intentions and its works, but also in its structures.
>
> The new Perónist Constitution will ensure the unity and continuity of the State in the person of its Head, located above the three institutional powers. It will ensure a genuine popular representation through intermediate communities and constituent bodies of the nation, provinces, unions, church, universities, armed forces, etc. It will respect and promote the autonomy and privileges of social groups and intermediate communities. Thus the State will be able to satisfactorily perform all functions.
>
> This assumes, of course, the total and final suppression of political parties that constitute instruments of demoliberal deception. The Community is organically made. Parties or a part of the nation, competing with others, cannot validly express the unitary historical intention. As a sovereign state, the mission is to lead the Community to its increasing assertion.[69]

Perón stated his aim: The organic state, where all sectors function as part of a national community. Political parties create artificial divisions, as do economic classes. When every sector of society is organised into its own syndicate, guild, corporation, union or whatever else one might wish to call it, that grouping looks after its members' interests. That is what Perón means when he states that such groups will remain autonomous.

XIII : Tomorrow: Community Now: In the final section of Perón's 1966 treatise he outlined radically new social and economic relationships. This is not merely a matter of improving conditions or arbitrating between capital and labour, but of eliminating the distinction between capital and labour, and between owner and worker. The concept is syndicalist, where

69 Ibid., XI.

the union assumes the function for the running of the economic unit, and through which profits are divided and management is organised:

> Considered in its functional aspect, the company is a hierarchical community of producers, variously specialised, that have joined forces to manufacture a particular article or provide a given service, supplying tools or machines.
>
> Considered, however, in its legal aspect, this same company does not pass today, as a mere purchaser of capital machinery, raw materials and labour. Pure fiction. Well, if with a magic wand the owners of capital were removed, the company would continue to operate without any disruption while it would stop and disappear if its producers were eliminated.[70]

Justicialism rejects communism as being 'state capitalism', and Perón next refers to the futility of transcending capitalist bosses only to create bureaucratic bosses functioning for the state. Rather, an economic unit would be organised as a workers' co-operative under the direction of the union:

> It is not enough, therefore, to improve the standard of living of the proletariat. It is not enough to give the producers the rightful place in the Community. Nothing will be solved by replacing the capitalist bourgeois oligarchy by a bureaucratic oligarchy. What is needed is to abolish wage labour, returning to the company in its organic reality, if possible, the ownership of capital and the free disposition of the fruits of labour.
>
> Any social-individual entity, group or community, has the natural right to own assets that are essential to survive and be fully realised. The municipality, for example, is

70 Ibid., XIII : Tomorrow: Community Now.

naturally entitled to ownership of the public highway or power line.... The company is also an independent social entity. It is the producers who must be the owners of the capital... This applies to both the industrial company and the agricultural enterprise... The land must be owned by those who work it, as machines are owned by those who work them. This principle does not, at all, cause the fragmentation of the ownership of the instruments of production, but the abolition of individualistic property ownership... [The aim is] the suppression of parasitism in all its forms.

Once capitalist parasitism disappear *ipso facto* classes will be eliminated. No more bourgeois or proletarian, but functionally and hierarchically organised producers in their companies.[71]

The integration of the union into the full economic functioning of the national economy means that the union loses its class struggle character, where it has served merely to eke out some extra rewards from capitalism. Rather, the union assumes a core position in the running of the economy. Furthermore, the union assumes functions hitherto left to the state: that of organising social welfare and of legislating labour conditions (since the syndicates will also be the units by which their members are represented in Government). The syndicates are involved in formulating and implementing the national economic plan:

The union will then lose the class character that has been imposed as a necessary struggle that takes no responsibility, and will [instead] become a federation of companies, with assets needed for care and the legislative and judicial powers to define their privileges. In each union, there will be bank credit distributed among companies within the framework of the planning and the economic leadership of the National Government.[72]

71 Ibid.

72 Ibid.

Ownership is assumed neither by the state nor by the individual but by the syndicate in which each member has a personal stake as a share-holder. The 'natural social order' is of the type that had existed for centuries, prior to the French Revolution, known as the guild in the medieval era and the corporation in ancient Rome. These trade and craft organisations ensured not only the rights but also the duties of their members, and held their professions to be a divine calling and not merely an economic drudgery.

> The Perónist revolution seeks therefore to reach a compromise between individualist capitalism and state capitalism, not just to 'improve relations between capital and labour'. The Perónist revolution entirely repudiates any form of exploitation of man by man and wants to return, in all fields, to the natural social order. This is the meaning of our THIRD POSITION. [73]

Perón had laid the foundations for syndicalism since his position in 1943 as Secretary of Labour and Social Welfare, by strengthening the labour movement, and labour representatives were brought into responsible positions in the Justicialist state. Syndicalism had since the 19th century been a part of the Left that rejected the statism of Marx, demanding instead that the foundation of the state would be a federation of syndicates. Elements of the Nationalist Right saw the potential of syndicalism as more than a weapon of class warfare, but as the basis for organising the organic national state, transcending class divisions by providing a means of political organisation that also eliminated the petty divisions of party politics. The result was a widespread emergence of 'national syndicalism' and 'corporatism' after the First World War. This worldwide movement was defeated by the alliance between plutocrats and communists during the Second World War. Perón remained committed to the doctrine that he had been formulating for decades. In 1951 he sought to lay the foundations of the syndicalist state by creating syndicalist

73 Ibid., XIII : Tomorrow: Community Now.

provinces at Chaco and La Pampa. This 1966 treatise shows that Perón never compromised on the need to establish the syndicalist state.

The Crisis in Socialism

What some of the Left demanded was a militant ethos, not a party platform. Chief among these was the leading French syndicalist philosopher Georges Sorel (1847-1922) who had adopted Marxism as a moral critique rather than as an economic programme. He wrote that 'nearly all the Marxists strongly regret the exaggeration with which, for a long time, the beauties of materialism had been lauded'.[74] Sorel had praised Charles Maurras, leader of the militant Royalist—Catholic-nationalist *Action francaise* for the inroads that were being made against democratic thought among educated youth.[75]

Both Sorel[76] and Maurras[77] looked at the doctrines of the 'anarchist'[78] philosopher Pierre Proudhon as offering an alternative socialism to that of Marx, who had despised Proudhon. That the French Right would look to Proudhon is not surprising: the Royalist regime prior to the Jacobin Revolution had been based on economic strictures regulated by the guilds. These had been abolished by Jacobinism, in the name of 'democracy', in pursuit of 'free trade'. Syndicalism and later corporatism were modernised forms of the guild. Hence, national tradition and social revolution converged in their rejection of bourgeoisie liberalism, free trade and the inadequacy of Marxian economics. This provided the basis for a national-social synthesis, or a national-syndical synthesis.

---

74 Georges Sorel, L'ethique du socialisme, 292, cited by Zeev Sternhell, *The Birth of Fascist Ideology* (New Jersey: Princeton University Press, 1994), 41.

75 Zeev Sternhell, ibid., 38.

76 Ibid., 44.

77 Ibid.

78 Not to be confused with the current puerile bourgeois versions of 'anarchism', whose slogan of 'no flags, no borders' is the same as that of international capitalism.

Sorel called Marxism 'an oversimplification of the labour movement', and stated that 'we know that things do not happen as simply as Marx supposed in 1847'.[79] This 'revision of Marxism' was adopted by the Italian revolutionary syndicalists, 'and became an essential element of early Italian fascism'.[80] The basis of revolution was the syndicates (unions), Sorel writing: 'Socialism is the organisation of revolt, and a syndicate with a revolutionary orientation is the thing that is most specifically socialist'.[81] Further, the syndicate and not the State would be the foundation of a socialist society. In 1897 Sorel condemned the socialist parties as merely wanting to take the mantle of power from the bourgeoisie without changing the basis of bourgeois society.[82] Sorel revived the concept of the organic society, in which 'the workers as a whole constitute a body', and the syndicates become 'social authorities', which create independent co-operatives in the running of the economic units, to replace bourgeoisie democratic institutions.[83]

The concept of the syndicalist state, which was also called the corporatist state, called for a federation of syndicates that would lead up through a pyramidal hierarchy to a syndicalist or corporatist legislative assembly that would replace the liberal-democratic parliaments that are a façade for plutocratic control.

From these beginnings what is generically called *fascism* emerged after the First World War, and although its first victory was in Italy, the impetus had largely come from France. In 1909 Sorel adopted the 'integral nationalism' of the Maurrasian Right. That year Sorel wrote an article for the Italian revolutionary syndicalist journal *Divenire sociale*, in praise of Maurras' ideology, which was reprinted in the Maurrasian movement's journal of the same name, *L'Action francaise*. The article referred to a convergence

79 Zeev Sternhell,op. cit., 47, citing Sorel, Idées socialistes et faits économiques, 401.

80 Zeev Sternhell, ibid., 47.

81 Ibid., citing Sorel, Idées socialistes et faits économiques, 401.

82 Sorel, L'avenir socialiste de syndicates; cited by Sternhell, ibid., 51.

83 Ibid.

of Maurrasian 'integral nationalism' and Sorelian revolutionary syndicalism.[84] For their part the Maurrasians praised Sorel effusively. In 1911 Georges Valois, who later founded the first French fascist organisation after the First World War, liaised with the non-Marxist Left for *L'Action francaise*. He declared at the Fourth Congress of *L'Action francaise*:

> It was not a mere accident if our friends encountered the militants of syndicalism. The nationalist movement and the syndicalist movement, alien to one another though they may seem, because of their present positions and orientations, have more than one common objective.[85]

Sorel and Valois had begun regular contact the previous year, with Sorel stating that there was unity of purpose in opposition to 'the stupid pride of democracy'. Declaring the aims of a projected but abortive journal[86] he stated that 'democracy is the greatest social danger for all classes of society, and especially the working class', as it allows financiers to dominate and exploit the producers. The answer was to organise institutions outside of democracy;[87] that is, through syndicates. From the workers around the journal *L'Indépendance* (1911-1913) Valois founded the Cercle Proudhon in 1911, which espoused syndicalism and nationalism, with major input from Sorel.[88]

It was in Italy that the national-syndicalist synthesis achieved its first victory via *Fascism* in 1922. In 1925 Valois founded the *Faisceau* in France.[89] Italian syndicalism had gone through similar developments as the French, and was also influenced by Sorel. In 1910 Italian socialists, encouraged by the convergence of syndicalism and nationalism in France, left the Socialist Party

84 Ibid., 78-79.

85 Valois, cited by Sternell, ibid., 83.

86 Another journal, *L'Indépendance*, was, however, successfully established.

87 Sorel and Valois cited by Sternhell, op. cit., 84.

88 Sternell, ibid., 87.

89 Ibid., 93.

and joined Enrico Corradini[90] when he established the Italian Nationalist Association that year, which fused with the Fascist party in 1923.[91] Corradini's nationalism was anti-bouregois and of a 'proletarian' orientation, describing Italy as a 'proletarian nation', 'materially and morally'.[92] It is at the first congress of the Italian Nationalist Association in 1910, a decade before Hitler, that Corradini referred to 'national socialism'.[93] Syndicalism was the theme of Corradini's speech to the Nationalist Convention in 1919. He stated that nationalism is the 'unifying force' between capital and labour, and the role of both is to serve the productivity of the nation, subordinating the private interests of both capital and labour. The most effective way of achieving economic organisation is 'by the formation of syndicates'. These would 'supercede the old political parties'.[94] Again, the aim was a syndicalist state, or what became the corporatist state under Italian Fascism, whereby syndical representation rises up from factory level, to local, provincial and finally national level, culminating as a syndical legislative assembly.[95]

Alfredo Rocco, a major intellectual influence in Corradini's Nationalist Association, who became Minister of Justice in Mussolini's Fascist regime during 1925-1932, introduced a Bill into the Chamber of Deputies in 1934 on the formation and functions of the corporations and syndicates. He pointed out that corporatism grew from the convergence of nationalism and syndicalism before the First World War, in what he called 'national syndicalism'.[96]

---

90 Ibid., 96.

91 George Steiner (editor) *Roots of the Right: Italian Fascism* (London: Jonathan Cape, 1973), 135.

92 Corradini, 'The Principles of Nationalism', report of the First Nationalist Congress, Florence, 3 December 1910; in Steiner, ibid., 146.

93 Corradini, ibid., 147.

94 Corradini, 'Nationalism and the Syndicates', speech at the Nationalist Convention, Rome, 16 March 1919, ibid., 159.

95 Ibid., 161.

96 The Spanish Falangists called themselves National Syndicalists.

The Fascist syndicates, when Mussolini assumed Office in 1922, formed themselves into corporations, and assumed their social functions in the economy by 1926. The 1934 law extended the functions of the corporations, in repudiating both 'liberal economics and socialist economics',[97] and assumed the organisation of production.[98] Within the State economic plan, the corporations were the 'self-government of the various categories of producers, employers and workers'.[99]

Charles Maurras' ideology influenced the Nacionalista in Argentina, the main organ of this trend being *La Voz Nacional* during 1927-1931.[100] Within this Nacionalismo also appeared support for Mussolini and Fascist Italy for having initiated a new social revolution that was progressive, traditional and patriotic. From Argentina's Spanish heritage, Argentine intellectuals started to look for a resurgence of the Hispanic culture from anti-liberal philosophers such as José Ortega y Gasset. They admired the progressive dictatorship of Primo de Rivera, whose son, José Antonio de Rivera, became leader of the National Syndicalist *Falangists*, and was summarily executed by the Republican authorities during the Spanish Civil War. Spain's ambassador to Argentina during the Primo regime, Ramiro de Maeztu, was seen as the potential link to unite Spain and Latin America into an anti-liberal, anti-Marxist bloc. The ambassador kept in close contact with Nacionalismo luminaries.[101]

---

97 Alfredo Rocco, 'The Formation and Functions of the Corporations', Chamber of Deputies, 16 January 1934, in Steiner, op. cit., 292-293.

98 Ibid., 294.

99 Ibid., 295.

100 Sandra McGee Deutsch, 'The Right Under Radicalism 1916-1930', in *The Argentine Right*, edited by Sandra McGee Deutsch and Ronald H Dolkart (Wilmington, Delaware: Scholarly Resources inc., 1993), 53.

101 Ibid., 52.

Juan and Eva Perón tour Mendoza province in 1952

Nacionalismo

One of the early Nacionalismo links within the milieu that brought Perón to Office was General José F. Uriburu, associated with the movement from 1925, who would lead the bloodless 1930 'September Revolution',[102] in which Perón was one of the military officers who took part.[103] The Uriburu regime was composed of conflicting views between old-line conservatives and Nacionalista, with Uriburu inclined towards the latter, and wanting to replace the rotten parliamentary system with a corporatist state.[104] Uriburu left Office in 1931. He died the following year. While he had encouraged the development of the Nacionalistas as a mass movement, Government policy stagnated after his death. However, the number of Nacionalista groups, including those of workers, professionals, youth, students, and women, proliferated during the 1930s,[105] and the general

102 Sandra McGee Deutsch, ibid., 53.

103 Rodney P. Carlisle (general editor), The Encyclopedia of Politics: The Left and the Right, Volume 2: The Right (Sage Publications, 2005), 525.

104 Ronald H. Dolkart, 'The Right in the Década Infame 1930-1943', citing Uriburu's October 1930 manifesto, in The Argentine Right, op. cit., 67.

105 Ronald H. Dolkart, ibid., 71.

tendency was that of corporatism rather than either one-man dictatorship or parliamentarianism. Enzo Valenti Ferro of the Legion Cívica Argentina, wrote a manifesto urging the protection of workers through a national workers relief programme, with medical care and accident compensation; and the conciliation of capital and labour through a state labour department.[106] What the Nacionalistas lacked however, with the demise of General Uriburu, was a charismatic leader. Perón would soon provide that leadership and fulfil that programme.

With the advent of the conservative Justo regime, the Nacionalistas became increasingly strident in their opposition. The Roca-Runciman Pact of 1933 increased Argentina's dependence on Britain, and prevented the development of an industrial base by imposing British manufactured goods on her. The opposition to British influence became a *cause celebre* for the Nacionalistas, and one that Perón would address. The pact was associated with the interests of the Argentine oligarchy. The result was that during the rest of the 1930s and early 1940s the Nacionalistas not only opposed British interests, but favoured Britain's enemies, National Socialist Germany and Fascist Italy.[107]

While the Left also campaigned against British dominance, Nacionalismo characterised the socialists and the communists as being just as foreign in inspiration as the oligarchy. Interestingly, the U.S. ambassador reported that the communists were 'almost entirely foreigners, some of whom are unable to speak Spanish'.[108] As in many other states, Jews were prominent in communist and other Marxist organisations. The Yevsektsiya, the Yiddish section of the Argentine Communist Party, was particularly conspicuous, 'Jewish Communists [being] the most avid readers (and publishers) of Party leaflets, newspapers, and magazines'. After the Uriburu regime outlawed the Communist Party, Yevsektsiya was the most significant of the underground

106 Ibid., 72.

107 Ibid.,75.

108 Ronald H. Dolkart, ibid. 77, quoting U.S. Embassy dispatches.

communist organisations. While the Argentine Communist movement lost most of its working class base to Perónism during the 1940s, the Jewish communists who left the party did so primarily because of their rise in economic status.[109] The Argentine Right had long identified communism with Jews, especially since the Semana Trágica of 1919.[110]

The Spanish Civil War during the 1930s further radicalised the Nacionalistas, who saw the stark choice for the world as being between Communism and Fascism. Conservatism would not suffice. While there had been a Partido Nacional Fascista as early as 1923, the Union Nacional Fascista had a significant following, and aligned with Nacionalistas.[111]

Although the Ortiz Government sympathised with the Allies during the Second World War, Argentina, like most states in the Western Hemisphere, was neutral. The Government and parliament condemned the pro-fascist Governor of Buenos Aries, Dr. Manuel Fresco, and he was obliged to purge his administration of pro-Fascist Nacionalistas. Fresco, who had been president of the Chamber of Deputies from 1934, was elected Governor of Buenos Aires province and served during 1936 to 1940. His administration was marked by the inauguration of public works, including roads, hospitals, schools, churches, another feature being the monumental futuristic character of public buildings of

109 Ariel Svarch, op. cit. 'Jewish Communist culture and Identity in Buenos Aires', 12 October 2008, Perush: An Online Journal of Jewish Scholarship and Interpretation, http://perush.cjs.ucla.edu/index.php/volume-2/jewish-urban-history-in-comparative-perspective-jewish-buenos-aires-and-jewish-los-angeles/-5-ariel-svarch-jewish-communist-culture-and-identity-in-buenos-aires-ideas-on-comparative-approaches

110 Semana Trágica (Tragic Week) was a series of riots that took place in Buenos Aries in January 1919, instigated by anarchists and communists and suppressed by the police and military. The violence began when a policeman was shot during a picket at a British owned factory. Strikes and violence quickly spread. A faction of a funeral procession, for example, broke into the Convent of the Sacred Heart and burnt the Church. While attacking a store, some of the group were killed by police fire. A general strike was called, and a revolutionary situation developed. A police raid on a meeting of the self-styled 'First Soviet of the Federal Republic of Argentine Soviets'discovered plans for a Communist revolt. Forty ring-leaders were detained, all of whom were Russian Jews.

111 Ronald H. Dolkart, op. cit., 79.

architect Francisco Salamone. Fresco resigned, and founded the Unión Nacional Argentina (UNA), also known as *Patria*. In 1942 he founded a newspaper, *Cabildo*. Fresco's legacy contributed to the foundations of Justicialismo, and Perón would later implement many of the governor's ideas on labour relations,[112] and public works. Fresco met with Perón in 1945, following the 17 October workers' mobilisation, and brought his UNA over to Perón, providing a founding constituent of the Justicialist party.

With the growing rift between the Nacionalistas and the Castilla Government, pro-Axis elements within the military, including Perón, formed the Grupo de Oficiales Unidos (GOU), instigating the seminal revolt of 4 June 1943,[113] which set Perón on his course to leadership. By this time the most active of the Nacionalistas were the Alianza Libertadora Nacionalista (ALN), a student based organisation that had been founded during the 1930s. The ALN remained aligned to Perón while other Nacionalista organisations went into opposition, because Perón would not be dominated by factions of either Right or Left.

The ALN doctrine was a social and national synthesis, and they militantly opposed capitalism and communism, the oligarchy and liberalism. Richard J. Walker of Washington University, states of the ALN:

> Rejecting both capitalism and communism, the Alianza proposed an authoritarian corporate state and national control over major economic activities. Setting itself apart from many other right-wing groups, the ALN called for agrarian reform and social justice, arguing that earlier Nacionalistas had been too elitist in their approach, ignoring the justifiable concerns and obvious needs of the working classes, and abandoning the workers to anarchists and communists. The ALN, holding rallies in working-class districts such as La Boca in Buenos Aires, sought to

112 Ibid., 90.

113 Ibid., 93.

> develop a broader base of support than had been the case for other Nacionalista organizations'.[114]

The Nacionalista determination that Argentina should remain neutral in the Second World War, buttressed by the patriotic resentment at Britain's influence over Argentina's economy, had a significant influence within the military, and especially in the GOU. In fact, the GOU coup was motivated by concern that President Ramón Castillo's handpicked successor, Robustiano Patrón Costas, would pursue a pro-Allied course, as well as by disgust at the ineptitude and corruption of democracy.[115]

Walker writes that Perón, once on the course to power, used and discarded Nacionalistas and Nacionalismo according to his own interests.[116] However, this is to assume that Perón was only guided by self-interest rather than by the development of a doctrine that would transcend both Left and Right in the new social-national synthesis of Justicialismo. As his subsequent life shows both in and out of power, he remained committed to that doctrine. While certain major Nacionalista elements did not achieve the authority under Perón that they had assumed, presumably with the prospect of controlling him, the most advanced of the Nacionalistas, the (ALN) remained loyal to Perón to the point of martyrdom in 1955.

Despite the inclusion in the Cabinet of provisional president General Pedro Ramírez, of an oligarch, Jorge Santamarina, as minister of finance, pro-Axis Nacionalistas dominated. The state investigated concessions to foreign capital during the previous regime, and nationalised some foreign owned companies. Land rents were lowered in the major agricultural provinces, and political parties and groups were dissolved, with the prospect of establishing a corporate state. Hence the groundwork was laid for the Perón revolution to build upon that work. Within the Ramírez

114 Richard J. Walker, 'The Right and the Perónists 1943-1955', in *The Argentine Right*, op. cit., 100.

115 Ibid., 101.

116 Ibid., 102.

Government Perón held the position of secretary to Minister of War Edelmiro Farrell. In October 1943, despite efforts to remove Perón, his ally, Farrell, became vice president while holding the war ministry, while Perón became head of the Labour Department. This provided Perón with the mass support base that would soon propel him to the leadership of Argentina. Perón made it clear that he aimed to integrate the workers into the national cause, which caused disquiet among the elitist faction of the regime.

When President Ramírez began succumbing to U.S. and British pressure to enter the war, and broke off diplomatic relations with Germany and Japan in January 1944, he was compelled to resign, and Farrell became the provisional president, with Perón succeeding him as Minister of War. Succumbing to Allied pressure the Argentine Government declared war on Germany in March 1945, for which Allied support for Argentina's international position in the post-war world had been promised. While the war was all but over by that time, Nacionalistas in government considered Perón to be a traitor. However, Perón never repudiated his pro-Axis views and for the rest of his life referred to the Axis fight against international finance.

It was the uneasy relationship between Perón and factions of the Nacionalistas that resulted in the latter joining with liberals in both the military and politics to oust him in October 1945. This however proved to be the start of the Perónist state, as workers responded with a mass demonstration of support on 17 October, which has henceforth been celebrated by Perónists as 'Loyalty Day'. Perón was released from detention and his presidential candidacy announced. The Partido Laborista was organised to support his candidacy. That was the beginning of the Partido Perónisat, which in turn became the Partido Justicialista. The Partido Laborista was able to draw from the trades union structure that Perón has encouraged when he headed the Labour Department. Perón also received the backing of the Catholic Church, due to his commitment to maintain religious instruction to the schools, an alliance that was eventually to have an unfortunate end.

Despite Nacionalista influence on the opposition to Perón, other Nacionalistas backed his presidential campaign, preferring him to José Tamborini, candidate for the Unión Democrática..[117] Of the Nacionalistas, it was the ALN that provided the primary, consistent and enduring support, including militant actions against Perón's communist opponents. Perón could mobilise the masses behind the cause of the homeland to the extent that the Nacionalistas could not.

F.O.R.J.A. - 'Radical Nationalism'

Among the intellectual antecedents native to Argentina, a precursor of Justicialism was the FORJA movement of Dr. Arturo Martín Jauretche, who began his political involvement as a supporter of the Radical Civic Union (UCR). This was aligned with the faction led by future President Hipólito Yrigoyen (1916-1922, 1928-1930), whose regimes were noted for their pioneering social reforms in favour of the menial workers. In 1928, at the beginning of the second Yrigoyen regime, Jauretche was appointed to the civil service. When the military coup led by General Uriburu ousted Yrigoyen in 1930, Jauretche fought with the resistance and was involved in political agitation. He was imprisoned for taking part in a failed uprising in Corrientes province in 1933. In 1934 Jauretche was among those who broke with the UCR, under the centrist leadership of Máximo Marcelo Torcuato de Alvear Pacheco, President of Argentina (1922-1928). Jauretche organised the faction into the *Fuerza de Orientación Radical de la Joven Argentina* (FORJA).[118] What is significant about FORJA is its doctrine of both nationalism and opposition to economic liberalism. Because FORJA was kept out of the political system, the organisation relied on street demonstrations and propaganda.

Jauretche, explaining the founding of FORJA, referred to the manner by which they were smeared as both 'Nazis' and 'Communists'. FORJA claimed to be the true guardian of

117 Richard J. Walker, ibid., 109.

118 Translating in English to 'Forge'.

Argentine radicalism. As for genuine 'democracy' it meant no more or less than government by the people whether this was achieved with or without a parliament. There were 'two Argentina's: Jauretche saw those who were claiming the mantle of radicalism as inherently 'conservative' insofar as they really did not want change. This is the Argentina that 'has no vitality, is a decrepit building, inertia exists in her'. The second was 'underground Argentina, young, vigorous, chaotic yet, but soon to be oriented, which is shifting despite the mess that introduced foreign factions within it, like communism and fascism. The majority of young people, communists or fascists, do not think in this way. They have not found radicalism and FORJA is slowly guiding and working with them'.[119]

FORJA condemned the Roca-Runciman treaty that subordinated Argentina further to Britain, and the creation of the Central Bank, which they rightly saw as yet another means of subordinating Argentina to international finance.

The bank had been set up on the advice of the Bank of England's globe trotting Otto Niemeyer. He was busily instigating the formation of such banks around the world. The purpose of these banks, including the USA's Federal Reserve Bank, controlled by private bond-holders, was to give the impression of being state banks, while serving to bring states into a world financial system run by the international bankers from The City of London and from Wall Street. Dr. Carroll Quigley, Professor of History at Harvard University, who studied the matter close-hand for decades, remarked that the purpose of such central banks was to form 'a single financial system on an international scale which manipulated the quantity and flow of money so that they [international bankers] were able to influence, if not control, governments on one side and industries on the other'.[120] This is the key to understanding history.[121]

119 Arturo M. Jauretche, 'Account of FORJA's birth', 1942.

120 Carroll Quigley, *Tragedy and Hope* (New York: Macmillan and Co., 1966), 51.

121 See K. R. Bolton, *The Banking Swindle* (London: Black House Publishing, 2013).

Arturo Martín Jauretche

A major focus of FORJA was to maintain Argentina's neutrality in the event of a war with the Axis, a significant feature of the GOU and the Nacionalistas.

FORJA synthesised two forces under its banner: 'the nationalist claim of the national and the demand of the people for popular reconciliation'.[122] This is the national and social synthesis that became Justicialism. Jauretche believed that 'fascism' – at least as it was portrayed by certain factions of the military – only sought the national principle, without attempting to integrate the totality of the people; while 'dry radicalism' only sought to proclaim itself in the name of the people, but has 'forgotten its initial position' in defence of nationalism. The regime sought to prevent the creation of an 'authentic nationalist formation'. FORJA stood for a new synthesis: 'radical nationalism'. 'Social justice is identified with nationalism'; there can be 'no possible conception of nationalism in a country that does not have an implicit demand for social justice'. A nationalist State owes to its people the 'fair distribution' of goods, otherwise Argentina remains under colonial status, and the state does not have control

122 Arturo M. Jauretche, 'Account of FORJA's birth', op. cit.

over the nation's resources.[123] It is this conception of social justice as the foundation of national unity and sovereignty that would define Justicialism.

Jauretche differentiated Argentine radical nationalism from Italian Fascism, which he saw as 'making man an instrument of the State', and of German National Socialism as making man an instrument of race, while Soviet communism made man the subject of dialectical materialism. In FORJA 'we aim to make a State the defender of the freedom of man', by ensuring that the owners of the economy are not able to 'infringe on the freedom of man'.

When the GOU coup ousted Pedro Pablo Ramírez over the issue of neutrality, Jauretche aligned himself with Perón. In 1946 Jauretche was named president of the Bank of the Province of Buenos Aires, which had been nationalised by Perón that year, along with General Domingo Mercante, who had mobilised the army and the workers to free Perón on 17 October 1945. Jauretche maintained the position until 1951, when Mercante broke with Perón, and Jauretche resigned. Jauretche initiated the Perónist doctrine of 'import substitution industrialisation', the aim of which was to replace imports with domestically produced manufactures. He was devoted to ending the class division between the menial workers and the middle class, seeing them as both sectors of a national community. The enemies of this community were the liberal and cosmopolitan intelligentsias.

Although Jauretche had not been in government since 1951, he maintained his support for Justicialism after Perón's ouster in 1955. He founded two periodicals, *El Líder* and *El '45* to defend what he called 'the ten years of popular government'. However, in 1956 he was exiled to Montevideo because of his condemnation of the economic policies of Raúl Prebisch, secretary of the Economic Commission of Latin America; whom Jauretche regarded as 'returning Argentina to colonialism'.[124]

---

123 Ibid.

124 Arturo M. Jauretche El Plan Prebisch: retorno al coloniaje (The Prebisch Plan: A Return to Colonialism, 1956).

In exile Jauretche refuted the smears against Perónism.[125] In an exchange with Argentine Marxist writer, painter and physicist, Ernesto Sábato, he wrote:

> What drove the masses to Perón was not resentment, but hope. Recall the crowds in October of '45, who took over the city for two days, who didn't break a single window and whose greatest crime was washing feet in the Plaza de Mayo... Recall those crowds, even in tragic times, and you will recall that they always sang together — something very unusual for us — and they remain such singers today, but have been banned by decree from singing. They were not resentful. They were happy *criollos* because they were willing to throw away their sandals to buy shoes and even books and records, to take vacations, to meet in restaurants, to be sure of bread and a place to live, to live something like the 'western' life which was denied to them even then.[126]

Despite his disputes as to the tactics of the Perónist party during Perón's time of exile, in 1973 Jauretche continued to maintain that the victory of Perónism was the victory of youth, and of those who thought youthfully. He saw as 'necessary' a clash between those whose thinking was youthful and those whose thought was old. He recalled the 'Democratic Union' - conservatives, oligarchs, socialists and communists - who had combined against Perón under the patronage of U.S. Ambassador Braden, and stated of them decades later: 'Those people had stopped in time. They did not understand that the country was in a leap forward; they did not understand that it was the young people'. He wrote that he hoped his old Perónista comrades would consider the victory of youth a cause for joy. He referred to the use of the word 'socialism' by the young as being a drawback. Although he also considered the use of the term 'national socialism' as a drawback for obvious reasons, and also because it was an imported term, he nonetheless

125 Arturo M. Jauretche Los profetas del odio (The Prophets of Hate, 1957).

126 Ibid.

regarded it as a more accurate description for Justicialism than socialism.[127]

Jauretche continues to be honoured by the official governing Partido Justicialista. The Government of Nestor Kirchner declared the birthday of Jauretche, 13 November, National Thinking Day. A University in Buenos Aires is named after him.

While the corporatist and national syndicalist ideologies that emerged in France, Spain, and Italy, influenced the Nationalist Right in Argentina, Left-wing syndicalism had a major impact on the Argentine labour movement. Syndicalism had a larger following among the trades unions than orthodox socialism. It was in response to the growing syndicalist labour movement that the government in a conciliatory move established the National Labour Department in 1907.[128] This is where Perón established his power base decades later, and began to develop his doctrine through his direct interaction with the unions.

127 Arturo M. Jauretche, 'Reflections on the Victory', *Quiz* Journal, No. 3, July 1973.

128 Luis Alberto Romero, *A History of Argentina in the Twentieth Century* (Pennsylvania State University, 2002), 21-22.

Third Position: Beyond Capitalism and Communism

During the Cold War, when states were being cajoled and scared into supporting one or another of the antagonists, Perón reiterated that Justicialism is as much opposed to capitalism as to communism, and beyond that is opposed to the imposition of great power hegemony. Already in 1950 Perón had described his doctrine as a 'Third Position' in a speech to parliament.[129]

Unlike other Latin American anti-communists, whose answer to communism was merely counter violence, Perón understood that an idea could only be defeated by a superior idea. Communism had merely been a reaction to capitalism; its mirror image, and both are anti-human. Both 'insectify' humanity; that is, both aim to reduce man to the level of a drone, rather than towards a higher – ultimately spiritual – meaning.

The rejection by Perónism of capitalism and Marxism, and of the 'Western bloc' headed by the USA, and the Eastern, headed by the USSR, which he saw as imperialism working in unison to run the world, placed Argentina in a 'third position' in the world of power politics.

Jill Hedges points out that this 'third position' was the forerunner of what would become the 'Third World'.[130] Salbuchi writes that the socio-economic doctrine of Justicialism was the basis of this 'third position' applied to the diplomatic and geopolitical realms: 'All these and many other government policies, measures and doctrines later went under the name of "Third Position", i.e., non-alignment with neither of the superpowers: U.S.-U.K. nor the USSR. PsyWar tactics later downgraded this concept to "Third World", which became synonymous with poverty and destitution'.[131]

In 1969 Perón, in referring to the division of the world between

129 Perón, Ménsaje al Parlamento, 1 May 1950.

130 Jill Hedges, op. cit., 132.

131 Adrian Salbuchi, op. cit.

the USA and the USSR described Justicialism as a 'Third Position' that rejected both:

> For a quarter of a century, the Justicialist Revolution in Argentina promoted a popular transformative movement without bloodshed that, responding to its evolution, has given birth to a 'third position' that is equally distant ideologically from the dominant imperialisms and from the system they tried to impose throughout the world. The international synarchy, that harbours the imperialist interests in both zones, has promoted a *modus vivendi* that in the name of 'coexistence', opposes any other evolution that is not within the ideologies or systems imposed by them. So, the reaction of both imperialisms is characterised by violent domination, whether it is economic, military, or both at the same time, as we have been given evidence for in Latin America, in the zone of the Russian satellite states, or more specifically in Santo Domingo and Czechoslovakia.[132]

Having regained leadership of Argentina after 18 years of exile, Perón reiterated Argentina's 'third position' vis-à-vis world politics in a message to the Fourth Conference of Non-Aligned Countries in 1973:

> As far as foreign policy is concerned, the terms of our actions are clear and precise. We argue, from the very moment of the birth of Perónism, as basic principles and objectives in the international [realm], the following:
>
> 1. The overall defence of national sovereignty across our land and especially over Argentine Antarctica, the Falkland Islands and its independent islands.
>
> 2. Exercise of the Policy of Social Justice, Economic Independence and Sovereignty, as premises to ensure every

132 Perón, Anuario Las Bases (1969), 25, cited in *El Libro Rojo de Perón* (Buenos Aires: A Peña Lillo, 1973).

Perón supporters in Plaza de Mayo, Buenos Aires 1951

> people in the world their own happiness, by conducting their own justice and their own freedom.
>
> 3. The Third Position as a universal solution to dogmatic Marxism and demoliberalism international capitalism, leading to the annulment of the entire imperialist domination in the world.[133]

Speaking to the General Confederation of Labour in 1973, as part of a weekly discourse to workers at CGT headquarters, Perón outlined the character of the Justicialist revolution vis-à-vis the world situation and the super-powers. At this time, it is evident that much of what Perón was saying was an attempt to clarify Justicialist doctrine after his exile had seen a bitter and even bloody rivalry develop between Left and Right factions of Perónism. In this lecture he avers to the conflict between the labour movement leadership, and the Leftist faction that he – interestingly – calls 'Trots'; that is, Trotskyites.

133 Perón, 'Message to the Fourth Conference of Non-Aligned Countries', Algeria, 9 July 1973.

> Today I would like to address an issue that is especially important for the moment we live. It is this apparent controversy that seems to have occurred in some sectors of Perónism, the fight that apparently has been raised between union bureaucracy on the one hand, and the *Trots,* on the other.[134]

After Perón's exile in 1955, when there was a long era of repression of everything and everyone associated with Perón, many of the young generation became Perónists based on the legends of their parents and grandparents, and engaged in guerrilla warfare. Perón's view, in exile, was that the various factions within Justicialism would be reconciled on his return to Argentina. What transpired was a bloody conflict between Perónist factions, marked by the shoot-out at Ezeiza airport between Leftist and Rightist factions awaiting Perón's return. The factions were not reconciled; the ultra-Left intensified its guerrilla warfare, prompting the army to overthrow Isabel Perón in 1976.[135]

Perón referred to the wide variety of views within the Justicialist movement, stating that: 'I have always handled the Perónist movement with greater tolerance in that sense, because I think that those who join and live in a mass movement such as the Perónist should have absolute freedom to think, to feel and to act for the benefit of the same movement'.[136] Perón identified three currents within the movement, which we might term ultra-Leftist, 'conservative', and those who are truly Perónists insofar as they have transcended the old dichotomy:

> Certainly, in all revolutionary movements there are three kinds of approaches: first, that of the hurried, who believe that everything is going slowly, not doing anything, because they do not break things or people are not being killed. Another sector is made up of latecomers, those who do

134 Perón, 'Character of the Perónist Revolution', talk to the General Confederation of Labour 30 July1973.

135 This will be considered in a later chapter.

136 Ibid.

> not want anything done, and then do everything possible so that this revolution is not made. Between these two extremes there is a balanced approach not to go further or stay longer, but to do everything possible for the benefit of the masses, who are the most deserving.[137]

It is relevant to note that Justicialist administrations since the death of Perón have been accused of veering one way or another: Menem to the so-called 'right',[138] and what is termed the 'Left' of the Kirchner administrations.

Perón defined 'revolution' as structural change according to the social development of humanity, drawing from the ancient Greek conception of affecting change harmoniously, and without recourse to methods that make the 'cure worse than the disease'. Again, it is a reference to the crypto-Trotskyite advocates of permanent revolution who were undermining the Perónist revolution in the name of Perón:

> Revolution is likely to be as old as the world, because the world has never been static, but has always been in constant evolution, and revolutions are always part of that evolution. Perhaps the inventors of organised revolution have been the Greeks, who gave us the Greek *demos* of the Plato Revolution. They, perhaps, were the inventors of organised revolution, but the Greece of that time, before launching the revolution, placed at the forefront of all its universities a phrase that indicates what the revolution should be. They said: 'Everything in its extent and harmoniously'. That is the revolution: the changes made to your needs harmoniously, not so that the remedy is worse than the disease.

137 Ibid.

138 Or more accurately to neoliberalism which is not Right-wing. For a discussion on the intrinsically anti-capitalist nature of the true Right, and why neoliberal economics is not Right-wing, see K. R. Bolton, 'Marx Contra Marx: A Conservative Interpretation of the Communist Manifesto', Traditional Britain Group, http://www.traditionalbritain.org/content/marx-contra-marx-conservative-interpretation-communist-manifesto

> When talking about revolution, some believe that force is made with bombs and bullets. Revolution, in its true sense, is the structural changes needed according to the evolution of humanity, which is controlling all changes to be made.[139]

Perón stated that man is really only a passive agent of revolution or social evolution insofar as it proceeds according to organic historical laws, or 'historical fatalism':

> Man often believes he is the one that produces the evolution. In this, as in many other things, man is a little *messenger.* Because evolution is what he has to accept and to which he must adapt. Consequently, all that man can do is to agree with this development that he does not dominate; it is the work of nature and historical fatalism. He is only an agent that creates a system to serve that evolution and is placed within it. It means that the revolution that we speak of is not a cause but an effect of these developments.[140]

Perón proceeds with his own historical dialectic. He states that man creates social and political systems according to the requirements thrown up by the dialectical, or 'fatal' laws of history. This is the same as stating that political, economic, philosophical and other systems emerge according to what the Germans coined as the *zeitgeist*; literally the 'spirit of the age'. Hence, that is why Perón states that man can only be a messenger of that spirit. He can only work within that 'spirit of the age', no matter how he might rant against it. That is why despite Marx's attempt to establish a historical dialectic that would overthrow capitalism, his own ideology was merely a reflection, like capitalism, of the same *zeitgeist* of the 19th century: namely, economics. Hence, Perón places Marxism within the same context as capitalism, and states that Marxism is just another 'capitalist system':

139 Perón, 'Character of the Perónist Revolution', op. cit.

140 Ibid.

> Therefore, synthetically [dialectally] considering history, we see in the corresponding medieval feudal system that the Middle Ages is a product of the evolution of mankind. The feudal system is what man created to be able to walk within that system.
>
> Then comes the stage of medieval nationalism, i.e. the formation of nationalities. And there are the demoliberal-born capitalist system and the communist system, because both are born in the eighteenth century and developed in this century and part of the nineteenth century. One is individualistic capitalism, and the other is state capitalism. In the background are two capitalist systems.
>
> However, these systems have served the nineteenth and early twentieth centuries, and today are already both outmoded. Not either one but both. And I'll say why they are outmoded, why they have been overcome by evolution: The demoliberal-capitalist system is outdated, because it was created to serve the stage of nationalities, which now is ending, to give birth to the [historical-dialectical] stage of *continentalism*. Today men are already grouped by continents and not by nations, and that [demoliberal] system was created for that.[141]

The Rightist philosopher-historian Oswald Spengler had pointed out (and it seems likely that a man of Perón's erudition would have long been well-read on Spengler):

> Capitalism and Socialism are both of an age, intimately related, produced by the same outlook and burdened with the same tendencies. Socialism is nothing but the capitalism of the lower classes.[142]

What Spengler, a 'revolutionary conservative' of Weimer era

141 Ibid.

142 Oswald Spengler, *The Hour of Decision* (New York: Alfred A. Knopf, 1962) 141.

Germany, advocated was what he called 'Prussian Socialism' as an 'ethical attitude', 'not as a materialistic, economic principle'.[143] Justicialism is concerned primarily with forging a new humanity by subjecting economics to the moral, spiritual and cultural, which can only proceed once the basic material needs are fully met. Hence, Justicialism embraces what Spengler called 'ethical Socialism' in overcoming the materialistic outlook that is as much part of orthodox socialism as it is of capitalism. The ultra-Left within Justicialism failed to transcend the old mode of socialism rooted in the capitalist era, and to embrace the new. In Justicialism, and other 'third position' doctrines, economics is a start, and a servant; in capitalism and Marxism economics is the end and the master.

Perón here alludes to his concept of *continentalism,* which will be considered in detail in a later chapter, as an historical development transcending the old concept of the nation-state in favour of geopolitical blocs. This was an advanced concept in keeping with the new spirit of 'post-fascism' of certain thinkers such as Sir Oswald Mosley and Jean Thiriart. Perón knew both of these thinkers and leaders, who advocated united Europe as a 'third position', going beyond the petty-nationalism of pre-war and wartime 'fascism'. Only such geopolitical blocs could resist the hegemonic super powers. The concept of *continentalism,* which was embraced also by Hugo Chavez, the late Perónist leader of Venezuela in his call for a Latin American 'Bolivarian bloc', is of much relevance today in opposing the 'new world order', which the petty-states are unable to do alone.[144]

Perón believed that the two systems of capitalism and communism, under the superpower politics of the USA and the USSR respectively, were converging at the expense of people who did not want to be subjected to either. His answer was a Latin American bloc that he had worked towards already

143 Ibid., footnote 3.

144 For present-day geopolitical thinking on such transnational blocs see K. R. Bolton, *Geopolitics of the Indo-Pacific* (London: Black House Publishing, 2013).

during the 1950s. He saw the two superpowers coming together to divide the post-war world and acquiescing to one another's colonial invasions. The Latin American geopolitical bloc would form a 'third world':

> We have seen that after the Second World War occurs the Yalta Conference, where the bourgeoisie and communism agree. Next comes Potsdam, where treaties are made that allow shortly after Santo Domingo to be occupied by forty thousand *Marines* of Yankee imperialism. Soon after Czechoslovakia was occupied by Warsaw Pact forces, by the Russians, but with the *okay* of the Yankees. If they did not agree, well, they hide it very well. A few days ago, Brezhnev made a friendly visit to President Nixon. Words are made demonstrating they are in agreement. I think it is constructive to agree, but more constructive is that we form a third world.[145]

The choice facing the nations is that of 'Yankee imperialism or Soviet imperialism, or a third world'... 'Only the formation of a third world could be a guarantee that humanity could enjoy a better world in the future. But for that, the third world has to be organised and strengthened'.[146]

Perón then alluded to the origins of the Justicialist 'third position' as far back as the 1940s, in advocating new alliances:

> Almost thirty years ago, we, from here, launched the famous third position, which then apparently fell into the void, because the world war was over. They laughed at us. But twenty-seven years have passed since then, and today three-quarters of the world is pushing to be in the third world.[147]

145 Perón, op. cit.

146 Ibid.

147 Ibid.

Perón urged the Justicialists to 'think big' and to look outwardly toward the world, 'in which we will make our destiny, or succumb to the same adversity that others succumb'.

> You cannot think with the smallness of the time when everyone wanted to enjoy and no one wanted to jeopardise their fate or their future happiness to associate with that of others. Working today for the happiness of your neighbour is working well for the happiness of everyone else.[148]

Perón returned to the immediate aim of uniting a Latin bloc, this *continentalism* being the current trend of historical development, where Europe, Asia and Africa were uniting into geopolitical blocs.

> I think this is the way of our revolution. If we understand that there will be another revolution that may be based on the objectives for which we stand, integrating the Latin American continent, which is the last that will be left to integrate. All others have. Europe has built almost on a policy of confederal association to defend a future that they see with tremendous clarity. Asia is being integrated, as is Africa. And we're the last region.[149]

Referring to the pioneering efforts for geopolitical integration that Perón initiated during his first presidency, he recalled:

> In 1948 we made a treaty of economic complementation in Chile, seeking to create the Latin American economic community. We were very successful initially, almost all Latin American countries except the known *sepoys*,[150] came together and joined the treaty of economic complementarity. We were quick in this, and Europe did it with the Treaty of Rome in 1958, ten years after us. And now we're twenty

148 Ibid.

149 Ibid.

150 Sepoy is a reference to those subservient to British and U.S. imperialism.

> years behind them. Undoubtedly, we fell under the rule of U.S. imperialism, which allowed these countries to join, while Latin America has been apart and always fighting against the other, so that unity does not occur.[151]

It is notable that Perón alludes to Europe uniting under U.S. terms and approval.[152] On the other hand, attempts to form 'third position' blocs by the Arab states and Latin America were aborted. Perón posed and answered the question as to why U.S. imperialism permitted the confederation of Europe, but not that of Arabia and Latin America:

> Why do they have [European integration]? Very simply, because they are running out of raw materials and are wanting to conserve as satellite countries those with large reserves of food and raw materials for the overcrowding that is already 25 or 30 years away. They want us to work for them and then give them our food and raw materials. Why? **Because overdeveloped countries are the poorest in the future and underdeveloped countries are the richest in the future;** they will have the raw materials and food.[153]

The near future would find states either united, or dominated by imperialism. Perón referred to the threat by the Middle East to shut off oil supplies at the time (the so-called 'oil crisis') with the threat of invasion from the USA in response. That is what the plutocrats would do to any states that came against them. Perón concluded his talk again with references to the ultra-Left youth that were threatening the stability of the state and the unity of the Justicialist movement:

---

151 Perón, '*Character of the Perónist Revolution*', op. cit.

152 The European Union is a far cry from the Europe-a-nation envisaged by Perón's friends, Mosley and Thiriart, who aimed to create a Europe of the spirit and not of money. For the origins of the current European Union and the role played by bankers and Freemasons, see K. R. Bolton, 'introduction' to Hilaire Belloc's *Europe and the Faith* (London: Black House Publishing, 2012), 26-32.

153 Perón, '*Character of the Perónist Revolution*', op. cit

Comrades, what we have maintained for the past thirty years has been the truth. And that's why we won. When we hurried and wanted to run too fast, we had an opposition that blocked our way. But the truth remained standing. What has triumphed is not Perónism, is not us, and not me. What has triumphed is the truth, which is what always wins. So I think, comrades, that all those who are revolutionary and they want to fight without necessity, are not thinking. **We, the Justicialists, we have already shown that we are patient, that we are prudent, we hold reason and truth, and we have never used violence to impose ourselves. We have suffered and endured violence, but we have not been violent, because we are opposed to these methods. He who has the truth does not need violence, and that violence has never had the truth.** So all those youth who hastily criticise because we do not hurry, because God forbid if the boys were not in a hurry, you have to tell them as the Greeks stated: 'Everything in its extent and harmoniously'. So arrive not by violent struggle: arrive by rational and intelligent action within its extent and harmoniously.[154]

154 Ibid.

The Perónist State

With the social principles
That Perón has established
The entire people are united
And cry from the heart:
Long Live Perón! Long Live Perón[155]

There were three regimes in which Perón served as president, and therefore these are the ones that most closely reflect Perónism, while it is a matter of contention as to how faithfully subsequent governments headed by the Justicialist Party have followed Perón's doctrine.

As we have seen in the opening chapter, Perón had already made his mark on Argentine politics during the 1940's. As Secretary of Labour, Perón established the National Institute for Social Insurance (INPS), converting voluntary pension schemes into compulsory insurance, which covered 80% of the population by 1955. The scheme was one of the few of the Perónist era that was retained by the post-1955 regimes. Employers were obliged to provide severance pay and accident compensation. Labour courts were established to hear grievances. In 1945 Perón introduced the *aguinaldo*, an end of year bonus that provided each worker with a lump sum of one-twelfth of the yearly wage; and the National Institute of Compensation, which implemented a minimum wage and collated data on wages, prices and living standards.

A recent summation of Argentine labour laws by the International Labour Organisation comments: 'Some of the most outstanding labour legislation in the country was first introduced by Decree-Laws between 1943 and 1945 by the then Secretary of Labour, Colonel Perón'.[156]

155 From Perónist youth anthem, 'The Perónist Boys' (Los Muchachos Perónistas).

156 Arturo Bronstein, 'National Labour Law Profile: Republic of Argentina', International Labour Organisation, http://www.ilo.org/ifpdial/information-resources/national-labour-law-profiles/WCMS_158890/lang--en/index.htm

Celina Andreassi states of the Perónist regime:

> The period 1946-1955 marked a turning point in the economic development of the country. Up until that point, the economy had been characterised by a model based around agricultural exports, dominated by large landowners and a strong intervention of foreign companies—British, and increasingly from the U.S. This model had started to weaken during the 1930's, but it was not until the mid-1940s that it was replaced by what became known as 'import substitution industrialisation' (ISI).
>
> This new economic paradigm was based around the development of labour-intensive light industry to create jobs and produce domestic goods for the internal market. The State played an important role in channelling income from agricultural exports to industry, raising import tariffs, and nationalising foreign-owned companies such as the railways, gas, phone and electricity.
>
> The political model that accompanied these economic changes was based on a class alliance between the workers, industrial employers, the Armed Forces and the Catholic Church. However, this alliance excluded the old landowners – 'the oligarchy' - who would become the number one enemy of the new government.[157]

157 Celina Andreassi, 'The History of Perónism' (Part I), *The Argentine Independent,* 11 October 2011.

Dr. Arturo Sampay and the 1949 Justicialist Constitution

The 1949 Justicialist Constitution is a key document not merely in terms of the legal governmental structure of Perón's Argentina, but because it incorporates the doctrine of Justicialism.

The legal and constitutional scholar, Dr. Arturo E. Sampay, drafted the Perónist Constitution. The Constitution decreed into law the principles of distributive justice, establishing the State as the 'manager of the common good'; nationalising essential services, banking, foreign exchange and trade. Family rights were enshrined as the 'primary and fundamental core of society'. Also enshrined were charters of rights for the elderly and for workers. The development of a 'national culture' was affirmed as a State duty.

Sampay was a scholar of international repute. His seminal book, *Introduction to the Theory of the State*, was widely read internationally. He wrote books on constitutionalism, two on the 1949 constitution being published in Paris. When President Charles de Gaulle sought to reform the institutions of France to establish the Fifth Republic, he turned to the Perónist Constitution for guidance. In 1971 aspects of the 1949 Constitution were even incorporated into the Constitution of Salvador Allende's Chile, where Sampay was invited to lecture. In 1952 Sampay left Argentina as a result of intrigues within the Perónist movement, but never relinquished Justicialism, and remains an honoured figure among Perónists.

The regime that ousted Perón, determined to obliterate every vestige of his work, abrogated the 1949 Constitution in 1956, and returned to 19th century principles of free trade. While the post-Perónist regime imposed a bloodthirsty tyranny, it also withdrew the state from all the productive and creative realms that had been enacted under Perónism. Sampay observed that the abrogation of the 1949 Constitution and the entry of Argentina into the International Monetary Fund were related issues, both leading

Dr Arturo Sampay drafted the 1949 Argentine Constitution which granted workers legal rights, and better working conditions.

to the destruction of Argentina as a sovereign and socially just nation. Sampay returned from exile in 1958, but his professional career was closed to him. With the return of Perón from exile, Sampay resumed his Chair at the University of Buenos Aires. He wrote further books, including *Constitution and People*, and *The Constitutions of Argentina.* He and his works were again suppressed with the overthrow of Isabel Perón.[158]

Sampay's own philosophical outlook accorded with the principles that Perón wished to fulfil. Sampay held that each state must find the legal and constitutional systems that accord with their own character through what he termed 'political realism'. His philosophy has been called 'Aristolean-Thomism', indicating the proximity his ideas had with Catholic social doctrine. He was educated by the noted Bishop Olgiati and by the Catholic philosopher Jacques Maritain.

158 Alberto R. Gonzalez Arzac, 'Tribute to Arturo Enrique Sampay', speech delivered on 4 May 2004 at the House of Representatives of the Province of Buenos Aires (La Plata). Arzac served as Secretary of the Interior of the province of Buenos Aires (1962-1963), professor of constitutional law at the University of Buenos Aires (1973-1976) , and inspector general of Justice of the Nation (1989-1990).

Sampay repudiated the liberal, 'Enlightenment' doctrines that had proceeded from revolutionary French Jacobinism and U.S. constitutionalism, and therefore rejected 'liberal democracy' as 'agnostic, relativistic', and 'leading fatally to Caesarian democracy'.[159] By the latter he meant that it is liberal-democracy that leads to tyranny in the name of the 'majority'. Certainly the result of liberal-democracy in France, under the slogan of 'Liberty, Equality, Fraternity', was the Jacobin tyranny and the 'Reign of Terror'. Bolshevism had arisen from the same origins. It was the result of a doctrine that dethroned God and the spiritual ; what Sampay saw as the agnostic and relativistic outlook of liberalism.

For Sampay the State is not something that arises from 'nature', as the drawing room intellectuals of 18th Century France perceived 'nature', but arose as a cultural entity from the people. Hence there is no 'universal law', or universal concept of the State, under which the entire world should be subjected, as in today's U.S. drive for a 'new world order'. Each people brings forth its own concept of the State, constitution and laws according to its historical and cultural circumstances. This is a rejection of internationalism, or 'globalisation' as it is now called.

In critiquing the 1853 Argentine Constitution, Sampay mounts a broad attack on Liberalism and its secular, agnostic dethroning of the spiritual and cultural, in favour of the economic. The political and the economic orders are rather, under Sampay's doctrine, and under Justicialism, based on cultural and moral laws that are ultimately based on the traditional place of God, before the 'Enlightenment' enthroned Man as the centre of the universe:

> Agnosticism, official philosophy of the liberal Argentine, is the negation of morality ... Being a human rather than institutional crisis, it is clear that without a reintegration

159 A. E. Sampay, *La crisis del estado de derecho liberal - burgués* (Buenos Aires, Losada: 1942).

> of Culture the highest values of Christianity will not be restored morally, and thus politically.[160]

'Universal human rights' which have been enshrined as a war code by the United Nations Organisation in its 'U.N. Universal Declaration on Human Rights', as a justification for U.S. and U.N. intervention in the affairs of states, stems from the Liberal concepts of law and rights as deriving from the human interpretation of what is 'natural', rather than from what is divine. Therefore, these Liberal laws and rights are held to be 'universal', and to be enforced on all states and peoples, regardless of their traditions and history. Politically this was expressed by Jacobinism[161] and by U.S. legalism[162]. The concept of the 'new world order' is an expression of it, as is the slogan on the 'Great Seal of the United States: *Novus Ordo Seclorum* (new secular order). Writing of these influences on the 1853 Constitution, Sampay stated:

> The declaration of natural rights acquired eminent Enlightenment political dimensions through the influence it exerts on the Declaration of Independence of the United States and the French Revolution ... The result is that the chapter on the Declarations, Rights and Guarantees [of the 1853 Argentine Constitution] meant the naturalism of the Enlightenment as the *a priori* forms or logos of all individual rights.[163]

Sampay traced the origin of the Liberal doctrines that had come to Argentina, and indeed one can say over much of Latin America, to 'Illuminism',[164] that is, the Order of the Illuminati, the crypto-Masonic secret society founded in Bavaria, in 1776,

160 A. E. Sampay, *The Philosophy of the Enlightenment in the Constitution of 1853*, (Buenos Aires: Ed Depalma, 1944), 11-12.

161 'Declaration on the Rights of Man and the Citizen'.

162 U.S. Constitution and Bill of Rights, and U.S. Declaration of Independence.

163 A. E. Sampay, *The Philosophy of the Enlightenment*, *op. cit.*, 26-28.

164 Ibid., 14.

by Professor Adam Weishaupt.[165] The Illuminati provided a doctrinal and organisational basis for the French Revolution, with the aim of destroying the traditional order and establishing a world state on communistic lines. It is notable that Perón referred to the influence of Freemasonry on the politics of Argentina, calling it part of an 'international synarchy'. We will consider this in a later chapter. Sampay also regarded the use of 'planned immigration using Protestants' as a means of changing the character of Argentina, since the Protestant work ethic was used as a religious justification for capitalist exploitation.[166]

The Freemasonic nature of Enlightenment doctrine, the French Revolution, and the various revolutions during the mid 1800s and early 1900s, was recognised by the Catholic Church. The encyclical of Pope Leo XIII written in 1884, entitled *Humanum Genus*[167] charges Masonry with being the revolutionary advocate of a 'naturalistic' religion, which is what Sampay was referring to. Many states prior to and during the Second World War exposed and prohibited Masonry as a subversive organisation, including Franquist Spain, Vichy France, Salazar's Portugal and the Axis states. A present day Perónist scholar, Alberto Buela, in explaining Sampay's doctrines, states of this that the 'naturalistic' religion of Masonry and Illuminism attributes 'human reason with absolute autonomy', creating a 'new god', the 'goddess of reason',[168] quoting Sampay that this 'carries the secularisation of

---

165 See Professor John Robison, Proofs of a Conspiracy (1798), text online at: http://www.sacred-texts.com/sro/pc/index.htm?utm_source=Gawker+Newsletter&utm_campaign=a7dc1e6416-UA-142218-2&utm_medium=email

166 *Sampay, op. cit., 13. For the capitalistic nature of Protestantism see Max Weber, The Protestant Ethic and the Spirit of Capitalism (1905), online at: http://www.d.umn.edu/cla/faculty/jhamlin/1095/The%20Protestant%20Ethic%20and%20the%20Spirit%20of%20Capitalism.pdf*

167 The Catholic Encyclopaedia, 1910, cites encyclicals by 17 Popes condemning Masonry, from Clement XII in 1738 to Leo XIII in 1890.

168 This 'goddess of reason', it might be noted, took tangible form as an actress paraded through the streets of Paris by Jacobin mobs, crowned, and enthroned on the altar of the Cathedral of Notre Dame, where the 'rationalists' and 'liberal-democrats' worshipped her as the embodiment of 'reason' on the ruins of Catholicism. The Statue of Liberty at New York represents the same 'goddess', having been a completely Masonic enterprise, designed by a Mason and consecrated at New York by the Masonic Lodge. (The architect of the statue, Frederic-Auguste Bartholdi, and the designer of the

intelligence which characterises modernity'.[169] The rationalist-liberal dogma is at the root of modernist doctrines that enthrone man-as-god. Among these are liberalism and both capitalism and communism.

Sampay stated that the individual was conflicted between self-interest and his development as a social being, and it was the aim of the State to balance these drives. He wrote that 'the political act as realism, being adapted to the local and historical circumstances, should tend to be an organic development of each country'.[170] The legal doctrine adopted by Perónism rejected internationalistic and liberal-humanist notions of law that attempt to impose a uniform international system over all states, culminating in a world state. Sampay regarded the concept of law and constitution as 'organic', as developing from the specific historical circumstances and characteristics of nations, and not as part of some nebulous universal theory of 'humanity'.

The 1949 constitution was a repudiation of the constitutional principles that had ruled Argentina since 1853. This reflected the liberalism of the time based, stated Sampay 'on an absolute concept of ownership and the belief that private action, driven by [self] interest alone would be able to automatically generate a just order'.[171] The Perónist political scientist Dr. Alfredo Calcagno comments:

---

structural framework, Gustave Eiffel, were both Masons). The principal architect of the pedestal was Bro. Richard M. Hunt. The Ceremony of Consecration of the statue was organised by the New York State Grand Lodge. On 28 October 1886, Edward M. L. Ehlers, Grand Secretary of Continental Lodge 287, read a list of items that were placed in a copper box in the cornerstone, among which was a parchment listing the Grand Lodge officers. A traditional Masonic ceremony was observed.

169 Alberto Buela, 'Sampay como pensador nacional, popular y católico', National Technological University, 22 March 2012; citing Sampay, *The philosophy of the Enlightenment, op. cit., 51.*

170 Quoted by Dr. Alfredo Eric Calcagno, 'Tribute to Arturo Sampay', Miradas al Sur, No. 186, 24 July 2011.

171 Quoted by Calcagno, 'The Basic Directions of the two Constitutions of 1853 and 1949', Miradas al Sur, No. 215, 1 July 2012.

> The basic dilemma was exclusion or inclusion. One of the worst results of liberalism, neoliberalism, was exclusion. In the opposite direction, the 1949 Constitution established, as Sampay stated, 'an economic order sustained by social justice and strengthening of the national consciousness as the basis of defence of our political sovereignty'.[172]

The Perónist constitution aimed at a policy of inclusion for every sector of Argentine society, social justice being the means of integrating the previously excluded classes into the totality of a new state, based on the development of a new national consciousness among all classes.

In speaking to the Constituent Assembly in 1949, Sampay cogently defined exactly what the Perónist conception of Justicialism is, stating: 'social justice is understood as that which orders the interrelationships of social groups, professional groups and classes with individual obligations, moving everyone to give to others in participation in the general welfare'.[173]

The 1949 Constitution established the economic principles of social justice that were to be incorporated into the running of society:

> Wealth, income and interest on capital are exclusive fruits of human labour,
>
> Capital must be at the service of the national economy and have welfare as its main object ; various forms of exploitation cannot thwart common welfare of the Argentine people,
>
> The organisation and use of wealth are intended for the welfare of the people, within an economic order in accordance with the principles of social justice.

172 Ibid.

173 Quoted by Felipe A. Arzac Gonzalez, former Associate Judge of the Supreme Court and Professor of Constitutional Law, Miradas al Sur, No. 129, 6 November 2010.

A present-day Perónist scholar, Dr. Alberto Buela, states of the Sampay Constitution, that it,

> rescues social rights of the working people, the social function of property, the direction of the economy in terms of the common good, the principle of reciprocity, the family as primary and indissoluble in society, the rights of the elderly, the principles of land reform, the moral illegitimacy of usurious activity, the nationalisation of energy sources such as public assets that may not be sold to individuals for exploitation, university training policy, child education in the practice of the personal, domestic, professional and civic virtues.[174]

Dr. Felipe Gonzalez defines the purpose of a 'company' under Justicialism, as defined by Sampay in the 1949 Constitution:

> The company as a service to the community and its members. Now, after explaining social justice and its relation to the distribution of business profits, [Sampay] made a brief report on the nature and function of companies. As explained by the text of the Perónist Constitution, the only source of wealth -after natural endowment - is human labour. Capital is also accumulated human labour. Then we must ask, what is the company? The company is a grouping which operates to meet human needs. The needs of the group members and others for whom the product is intended. This means that the legitimacy of the company is given because its purpose is to meet human needs and the legitimacy of the benefit is to meet the needs of the group working in the company, from the members dedicated to organising production, to those who operate the machines, to those who clean the floor, all of whom deserve to be considered with dignity and consideration that their work as a whole constitutes the company product.[175]

174 Alberto Buela, 'Sampay como pensador nacional, popular y católico', National Technological University, 22 March 2012.

175 Felipe A. Arzac Gonzalez, 'The Participation of Workers: Analysis of one of the

Again, the premise is corporatist in nature, in this instance, the business company becomes more than an economic entity serving the sole interests of its owner or outside shareholders. The company itself is an organic entity, with each individual a vital component for the working of the whole. Workers receive a share of the corporate profits.

Workers' Bill of Rights

One of the first measures of the Perónist regime was to enact a 'Bill of Rights of the Workers', which was incorporated into the 1949 Constitution. At this early stage, the doctrine of Justicialism had already been formulated. Within this workers' Bill of Rights are all the primary features of Justicialism: the 'humanisation of capital', and the harmonisation of the different productive and creative elements into a national community. In particular, economics was subordinated to spiritual and moral values. This Bill of Rights, and the socio-economic programme that it initiated is therefore much more than a party programme for the implementation of a welfare state. Welfarism under social democracy is an end in itself and geared entirely to economic motives; the social justice of Perónism is something of a different character. The Bill of Rights of the Worker states:

> Proclaimed by His Excellency the President of the Argentine Republic, General Juan Perón, at Buenos Aires, on February 24th 1947.
>
> The President of the Argentine Republic, true interpreter of the aspiration for social justice cherished by the peoples, and bearing in mind that the rights deriving from work, as also the individual liberties, constitute the natural, inalienable and imprescriptable attributes of human beings, and that if these rights are ignored or injured they result in social antagonisms, struggles and unrest, considers it necessary

most recent projects that drove President Néstor Kirchner', Miradas al Sur, No. 129, 6 November 2010.

and advisable to expressly state them in a declaration, so that, in the present and in the future, this declaration may serve as a rule to guide the action of individuals and public powers tending to raise the standard of social culture, to dignify labour and to humanise capital as the best means of establishing a balance among the concurrent forces of economy and to strengthen, in a new juridical organisation, the principles which inspire social legislation. For all these reasons, and in accordance with the preceding aims and purposes, he solemnly sets forth the following.

I - The Right To Work

Work is the indispensable means to satisfy the spiritual and material needs of the individual and their community, the cause of all the conquests of civilisation and the foundation of general prosperity; therefore, the right of work must be protected by society, which must consider it with the dignity it deserves and must provide employment to all those in need of it.

II - The Right To A Fair Remuneration

Wealth, income and interest of capital being the exclusive outcome of human labour, the community must organise and reactivate the sources of production in such a manner as to make possible and ensure for the worker a moral and material remuneration which not only satisfies his vital needs but also compensates for the results obtained and the efforts carried out.

III - The Right To Capacitation

The improvement of the human condition and the preeminence of spiritual values impose the necessity of promoting the raising of the standard of culture and professional capability, endeavouring that all minds must be guided towards every field of knowledge; society must stimulate the individual effort providing the means by which, afforded the same opportunities, any individual may exercise his right to learn and perfect himself.

Workers in Buenos Aires celebrate the Justicialist Constitution 1949.

IV - The Right To Appropriate Working Conditions

From the considerations due to the human being, the importance of work as a social function, and the mutual respect among the concurrent factors of production, arises the rights of individuals to demand fair and appropriate conditions for the development of their activities and the obligation of society to watch over the strict observance of the precepts under which these conditions have been established and regulated.

V - The Right To The Preservation Of Health

The care of the physical and moral health of individuals must be one of society's principal and constant concerns. Society must see to it that the working regimes meet the necessary requirements of safety and hygiene, that they do not exceed the normal possibilities of human effort, and that they afford due periods for rest for recovery.

VI - The Right To Welfare

The right of workers to welfare, which may be summed up in the possibilities to obtain adequate dwelling, clothing and food, and to satisfy their own needs and those of their families without undue distress, so that they may work with pleasure, rest without worry, and enjoy in moderation spiritual and material expansions, imposes the social obligation of raising the standard of living and of work by means of the direct and indirect resources allowed by economic development.

VII - The Right To Social Security

The right of individuals to protection in cases of decrease, discontinuance or loss of their working capacity, imposes upon society the obligation of taking into its charge, unilaterally, the corresponding measures of compensation or of promoting systems of obligatory mutual aid, destined, both of them, to cover or to supplement the insufficiencies or inabilities proper to certain periods of life or those resulting from misfortunes arising from eventual risks.

VIII - The Right To The Protection Of His Family

The protection of the family is born from a natural feeling of the individual, since the family is the source of his highest sentiments of affection, and any effort tending to ensure its welfare must be encouraged and stimulated by the community as the most favourable means of achieving the improvement of mankind and the consolidation of the spiritual and moral principles which are the very essence of social relationship.

IX - The Right To Better Economic Conditions

Productive capacity and man's ambition to surpass himself find a natural incentive in the possibility of improving economic conditions, hence, society must support and encourage any individual initiative tending to achieve this aim, and stimulate the formation and utilization of capitals insofar as they constitute active elements of production and contribute to general prosperity.

X - The Right To The Defence Of Professional Interests

The right to unionise freely and to participate in other lawful activities devoted to the defence of professional interests constitute essential rights of the workers which society must respect, ensuring their free exercise and repressing any action which might impair or prevent it.

The Twenty Justicialist Principles

In 1950 Perón summarised Justicialism in twenty principles:

1. True democracy is the system where the Government carries out the will of the people defending a single objective: the interests of the people.

2. Perónism is an eminently popular movement. Every political clique is opposed to the popular interest and, therefore, it cannot be a Perónist organisation.

3. A Perónist must be at the service of the cause. He who, invoking the name of this cause, is really at the service of a political clique or a 'caudillo' (local political leader) is a Perónist by name only.

4. There is only one class of men for the Perónist cause: the workers.

5. In the New Argentina, work is a right which dignifies man and a duty, because it is only fair that each should produce at least what he consumes.

6. There can be nothing better for a Perónist than another Perónist.

7. No Perónist should presume to be more than he really is, nor should he adopt a position inferior to what his social status should be. When a Perónist starts to think that he is more important than he really is, he is about to become one of the oligarchy.

8. With reference to political action the scale of values for all Perónists is as follows: First, the Homeland; afterwards the cause, and then, the men themselves.

9. Politics do not constitute for us a definite objective but only a means of achieving the Homeland's welfare, represented by the happiness of the people and the greatness of the nation.

10. The two main branches of Perónism are Social Justice and Social Welfare. With these we envelop the people in an embrace of justice and love.

11. Perónism desires the establishment of national unity and the abolition of civil strife. It welcomes heroes but does not want martyrs.

12. In the New Argentina the only privileged ones are the children.

13. A Government without a doctrine is a body without a soul. That is why Perónism has established its own political, economic and social doctrine: Justicialism.

14. Justicialism is a new philosophical school of life. It is simple, practical, popular and endowed with deeply Christian and humanitarian sentiments.

15. As a political doctrine, Justicialism establishes a fair balance between the rights of the individual and those of the community.

16. As an economic doctrine, Justicialism achieves a true form of social economy by placing capital at the service of the national economy and this at the service of social welfare.

17. As a social doctrine, Justicialism presides over an adequate distribution of Social Justice, giving to each person the social rights he is entitled to.

18. We want a socially just, an economically free and a politically independent Argentina.

19. We are an organised State and a free people ruled by a centralised government.

20. The best of this land of ours is its people.[176]

A further Twenty Principles summarising Justicialism was formulated in 1955, and published in the periodical, *Mundo Perónista*, with the suggestion that readers make the axioms into a booklet that can be carried about and studied. The simple quotes from Perón nonetheless reflect the depth of Perónist doctrine. The premises are that the economic policy of social justice is but a means of achieving the elevation of the Argentine culture and people, which can only be accomplished if the nation is sovereign. The working masses are an integral a part of the nation-people-culture of the new Argentina. Capital and labour are reconciled in this unity by the role of the State in ensuring that capital works in the service of the nation and people, and not as the master. Justicialism is a national manifestation of a universal principle, which Perón called 'national socialism' and a 'Third Position' (Point 13). The underlying ethos is that of Christianity. The aim is to satisfy the material needs of man not as the end, but as the starting point for the elevation of the human culture and spirit.

Social Justice In The Living Thoughts Of Perón

1. Social Justice and Democracy - I understand that there is no integral democracy without social justice. (*A Docentes*, 21-2-45).

2. Trilogy of Social Justice - The Revolution to achieve perfect social justice has arrived at an understanding of the true trilogy: the worker, the patria, and the State. (*Al sindicato del vidrio*, 10-6-45).

3. Basic Postulates of Social Justice - We are forming a social conscience based on the three postulates of our social justice: in ethics, firstly, the elevation of social culture, secondly, bestowing dignity on labour, and thirdly, the

176 Perón, *speech at the Plaza de Mayo, 17 October 1950.*

humanisation of capital. (*A obreros maderos*, 24-9-45)

4. Social Justice and Government - The government should not view justice as an innate sentiment, but rather should ensure it. (*A Empleados*, 4-12-46)

5. Social Justice and Internal Peace - Argentina should set its internal peace on the rock base of social justice. (*En la concentración de Montjuich*, 23-6-47)

6. Social Justice and Economic Independence - I affirm that without economic independence there is no hope of social justice. (*Al Congreso de Organismos Sinicales*, 9-7-47)/

7. Social Justice and National Unity - Through social justice we have united all Argentines (*En Córdoba*, 23-2-48)

8. Social Justice and Universal Peace - Universal peace will only be possible when social justice rules over every people. (*Mensaje al Parlamento*, 1-5-48)

9. Concept of Social Justice - When we say social justice we desire that no one forgoes that which they deserve; that there won't be the exercise of power in excess; that everyone receives the compensation that their efforts deserve. (*A obreros vitivinicolas*, 1-8-49)

10. Requisites of Social Justice - To ensure justice the only thing one has to have is a little virtue in the heart and a little truth in the mind. (*A estudiantes chileños*, 17-9-49)

11. Limits of Social Justice - I promised to my people social justice and this has been achieved without any limit but that of justice itself. (*En Plaza Mayo*, 17-10-49)

12. Social Justice and Cooperativism - The cooperative spirit is the triumph of social justice and of the social conscience

of the Argentine people. (*A Cooperativas Agrarias*, 5-3-50)

13. Social Justice and the Third Position - In the social order, the third position between individualism and collectivism is the adoption of an intermediary system whose basic instrument is social justice. (*Ménsaje al Parlamento*, 1-5-50)

14. Social Justice and the Exploitation of Man -We only accept fully developed social justice in a Justicialist State that punishes the exploitation of man by man and doesn't accept the exploitation of man by the state. (*A la Unión Ferroviaria*, 31-7-50)

15. Social Justice and Liberty - Individual liberty formulates itself on the base of justice. (*En el Salón Blanco*, 26-9-50)

16. The arms of Perónism - The two arms of Perónism are social justice and social welfare. (*En Plaza Mayo*, 17-10-50)

17. Social Justice and Social Security - Social security is certainly a fundamental part of social justice, one of its most brilliant consequences. (*III Reunión Interamericana de Seguridad Social*, 12-3-51)

18. The Just and the Justicial - The old individualistic concept of the just has been for us converted into the new concept of the justicial, according to which each one should give one's self to everyone, but within a social function. (*Mundo Perónista*, 15-12-51)

19. Social Justice and Christianity - We have wisely understood the old Christian message of love, building a fraternal community organised upon the monolithic pedestal of justice. (*Mensaje de fin de año*, 31-12-51)

20. Goals of Social Justice - Our social justice does not only desire an equitable distribution of material values, but also a corresponding and just distribution of spiritual and moral goods. (*Mensaje al Parlamento*, 1-5-52)

The transcendent and redemptive character of Justicialism as part of a more universal doctrine aiming to create a new humanity puts Justicialism beyond mere 'popularism'. It is the doctrine that makes Perón enduring as a philosopher, that sustained the strength of Justicialism during decades of severe repression, and that, being a faith beyond mere politics, much less a party, suffers more damage from within, from traitors, opportunists, careerists and infiltrators, who have been unable or unwilling to carry forward the new synthesis.

Body, Mind and Soul: A Return to the Classical Ethos

Social justice, the harnessing of the economy and control of banking were means to an end under Perónism. Once the necessities of life were met, and more than met, providing a just reward for one's labour, life is granted the opportunity to go beyond the economic and material considerations that are the be-all and end-all of capitalism and Marxism. Justicialism achieved in practical terms what the Left-wing existential philosophers and psychologists could only theorise about: If the primary biological drives of human existence are satisfied, the individual is free to proceed to what the 1960s psychologists and existentialists were calling 'self-actualisation'. While this came to nothing more than a banal and easily controlled 'youth rebellion' in the USA and Western Europe, that ended up being self-destructive,[177] Perón's Argentina had met the material needs of its people, and opened up a new road to cultural and spiritual ascent towards the formation of a new humanity. This is what makes Perónism, like other variations of the 'third position', more than just a political or an economic doctrine. The Perónist became a spiritual fighter.

Perón's British contact, Sir Oswald Mosley, describing the new post-fascist doctrine that he called 'The Doctrine of Higher Forms', wrote:

> What then, is the purpose of it all? Is it just material achievement? Will the whole urge be satisfied when everyone has plenty to eat and drink, every possible assurance against sickness and old age, a house, a television set and a long seaside holiday each year? … …The ideal of creating a higher form on earth can now rise before men with the power of a spiritual purpose, which is not simply a philosophic abstraction but a concrete expression of a deep human desire.[178]

177 K. R. Bolton, *The Psychotic Left* (London: Black House Publishing, 2013), 148-234.

178 Oswald Mosley, *Europe: Faith and Plan* (Essex: Euphorion Books, 1958), 143, 146.

This is in contrast to the economic-driven conception of life that sees nothing beyond the satisfaction of humanity's material needs, to which Mosley posed the question: then what? He pointed out that communism has no answer, and wondered whether the orbiting of the *sputnik* satellite would be sufficient to relieve the tedium of communism?[179]

Perón wrote of wider cultural and spiritual implications, which also incorporated the importance of 'sports culture', that was to be implemented by the 1955-1960 Five Year Plan. The Justicialist doctrine is explained as one striving for individual and collective harmony and balance in mind, body and soul; the ancient Greek philosophy of the state. In fact Perón specifically refers to the classical Greek inspiration:

> In the government's Five-Year Plan we have established a definitive guidance for Argentina culture, a premise as old as the culture itself. This establishes that the educated man must have developed to being harmonious and balanced in both his intelligence and his soul and his body. We believe that all teaching or any culture that does not tend to balance wisdom with goodness and health in education is inharmonious, and, therefore, counterproductive to man.
>
> We want intelligence to be in the service of a good soul and a strong man. In this we are not inventing anything, we are going back to the Greeks who were able to establish that perfect balance in their men in the most glorious period of its history. So I said that this principle is as old as the culture itself. Unfortunately, men have abandoned those roads, but we want them back, because we believe that's the truth and because we believe that is the path that will lead our people to greatness and happiness because they fight.
>
> Undoubtedly, to set a goal and set a plan is not a work of

179 Ibid., 143-144.

art but a process of understanding. We have set this goal and have set a plan. The artwork consists of performing these goals, because reality and realisation are always on the design and planning. You will be the architects of the realisation of that goal and that plan, gentlemen. The credit will only be yours, since the conception of an objective as simple and the planning of such a simple idea, can only be carried out with the tenacity and perseverance to succeed.

As I say, the goal is simple. That the Argentine people harmoniously develop a comprehensive culture. What we need now is to reach the family and life itself to educate the soul. It is necessary to go to the family, the state, society and the people to reach the soul. We aspire that intelligence awakens in a healthy and vigorous body. We believe in a short-term aim that the country has five million athletes, not because this is a final goal, but it is the first objective to enable the ultimate goal that leads to the Argentina Republic being composed of twenty million athletes. Of course it's a matter of time. We will set the initial milestone, striving to reach that target with the youth first, because we believe that it would be difficult for us to start with elderly or mature men in the art of sport. It will be necessary for us to take the youth, to ripen in the heat of the health of sport and the bonhomie of sporting action.

For this reason, gentlemen, we have established a simple plan, simple, so that it can be achieved. Previously we made things too complicated to do them well.

Let's get to work to train athletes. Who is going to work? The State only? The people only? Only the family alone? Teachers alone? No, we will work with them all because if we do not do so we will not get anywhere. In this we need to put all government, people, teachers, army, all the forces of the nation, in the task of forming men strong and good, to succeed.

For that reason, gentlemen, the plan is very simple:. we will devote all teaching instruments to having a sporting outlook.

The Ministry of Education should organise children and youth, to enlighten their knowledge, strengthen them with sports and gymnastics, and make them useful men, wise and prudent, balanced individuals complete in their culture.

All that is up to the Ministry of Education which has to establish a plan for children, one for youth and one for the university, by category, in which each activity is to be performed. It is necessary to abandon the outdated forms of the gym - unfortunately we have all done gym at school, because that is where we learned to hate the gym, never to do it during the rest of our days – it was so bad. Fathers and mothers used to see a man or a woman who had no interest in teaching there and none of those who were there had any interest in learning… instead of engaging these children in healthy outdoor activity and the sun, which is the primary condition for sport and gymnastics. You have to take the field, the air and the sun, to take fresh air and strengthen your body, especially your lungs. So we have established that the Ministry of Education is to eliminate this type of gym and instead take the children two or three times a week to games, clubs, the outdoors, to do what they wish, because it is difficult at this age to induce them with more or less coercive measures. We are in favour of the child doing what he pleases in the sporting order, because that is where they will choose their destination as athletes.

We could talk about this at extraordinary length. We could speak of gymnastics in its entirety, and the same of sport. We would not say anything but repeat what has been said for millennia. What we have to do are exercises; exercises for body and soul.

What exercises? There are so many forms of exercise. Gymnastics is an activity that is not directed only at the body but also the soul of the individual. It is necessary that the soul is the determinant of the activity that they are going to practice.

But what I can say is that in our country we have to be eminently dedicated to sport, because that is the gateway for all bodily and spiritual activity of our young athletes.

We have like all peoples, an idiosyncrasy that is absolutely particular to us. We have to practice our activities in accordance with our idiosyncrasy.

With respect to adults, they belong to the Argentina Confederation of Sports, with all its organisations, federations, clubs, etc.

But there is one sector, the youth who for some reason does not study and therefore is not under the organisation of the Ministry of Education. That youth is scattered throughout the territory of the Republic and is much larger than we can imagine. That's where the Eva Perón Foundation acts. The Foundation, in this plan, has the mission to develop sport among this youth, where it is not directed by the Ministry of Education, or controlled or directed by the Argentina Confederation of Sports.

Also, we will enable adults to practice within student organisations or those of the Foundation and, finally, that the children can compete with adults in the competitions of the Argentina Confederation of Sports.

All this organisation has been launched. The government is currently, through the Ministry of Education, establishing an extensive network of youth clubs, which belong to the Department of Social Services for students. This is a social service. Just as in the Ministry there is a social service for employees and workers, there is also a social service for students, which is more natural and logical.

Some have criticized the appointment of spiritual counsellors in schools. What is the role the spiritual director must take everywhere, even in the family? It's very simple. What child has not had a problem, a complex or pain in life? The smaller is perhaps the more serious. And how many have had somewhere to turn to in times of sorrow or trouble? We want to systematise that the child always has a decent and good person to turn to at times of need. This will connect well with the Foundation and social services.

We have been in schools in which boys were taught 'Morals' as a subject, where the virtue of honesty was taught, but they were not taught to be honest, good and decent. They were taught virtues theoretically. And so we had a gang of bandits who knew a lot of about moral theory, but it was not practiced. We do not want to teach but to inculcate virtues. Children are taught to know a lot about honesty and then steal and commit all possible crimes. We have a different view of life. We have been working with the souls of men and we aim to have these spiritual advisors. To get to the soul of man is not to approach him when he is happy but when he is troubled by a problem that cannot be solved by himself alone. That's when you have to give a hand and some advice, because that's when the counsel meets its purpose. That is more beautiful, more real and more in tune with life.

I say this because I want to bring to the spirit of the delegates that this comprehensive work is the process of reform in which we are engaged. We are solving all those old habits, good and bad, to purify, to activate learning, to work with the human body, real and objectively, and not keep dreaming theoretically of chimeras never performed or later materialized.

We want people with these characteristics, but we should all be builders in the same task and the same responsibility. The more modest sports leader in the most remote place in the Republic, if fulfilling his duty well, has more value than the highest of the citizens or officials who cannot meet theirs. So I want to ask you, with the simplicity with which I always say these things, to work with us across the country implementing those wonderful papers that were presented at this conference and carried out with the full force of your souls and convictions. We have to provide support institutionally from the government and from the state.

Virtue conquers both a sports field and in the classroom or in every day life. And that virtue is what calls us. We will not take sport and gymnastics as an end but as a means to train men. And against this aspiration to train men to give the country and offer them to our future, we all have a common responsibility.

Therefore, on behalf of the government, I express my deep gratitude, gratitude to the humble citizens, modest, as you give of yourselves what the powerful and the potentates were never able to give.

And on behalf of the Foundation, ladies and gentlemen, I also express my deep appreciation. In this task I recognise that without your patriotism and selflessness throughout the Republic, perhaps we would not have been able to fulfil our duty to carry on the work of the Foundation.

I wish to ask you on behalf of the Foundation, that each of us continues to work tenaciously, with honesty and selflessness with which you have done so far. We continue to strive for the Foundation and to honour our homeland. So we can offer the world the example of a people who work and sacrifice to be better every day, to go conquering the human scale, that men deserve only the good and

> strong, so that sport is conducting those ideals of which we dream, for you to be the teachers who direct and channel these activities.[180]

Perón was a notable sportsman in a number of areas. In what is evidently a speech to a teachers congress not long prior to his ouster, Perón laid down numerous elements of Justicialist theory and practice:

- The duty of the State was to encourage the forging of a new Argentine after the classical Greek ideal of a balanced and harmonious individual, in mind, body and soul.
- The focus would be on inculcating in the youth a sense of civic virtue that would guide his life, and sports would play a major role in this, in developing the physical health as a basis of mental and spiritual health.
- Sports and athletics would be centrally directed and co-ordinated under State jurisdiction through organisations such as the Eva Perón Foundation and the Ministry of Education, working with the Argentina Confederation of Sports.
- Options for sports and athletics would be opened up rather than imposed, to make the activities joyful rather than burdensome.
- Spiritual counsellors would mentor the young to ensure that their problems, big and small, are addressed.

As in much else, these final months of Perón's presidency held out the prospect of a radical transformation, of which the previous years were a prelude. This however was cut short with the military coup. Much had already been achieved in inculcating civil virtues among the young, where the Justicialist ethos was taught to children from the earliest years of their education. As for sports, this had also been a feature of Perón's Argentina.

180 Perón, '*Towards the formation of a spiritually and physically healthy people*', 1955.

Poster for 1951 Pan American Games

Of the sporting events hosted by Argentina during Perón's presidency: The 1948 FIBA South American women's basketball championships resulted in Argentina's first ranking. In the 1949 world shooting championships, Argentina came third place, with 5 Gold medals.. In 1950 Argentina hosted the World Basketball Championship, wining the gold medal, beating the USA 64-50. In the final rounds Argentina had beaten Brazil 40-35, Chile 62-41, France 66-41, Egypt 68-33. At the 1950 Buenos Aires Grand Prix, Argentina won third behind first and second places for Italy. The 1953 Grand Prix put Argentina second place, behind Italy.

The Pan American Games of 1951, with 21 nations participating, was another resounding success for Argentina, winning 68 Gold medals, 47 Silver, and 39 Bronze. The USA in second place won 46 Gold, 33 Silver, and 19 Bronze. Argentina' total medal count was 154, the USA's 98, and Chile 39. The South American Championship in Athletics put Argentina in first ranking with 12 Gold, 10 Silver, 6 Bronze; while the runner-up, Brazil, had 10 Gold, 6 Silver, and 12 Bronze; each with a total of 28 medals.

At the 1955 Pan American Games held in March at Mexico City, the last games in which Perónist Argentina contested, Argentina ranked second among 22 nations, with the USA leading with 88 gold medal, followed by Argentina's 27 and Mexico's 17.

However, the large amount expended by the Perónist

administrations on sports and athletics was not for the purpose of demonstrating Argentines prowess in competitions with other states, nor in providing the masses with a harmless distraction from political realities. Clearly from Perón's detailed remarks in his 1955 speech he viewed sports and athletics as being for a higher purpose; that of instilling a renewed Classical ethos of balance and harmony within young generations of Argentineans: the manifestation of the Olympian spirit on the American continent.

The Role of Catholicism

The position of Catholicism that had been affirmed since 1946 was formalised. In March 1947 a state decree made religious instruction in primary and secondary schools compulsory. In July the Dirección General de Enseñanza Religiosa was established under the direction of two priests, to oversee education, appoint teachers and approve religious texts.

The 1949 Constitution upheld the social function of private property, providing for state expropriation if it failed to fulfil that function. Jill Hedges alludes to this measure as being regarded as 'quasi-communist'. Indeed, Spruille Braden in later years referred to Perón alternately as a 'fascist' and a 'communist'. This is to totally misunderstand or misinterpret the origins and aims of property as a social function. The principles are expounded in traditional Catholic social doctrine, particularly the Encyclicals of Leo and Pius, previously cited.

At a ceremony held on 10 April 1948, Carlo Bishop Nicholas, Bishop of Resistencia Chaco, presented Perón with the pectoral cross in recognition of his Christian social work. During the ceremony, attended by the Argentine Episcopate, Perón outlined the role of the Church and of Catholic doctrine in the State. He pointed out that even the drafters of the liberal constitution of 1853 had been obliged to recognise the role of the Church in Argentina. Nonetheless, Christ Himself had established the division of powers between temporal and spiritual authorities when he had advised: 'render unto Caesar that which is Caesar's and unto God that which is God's'. The Perónist state was guided by Catholic doctrines, but not dictated to by the Church hierarchy. That difference was to be a cause of Perón's ouster in 1955, when his political opponents exploited the breach. As stated previously, the Justicialist Constitution enacted the following year, was primarily the work of Dr. Arturo Sampay, a Catholic-inspired legal scholar.. Perón stated at the award ceremony:

> The Constitution of Argentina requires the elected

President to belong to the Roman Catholic Communion. This requirement, which has been much discussed, has, however, in my view, a clear sense that harmonises with the constitutional obligation, and to sustain the religion and is not in any way incompatible with the equally recognised right of freedom of religions. The President is the President of all the inhabitants of the country, whatever the religion they profess or even if they profess none. Therefore, the provisions to which I have referred cannot establish a submission of executive power, executive power as such, that is, as ruler of the state, to any other authority. Not submission, but the simple influence of the Church in the functions of government. Anything else would be to ignore the mandates of the Divine Master that in proposing to give unto God that which is God's and to Caesar what which is Caesar's, to establish a transparent distinction between the spiritual and civil jurisdictions. In that sense the government of the people is the more wonderful because of the recognition that Christ proclaimed the earthly power of Caesar when Caesar was hostile to his preaching and proselytising work.

But - and this conclusion is connected with my previous words - the fact that the Church does not have to obey the head of state, that is, to keep the division of powers, does not mean that the state would have to do without the Church. **The obligation to uphold the Catholic religion, and the President as belonging to Catholic worship, is one of the most commendable aspects of our Constitution,** because those who sanctioned this, despite the liberal inspiration reflected in all its rules, could not deny that the government of the people must be based on moral standards and **moral standards are rooted and based on religious precepts.** That idea is not indifferent to the progress of the Nation because even if there were moral rules common to several religions other differences undoubtedly exist. Equal treatment of women and men within the family, the sacramental character of marriage, respect for individual freedom, certain concepts of property and labour relations, as well as many other Christian standards are not shared by all religions. So clear is this that the so-called Western civilisation stems from the expansion of Christianity in Europe and then in America and Eastern civilisation is supported by other moral standards born of other religions.

And if all men need to govern on the basis of morals, the people whose growth is significant partly through immigration from different countries and continents, need the moral constitution by which they are governed, and that Argentina has to be, for obvious reasons, Catholic. Hence, the President is to be Catholic.

Because of my Catholic faith I put this into the constitutional requirement. I would also point out that I've always wanted to be inspired by the teachings of Christ. It should be noted that just like not all who call themselves democrats, are in fact, not all who call themselves Catholics are inspired by Christian doctrines.

Our religion is a religion of humility, renunciation, of exaltation of spiritual values over material. It is the religion of the poor who feel hunger and thirst for righteousness, of the disinherited. Only for reasons well known, it was possible to subvert these values and to allow the take over of the temple by merchants and the powerful.

As to the Justicialist Constitution that replaced the 1853 constitution, Perónist legal and constitutional scholar, Professor Felipe A. Gonzalez, commented on the 1949 constitution:

The interpretation of social reality and the concept of justice had expressed the ethical foundation by Pope Pius XI in his encyclical *Quadragesimo Anno*, whose clear concepts stated that the law of social justice 'prohibits

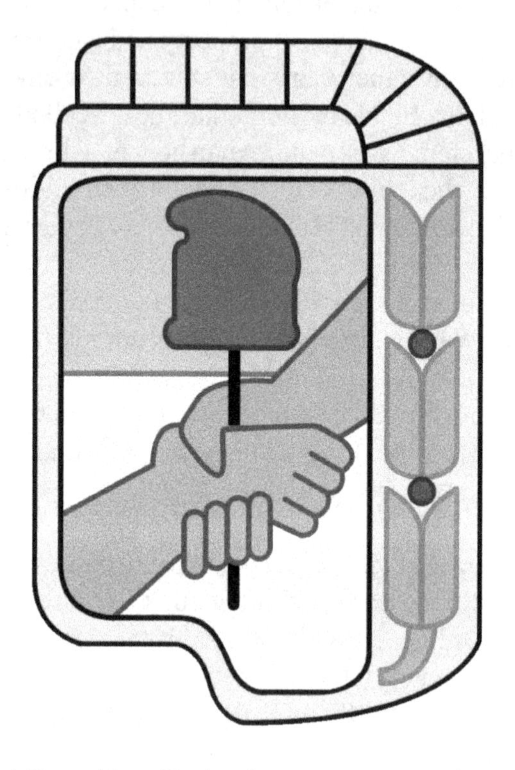

Justicialist emblem. The hands represent national union, the higher economic class is shown reaching out to the poor.

> the exclusion of by one class of the other class from the benefit of sharing', and 'give yourself, because each part of property belongs to the common good and the distribution conforms to the norms of the common good or social justice'. The encyclical is from 1931, that is, eighteen years previous to 1949.[181]

Gonzalez specifically related the 1949 Constitution to the principles of Pope Pius XI's encyclical *Quadragesimo Anno*, which inspired corporatist movements and States around the world.

181 Felipe A. Arzac Gonzalez, 'The Participation of Workers: Analysis of one of the most recent projects that drove President Néstor Kirchner', Miradas al Sur, No. 129, 6 November 2010.

The origins of the breach may be seen, ironically, in the 1949 Constitution, which while ratifying the status of the Church, dealt a blow to the political ambitions of provincial governor Domingo Mercante (whose power-base was that of the militant Acción Católica, which became avidly anti-Perónist) by allowing the incumbent president to run for a second term. It was widely assumed by Catholic political activists that Mercante would replace Perón after his term.[182] Also, the new constitution placed the state in the central role of family and educational issues that had previously been the domain of the Church, declaring that the state would 'orient official education and control private education', to 'create in young people virtues in line with Christian paradigms'.

What can be said of Church social doctrine today and for the last several decades is, however, quite different from that of its traditional doctrine, conceived as an alternative to the Godless creeds of Marxism and capitalism. Alberto Buela cogently described the situation, when comparing the doctrine that inspired Sampay:

> Today it sounds like a drag to characterise someone as a 'Catholic thinker', because Catholicism especially after Vatican II, became part of the 'thinking' mixture of social democracy, liberalism, neoliberalism and what remains of Marxism, which rules the Western intellectual and spiritual destinies. Sure there are exceptions. But seventy or eighty years ago, being a Catholic thinker was a pride for he who held that title. A sign for which Sampay always felt as his own identity.[183]

Despite the Catholic foundations of the Argentine State, and the application of Catholic social doctrine in all of its essentials by Justicialism, a breach between the Perónists and the Church was a major factor in the ouster of Perón in 1955 by the navy

182 Jill Hedges, op. cit., 129.

183 Alberto Buela, op. cit.

and anti-Perónist political agitators. While Perón sought to calm the increasingly chaotic situation, there seems to have been essentially non-Perónist elements claiming to be Justicialists, who ensured that the situation was aggravated. We will consider this situation in the chapter on the 'international synarchy'.

Fundación Eva Perón

The groundwork for the Fundación Eva Perón had been laid while Perón was Secretary of Labour during 1943-45, when he established direct, personal contact with the masses of people, starting the process of meeting individual petitioners for assistance. When Perón assumed the presidency this work was continued tirelessly by Eva. The workers and mothers, missing the contact with Perón at the buildings of the Secretariat of Labour, started calling on Perón at the front door of the Presidential Residence in Buenos Aires. Within several months Perón was receiving 3,000 letters a day. Long cues formed outside his residence waiting to see him. The labour unions began to send large amounts of goods, food clothing, and toys to the presidential residence to assist with the pleas for social aid. Eva also purchased items with her own money.

After Perón retired each evening, Eva would go to the residential garage, where the donated goods were stored for social aid, and with the help of her secretary, Atilio Renzi; her maid, Irma Ferrari; the cook, Bartolo; and two waiters, Sánchez and Fernández, they would work to dawn preparing packages for the needy.

In September 1946, Eva occupied the office where her husband had met the lines of petitioners in the Secretariat of Labour. One of the purposes of her 1947 tour of Europe was to learn how the welfare states of the social democracies cared for their citizens. She was disappointed with what she found. On her return she told Perón that what she saw in Europe of 'social aid' 'was just enough so that I would not roll up my sleeves myself'. She remarked that the palaces would be good places to build hospitals.[184] She returned to Argentina determined to create a social aid system that would value the workers, the poor and the orphaned, as much as anyone else within the nation. She

184 Ortiz, op. cit., 229.

Fundación Eva Perón. The building was closed and the statues to Argentine workers, by the Italian sculptor Leone Tommasi, were destroyed by the military junta in 1956.

had also seen the frenetic animosity her visit to Europe had aroused among the Communists in Italy and France; she was the representative of a state and a doctrine that had shown that social justice is achieved by the nation and not by the mere rhetoric of international proletarian solidarity.

On 19 June 1948, decree number 220.564 of Congress established the María Eva Duarte Social Help Foundation. The name was simplified into the Fundación Eva Perón in 1950. The Fundación had five aims:

1. To loan money, provide tools, and establish scholarships for deserving people who lack resources.
2. Construct housing for needy families.
3. Construct educational establishments, hospitals, recreational facilities and/or any other edifice which the Foundation considers necessary.
4. Construct buildings for the common good which can be transferred with or without charge to National, Provincial or Municipal governments.

5. Contribute or collaborate by any means available to the realisation of works constructed for the common good and which help meet the basic needs of the least favoured social classes.[185]

The initial fund was comprised of 10,000 *pesos* of Eva's own money.

From this start the Fundación became the primary social aid organisation of Argentina, unencumbered by bureaucracy and reaching out directly to those it helped. The Fundación moved into a six-storey building, which it filled with goods for distribution; then into an eleven-storey building. Eva personally opened and inspected many of the projects of the Fundación. She would often visit hospitals and others institutions at odd hours, disguised, to see how they really functioned. Other buildings catered for specific needs, such as the 140 grocery stores established and subsidised by the Fundación throughout Buenos Aires. There were also the schools, homes and hospitals established by the Fundación, which are considered below.

Emergency Homes

In 1948 the Fundación started by opening three *Hogares de Tránsito*, or temporary homes, for those who needed a place to live until their difficulties could be solved, whether in terms of housing, employment or health. Although open to anyone who needed assistance, priority was given to mothers with young children, who were unwed, separated, widowed, or abandoned.

The three *Hogares*, housing 700 individuals between them, were previously dilapidated mansions that had been renovated. 'Once renovated, they were luminous, comfortable and inviting, with spacious patios for the children to play in, libraries, dining rooms with individual tables (so families could eat together) and many

185 Dolane Larson, 'Eva Perón Foundation: Hogares de Tránsito', Evita Perón Historical Research Foundation, http://www.evitaPerón.org/social_work_eva_Perón.htm

other amenities'.[186] What is of added interest is that,given that Eva is often smeared as having lived an opulent lifestyle, with mountainous gifts, the many gifts she had been given during her 1947 European tour were given to these homes, including 'furniture, tapestries, fine paintings, rugs, porcelain and other objects d'art'.[187]

'Residents stayed for an average of about eight days or until the Fundación's social workers had solved their housing, employment, or medical problems'. When Eva inaugurated the second home she stated that these homes would provide 'lodging with dignity, excellent food, spiritual, material and moral support'. There would be sewing and typing classes for women, and movies and crafts for children. 'Everything they need' would be given freely.[188] This aid included: finding employment, providing transportation, helping those who needed hospitalisation, medicine or medical treatment; providing clothes and money; and providing for the needs of babies. A 'clothing section' at each of the *Hogares* enabled guests to choose their own clothes. Children had fully equipped outdoor playgrounds, supervised by licensed caregivers.

After Perón's ouster in 1955, the valuable gifts from Eva were privately auctioned, and the *Hogares* were closed.

Homes For The Elderly

The elderly were cared for equally as well. As a little girl Eva and her sister Erminda had been greeted every day by an elderly gentleman at his town, whom Eva called 'el señor Buen Día'. Such was his need that he would ask for a coin, and Eva and her sister would run to their mother to ask for something to give to him. Even after their father died, and their mother worked as a seamstress, they would always give the old man a few coins.

186 Ibid.

187 Ibid.

188 Ibid.

Erminda recalled twenty years after Eva's death that the old man was the first abandoned elderly person they had come into contact with, and that he awakened in Eva 'the need to help'.

On 28 August 1948, Eva proclaimed the 'Decalogue of the Rights of Seniors' and this charter, along with the workers' charter, were included in the 1949 Justicialist Constitution. The 'decalogue' guaranteed:

1. The right to assistance and to protection
2. The right to housing
3. The right to food
4. The right to clothing
5. The right to health care
6. The right to spiritual care
7. The right to entertainment
8. The right to work
9. The right to tranquillity, free from anguish and worry
10. The right to respect

In 1950, at the urging of the Fundación Eva Perón, Congress provided the first pensions to senior citizens. Prior to 1950, the Perónist regime, through the Fundación, ensured that the needs of the elderly were met. In 1949 the Fundación provided its own grants to those elderly in need over the age of 60.

On 17 October 1948, 'Loyalty Day' on the Perónist calendar, Eva opened the senior citizen's home, *Hogar Colonel Perón*, in Burzaco, Buenos Aires. This covered almost eighty acres of rolling hills. The facilities included a cinema, library, and workshops. Residence could choose paid employment, and about 80% did so. Options included an ecologically managed farm, a print shop, weaving and other craft shops and voluntary work as librarians, and musicians. When Perón was ousted in 1955 work on building three homes for seniors was halted.[189]

189 Larson, 'Senior Citizens' Homes', ibid.

Homes For Women Employees

In December 1949 Eva, on behalf of the Fundación, opened the General San Martín Home for Women Employees (*Hogar de la Empleada General San Martín*). Eva knew from her experiences the difficulties faced by young women coming to the city from rural areas, to find work. *Hogar de la Empleada* homed 500 women.

Each suite consisted of a spacious bedroom with wide windows, a bathroom and sitting room. The second floor of the *Hogar* comprised a library, a music room and a sewing room. The music room had crystal chandeliers, columns, mirrors, statues, and tapestries. Again, as with other such social establishments, these had been gifts to Eva from her 1947 tour of Europe. Well-equipped sewing rooms allowed the women to sew clothes for their children and themselves, and to learn the skill to find work. The homes included solariums and full, free medical and dental facilities, boutiques, self-service kitchens, and subsidised restaurants.

With the removal of Perón, the government shut down the Homes for Women Employees, and privately auctioned the gifts from Eva among their supporters. [190]

Highly Trained Nurses

The Perónist regime established a centralised, coherent health plan, run under the auspices of the Fundación. This was based on the 1947 blueprint of Dr. Ramon Carrillo, 'Plan Analítico de Salud Pública'. Dr. Carrillo, Perón's Minister of Health, stated that 20,000 nurses were needed to deal with the primary issues: infant mortality, tuberculosis, venereal disease, mental health, epidemics, the disabled, and increasing the life expectancy. Teresa Adelina Fiora, secretary to the Nursing School in the Peralta

190 Larson, '*Hogar de la Empleada General San Martín*', ibid.

Ramos Hospital, suggested that all nursing schools be centralised and their curricula updated. Within a year Fiora, supported by Eva's doctor, Jorge Albertelli, had established the Eva Perón School of Nursing. Previously nurses had merely undertaken chores without medical training. Under the new regime, a two year course instructed in hygiene and epidemiology, anatomy and physiology, semiology, general pathology and therapeutics, national defence and public disasters, first aid, infirmary (medical and surgical) obstetrics, gynaecology, paediatrics, dietetics, and social medicine. Post graduate studies over another two years included residence training at the Hospital Presidente Perón in Avellaneda, and other new Fundación hospitals in Lanus, San Martin, and Ramos Mejia. Here nurses specialised in laboratory technology, neonatology and psychiatry, and other areas. An aim was to teach nurses to work in remote areas without doctors, if necessary. Nurses were taught to drive hospital ambulances (which included ten beds and an operating theatre), ambulances equipped for emergency surgery, jeeps, motorcycles, and vehicles used for general transport.

Students who could not afford fees were subsidised by the Fundación. During 1950-1951 the Nursing School, la Escuela de Enfermeras, trained 5,000 nurses. Nurses were involved in the army campaign against malaria, and were sent around the world to help countries struck by natural disasters.[191]

Policlínics

Another part of the Carrillo plan was the establishment of the Policlínico Presidente Perón , in the working class city of Avellaneda, Buenos Aires Province. The hospital included a complex of five wings, each six stories high (ground floor plus five stories) with a capacity for 600 beds. The ground floor comprised a library, pharmacy, sterilization equipment and laboratories for clinical analysis, bacteriology and research. The first floor

191 Health and Safety Net: School of Nursing', Evita Perón Historical Research Foundation, http://www.evitaPerón.org/health_eva_Perón.htm

had a large terrace where patients and their families could relax, and departments for ear, nose and throat; rheumatology, neurology, neuropsychiatry, dental science, hematherapy, x-rays, ultrasound and physical therapy. The patient wards were on the second floor. On the third floor there were pre- and post-operative facilities, a special children's room, and on this floor social workers helped families and patients set specific goals and learn about preventive medicine. The fourth floor comprised the departments for gynaecology, obstetrics, neonatology and paediatrics. Nurses worked especially with first-time mothers. The fifth floor had four operating theatres. Another wing housed the outpatient clinics for paediatrics, gynaecology, obstetrics, dietetics, orthopaedics, dermatology and general medicine.

The Policlínico Presidente Perón specialized in pneumology, haematology and orthopaedics, employing 1,500 people, 218 of which were doctors and 491 of which were nurses, 32 kitchen workers, and carpenters, plumbers, electricians, gardeners, and administrators. The Policlínico contracted outside teachers (to keep children on track with their schooling) and home health care workers to assist in the homes of patients who were chronically ill or who could recover at home under medical supervision.

The three policlíncos in the Province of Buenos Aires, plus the Presidente Perón in Avellaneda, and Eva Perón in Lanús and Evita in San Martín, were all very similar. There were also thirteen other regional policlíncos. Additionally the Eva Perón Foundation established specialised hospitals, including: the Burn Institute in Buenos Aires, the Infectious Diseases Hospital in Haedo, the Thorax Surgery Hospital in Ramos Mejía, and 22 de Agosto Policlínico in Ezeiza.

High in the mountains of Jujuy, in Terma de Reyes, the Fundación set up a complex for children with kidney, rheumatic fever or nervous system problems. The complex catered for 144 children. It had a large swimming pool, and smaller baths with thermal mineral waters from the Andes Mountains. After the 1955 coup, the children were evicted and the hospital turned into a casino and a hotel for military personnel and their families. In Buenos Aires, the Fundación nearly completed what would have been the largest children's hospital in Latin America. The coup ordered the construction halted in 1955. The building was abandoned and became a hang-out for derelicts and criminals, and sometimes dead bodies were thrown over the wall into the neighbouring school yard. In 1976 the Videla regime turned the building into a concentration camp.[192]

El Tren Sanitario

In 1952 the Fundación set up el Tren Sanitario, the 'Health Care Train', to reach those Argentines who were unable to reach medical facilities. This had twelve cars carrying 46 health care specialists, which travelled throughout the entirety of Argentina over four months. One car was set up as a theatre to show films on hygiene and preventive medicine. The train had its own accommodation for personnel, generator, pharmacy, laboratories, x-ray rooms, and a waiting room, operating theatre, and a delivery room. Medical and dental examinations, x-rays, vaccinations, medicine, obstetrics and gynaecology, were offered as free services.[193]

Education

Prior to the Perón regime, School Homes were run by the Society of Beneficence. They were drafty, austere places, where opaque windows meant that one could not see inside or outside of the buildings. The children were called by the numbers sewn on their drab uniforms. The schools were run as sweatshops where the children sewed for the wealthy matrons of the Society. They were generally allowed out of the schools only during Christmas, to beg for money for the Society. Ninety-five percent of the money

192 Larson, 'Policlinics', ibid.

193 Larson, 'The Health Care Train', ibid.

received by the Society was expended on the salaries of its matrons. On the other hand, according to a 1939 Congressional report, employees of the Society worked in sweatshop conditions like the children, working 12 to 14 hours per day, with one day's holiday per fortnight.

Eva wanted to create real *homes* for children. The Fundación established 20 *Hogares Escuela* during its seven years existence. These homes were open; the hedges around them were small, so as not to block them from the rest of society. Family connections with those children who had to board at the schools were promoted. The homes were built in 'California mission style'; 'wide and airy, full of light, with red tiled roofs, white walls and lawns'.[194] The beds were made of oak. Bright tablecloths, an abundance of flowers, murals, books and toys gave the homes a cheerful atmosphere.

The homes were built where economic need was greatest, and took in 16,000 children. They were open to those children whose parents personally wrote to Eva telling of their needs, or children who were orphaned or neglected. Social workers were assigned to each family before and during the child's stay at a home. On admittance each child received a medical check-up and this continued thereafter every two months. They wore clothes of their choice. After Perón's ouster the home schools returned to their dismal existence. The regime's commission investigating the Fundación was shocked that such low class children were treated with such consideration, reporting:

> The attention given to the minors was varied and almost sumptuous. We can even say that it was excessive and not at all in accordance with the norms of the sobriety of a Republic which should form its children in austerity. Poultry and fish were included in the varied daily menus. As for the [children's] clothing, it was renewed every six months and the old clothing destroyed.[195]

194 Larson, 'Education', ibid.

195 Néstor Ferioli, La Fundación Eva Perón / 2. (Buenos Aires: Centro Editor de América

La Ciudad Infanti

The Children's City functioned like the Hogares Escuelas, where children could stay for the day or could reside there. Its purpose was to provide long or short-term care for children whose parents were in difficulty. On average the Ciudad took 300 children, and covered two blocks in the centre of Buenos Aires.

The aim of the Ciudad was to socialise marginalised children through play. Part of the Ciudad was precisely that, a city in miniature, with child-sized buildings, a plaza and fountain, a little service station where pedal cars could be stopped to 'fill up', where children all took turns at being a mayor, a banker, a chemist, a mechanic… A playground had a miniature train, and merry-go-rounds. There was a swimming pool and solariums.

The walls of the buildings were adorned with murals of children's stories such as Little Red Riding Hood, Cinderella, the Three Little Pigs, and circus animals. The types of meals were determined by the children's height and weight, and the requirements of a healthy life.

After the 1955 coup, the children were evicted, and the city was turned into a nursery for children of the wealthy. The miniature city was bulldozed in 1964, for a parking lot.[196]

La Ciudad Estudiantil

The Students' City was located next to the Children's City, and covered four blocks. The focus was on technology. The high school education here was so advanced that when the 1955 coup closed the facilities, the students were awarded scholarships to study in other countries. Another primary function was to

---

Latina, 199), 87.

196 Larson, 'The Amanda Allen Children's City', http://www.evitaPerón.org/education_eva_Perón.htm

Students at the Ciudad Estudiantil (Students City) 1951

Children's party at Ciudad Infantil (Children's City) 1951

prepare working-class children for future leadership positions, by involving them in decision-making, and a 'city' governing body was formed among the students, with its own president, ministers and diplomats. Every student had a job in the 'city'.

A social ethos was imbued there, Eva stating: 'They were to work towards the common good of the community but not let themselves become the tool of someone else's ambition'. The way the 'city' was run, with everyone having a job and responsibilities, and camaraderie in sports, encouraged students to form an integral community regardless of class or locale. During the evenings students would gather around bonfires and drink *mate* tea.

As we have seen, physical fitness was a feature of the Perónist regime, and physical education was therefore a major part of the student city. Each student could belong to one gym and two sports such as soccer, sword fighting, basketball, callisthenics, running, swimming, diving, water polo, and others.

After the 1955 coup the 'city' was turned into a detention centre for Perónists and Justicialist government members. [197]

University Cities

In 1953 the Fundación started the construction of two university cities in the provinces of Córdoba and Mendoza. The constructions were halted after the 1955 coup.[198]

'Social Aid' Not Welfarism Or Charity

From the start Eva Perón asked what role she could play in serving Argentina under the Justicialist administration. The people answered by calling on her directly, and results were had without bureaucracy and delay. Within the first month of 1947 among her

197 Larson, 'The President Perón Student City', ibid.

198 Néstor Ferioli, op. cit., 78-79.

first acts was a children's' tourism programme where workers' children could go from the cities and holiday among the hills of Córdoba. Already at the beginning of the year she negotiated and gave subsidies for the construction of 'policlínics' for workers in the textile and glass industries; the start of a programme that would see the building of many clinics and hospitals. Within the same month she had gained state social aid for 500 destitute families. A delegation from the slum, Villa Soldati, visited her to tell her of the conditions there. On the same day, she visited the neighbourhood and supervised the implementation of health care, social services and new housing. Within a month all of the families had been provided with new homes.[199]

In late 1949 Eva outlined the achievements of the first Perónist state at the Hall of the Ministry of Labour and Welfare, in which she spoke as the head of the Fund of Social Aid. She was speaking at the invitation of the Congress of Industrial Medicine, which was involved in ensuring the health of the industrial population in association with the Fund of Social Aid.

Eva stated that the basis of all the social aid work was the declaration of the 'Rights of the Worker', which had been incorporated into the Constitution.

She described the aims and work of the Fund of Social Aid, stating that hitherto there had been no national state organisation to deal with the deficiencies in welfare. Moreover, unlike the welfare states still being enacted by social democracies, the Fund, the precursor of the famous Eva Perón Foundation, was organised to take 'swift, direct and efficacious action', unencumbered by the bureaucracy and pettiness that plagued welfare states, then as now. The Perónist state was much more than a welfare state, however. Perónism recognised the creative role of the state in the formation of a people, nation and culture. Social aid was a duty of state, not a reluctant charity for which the recipients are

199 'To be Evita', Part II, *Evita Perón* Historical Research Foundation, http://www.evitaPerón.org/part2.htm

made to feel humbled and humiliated; an increasing condition of beneficiaries of the current social democracies. In fact Mrs. Perón specifically rejected the notion of 'charity', stating that:

> The donations, which I receive every day, sent in to the Fund by workmen, prove that the poor are those who are ready to do the most to help the poor. That is why I have always been opposed to charity. Charity satisfies the person who dispenses it. Social Aid satisfies the people themselves, inasmuch as they make it effective. Charity is degrading while Social Aid ennobles. Give us Social Aid, because it implies something fair and just. Out with charity![200]

One might be reminded by the admonition of Jesus in regard to the Pharisees who made a great public showing of their alms-giving in order to boast of how generous they were and to boost their own pride. Perónist 'social aid' is therefore quite different from our past and present notions of welfarism, whose recipients are regarded with disdain. 'Social aid' ennobled because it was based on contributions from fellow citizens, and not levied directly by state taxes in an impersonal manner. Trades unions, employees and employers, contributed to the social aid fund as part of a duty towards the common interest. This 'social aid' also had another significant factor; by eliciting donations from trades unions and employers, it was a practical means of helping to create Argentina as an organic society, where all citizens, regardless of their social background, contributed to the common interest. This is contrary to the effects of social democratic welfarism, where there is increasing miserly resentment at being taxed for welfare beneficiaries; a symptom that the bourgeoisie outlook is increasing rather than, as Marx had thought, decreasing. Mrs. Perón, towards the end of her talk, referred to the work of Social Aid, 'not as almsgiving or charity, but as pure justice, something well earned and which has been denied to [the 'shirtless ones'] for so long'.

200 Eva Perón, 'My Labour in the Field of Social Aid', 5 December 1949.

Eva wrote that her work was 'strict justice. What made me most indignant when I commenced it was having it classified as "alms" or "benevolence"'. 'Alms' was always 'a pleasure of the rich: the soulless pleasure of exciting the desires of the poor without ever having satisfied them. And so that alms should even be meaner and crueller, they invented "benevolence", and so added to the perverse pleasure of giving alms the pleasure of enjoying themselves happily with the pretext of helping the poor. Alms and benevolence are to me an ostentation of riches, and power to humiliate the humble.'[201]

Eva condemned the concept of 'charity' as the height of hypocrisy, given by the rich in the name of God. 'I think that God must be ashamed of what the poor receive in His name!'.[202] Eva recalled in her time what is today increasingly common among the modern Western states: 'all "social service" of the century that preceded us was cold, sordid, mean and selfish'.[203]

Perónism promised social justice for all Argentines. If there were shortfalls while state policies were being implemented, then it was the duty of the state to ensure that the citizens did not suffer as a consequence. Eva stated:

> The Fund was started to mitigate urgent needs and improve and consolidate family life, that is the life of all those inhabitants of Argentina who endure suffering and are anxiously awaiting the tangible benefits which our great President is dispensing from day to day. And furthermore we desired to supplement Government action and supply what was lacking to the solution of the problems of each individual.[204]

Addressing specifics, Mrs. Perón first turned her attention to

201 Eva Duarte Perón, *Evita by Evita* (London: Proteus Publishing, 1978), 121-122. Original title: *La Razon De Mi Vida*, Buenos Aires, 1953

202 Ibid., 122.

203 Ibid., 140.

204 Eva Perón, '*My Labour in the Field of Social Aid*', op. cit.

housing. In Buenos Aires province 118 groups of houses had been constructed. The new city, 'Evita', included 15,000 houses. Three 'model villages' had been built: President Perón, Los Perales and Primero de Marzo. 'Other groups of working class houses and modern villages have been built in Córdoba, Mendoza, Santiago del Estero, Tucumán and Corrientes, not to speak of other Provinces and Territories where similar work has been done'.

On child welfare, Perón had declared children as the 'only privileged' in Argentina. The Social Aid Fund had as of late 1949, started the construction of 'a Children's Polyclinic, with 1,000 beds'; an institution for newborn infants with a capacity of 1,000; and a section for contagious diseases, with 500 beds. The Social Aid Fund would be handing over 2,500 hospital beds for children for the city of Buenos Aires. Mrs. Perón referred to the 'policlínics' that were in the process of being built by the Social Aid Fund: 'The President Perón Policlinic in Avellaneda with 500 beds for clinical, surgical, and maternity cases; the Colonel Perón Policlinic at San Martin, likewise with 500 beds for clinical and surgical cases, and also with policlínics of 350 beds each in Santiago del Estero, Salta, Jujuy, Paso de los Libres (Province of Corrientes), Mendoza, San Juan, Córdoba and Rosario'. Tuberculosis clinics for men and women, each with 300 beds were being constructed.[205]

Women In The Perónist State

Women were integrated into the Justicialist 'organised community' as much as every other creative sector, which here too meant a radical change in socio-economic and cultural relations. Already in 1944, in his position as head of the labour and social welfare department, Perón established the Women's Division of Work and Assistance. Unlike the communist and demoliberal aim of integrating women as factory fodder into the economy by their removal from the home and family in the name of 'liberation' and 'feminism', Perón saw the family as the

205 The policlínics and other works, as considered previously.

foundation of the national community, and the central role of women within that. He stated:

> Dignifying women morally and materially is the equivalent of strengthening the family. To strengthen the family is to fortify the nation because the family is its first cell. To create a true social order one must begin with this basic cell, the Christian and rational basis for all human groups.[206]

On 25 July 1945 Perón stated his support for women's suffrage in a debate before the Chamber of Deputies. During late 1945 and early 1946 Eva's key role beside Perón in his electoral campaigning brought an uncharacteristic presence of a woman to politics. Women's suffrage was incorporated into the First Five Year Plan in October 1946. On 23 September 1947 the right of the women's vote was passed into law.[207] Eva was given the responsibility for mobilising women politically. Like Perón, Eva affirmed the family as the basis of the nation, and women's importance in that, stating on 27 February 1946:

> Women must vote. A woman is the moral foundation of her home and she must occupy a place in the complex social framework of her people. The new necessity of organising more extensive and reformatted groups demands it. The transformation of the concept of what it means to be a woman demands it because women have made more and more sacrifices in order to meet their obligations without asking for even minimum of rights.[208]

In September 1947 the Partido Perónista Feminino (PPF) was established to provide women with their own representative organisation. The PPF held its first National Assembly on 26 July 1949, at which Eva was elected the party's first president.

206 Juan Perón, 3 October 1944.

207 Pablo A. Vázquez, 'Evita Perón and Women's Participation in Politics', Evita Historical Research Foundation, http://www.evitaPerón.org/evita_Perón_instituto.htm

208 Eva Perón, 27 February 1946.

Eva Perón addressing women voters in 1950

In keeping with the organic, corporatist nature of the Justicialist State, the PPF was more than an electoral body: the party established *unidades básicas*, neighbourhood sections to implement social aid, and worked closely with the Ministry of Health and the Fundación Eva Perón.[209]

During the 11 November 1951 elections 3,816,654 women voted; 63.9% for the Perón-Quijano presidential ticket. The elections resulted in 23 women Deputies and 6 Senators entering Congress in 1952.[210]

Eva defined the Justicialist perception of women in a way that, despite her achievements for women that far outshine possibly any other female leader, has made her *persona non grata*, at best, among the oddly named 'feminists' of Left-wing disposition. Leftist 'feminism', like other forms of Leftism, generally serves capitalism. Elsewhere, I have detailed and documented the funding of 'feminists' and 'feminism' by the CIA and plutocratic Foundations.[211] I have

209 Pablo A. Vázquez, op. cit.

210 Ibid.

211 K. R. Bolton, Revolution from Above, op. cit.,160-200.

shown that feminism is a means by which women can be divorced from home and family, and behind the façade' of 'liberation', fully integrated into the global workforce. The capitalist outlook is essentially the same as that of Bolshevism, when, before Stalin restored the family, the ideal was to have children raised in factory crèches, and family life was to be replaced by communal life centered on the factory. This is regarded by orthodox Bolsheviks, and particularly by Trotskyites, as epitomising 'socialism', as the family, along with religious faith, must be eliminated.[212] Eva accurately discerned all of this sixty years ago. She wrote:

> Every day thousands of women forsake the feminine camp and begin to live like men. They work like them. They prefer, like them, the street to the home. They are not resigned to being either mothers or wives. They substitute for men everywhere. Is this 'feminism'? I think, rather, that it must be the 'masculinisation' of our sex.
>
> And I wonder if all this change has solved our problem? But no, all the old ills continue rampant, and new ones too, appear. The number of women who look down upon the occupation of homemaking increases every day. And yet that is what we are born for. We feel that we are born for the home, and the home is too great a burden for our shoulders. Then we give up the home… go out to find a solution… feel that the answer lies in obtaining economic independence and working somewhere. But that work makes us equal to men and – no! We are not like them! We feel the need of giving rather than receiving. Can't we work for anything else than earning wages like men?[213]

The answer of Justicialist feminism was to secure the position of women as wives and mothers within their homes. Hitherto, 'the mother of a family [had been] left out of all security measures'.

212 K. R. Bolton, Stalin: The Enduring Legacy (London: Black House Publishing, 21012), 13-20.

213 Eva Duarte Perón, Evita by Evita, op. cit., 183.

'The first objective of a feminine movement which wishes to improve things for women – which does not aim at changing them into men – should be the home', including economic security.[214] Eva suggested that every married woman be given a monthly state allowance from the day of her marriage, drawn from the earnings of all workers, including women. This would, to start, amount to half the average annual salary. Child allowances would be added, and an added allowance for those who are widowed and without work.[215]

In founding the PPF Eva stated that 'only women can be the salvation of women'. Starting with just thirty members, the party was constructed separately because it was up to women to attain for themselves the justice inherent in Perónism. As with the Perónist Party, the women's party was organised into 'basic units'. They were more than political. As localised cells, they could interact with each member. Hence, they became part of Eva's aim of elevating the culture of women: 'Libraries are organised in the units, cultural lectures are given, and, although I did not establish it expressly, they were early converted into centers of help and of social aid'.[216]

With the 1955 coup the homes and hospitals were closed, construction of new projects halted, buildings left derelict or taken over for personal use, and the art works and décor valuables, much of which had been donated by Evita from gifts she had received, were auctioned off among the friends of the new regime. This was part of a decades' long process, undertaken with religious fervour, to expunge every memory of the Peróns. A major part of the process was to smear the names of Perón and Evita, and try to destroy the love the people had for them. The smears have continued, and some have become popularly assumed, such as allegations of corruption and even charges that Evita enriched herself. By the time the coup ousted

214 Ibid., 184.

215 Ibid., 186.

216 Ibid., 194-195.

Perón in October 1955, the Fundación had amassed over three billion pesos. Seventy per cent of the funds had been donated by labour unions. Ferioli, in his definitive study on the Fundación, states that the sources of money comprised:

- Labour union contributions stipulated by law
- Spontaneous donations given by affiliated or unionised workers
- Percentages deducted under collective bargaining agreements
- State, provincial or municipal subsidies
- Donations from businesses
- Donations from individuals
- Incidental resources[217]

Much of the State funding came from racetrack revenue. A one off percentage from pay rises was often given to the Fundación, as it was Evita who regularly brokered the labour agreements between workers and employers. The wealthy often donated considerable amounts.

The story is now common that Evita extorted money from businesses. With the 1955 coup the commission of enquiry into the Fundación, which was supposed to expose it, and Evita, as corrupt, invited businessmen to testify. However, only one complaint was made – by the furniture company Sagasti – and this was not upheld. Sagasti had not been paid for beds that had been made of poor quality wood and not to the requested specifications.[218]

After Evita's death in 1952, Perón undertook the presidency of the Fundación, as head of a nine member council, composed of five workers and four state delegates, which met every fifteen days.

217 Nestor Ferioli, *La Fundación Eva Perón*, (Centro Editor de America Latina, 1990), Vol. 1, 41.

218 Ibid., Vol. 2, 161-162.

After the 1955 coup blood banks in Fundación hospitals were smashed because each container of blood carried the seal Fundación Eva Perón. Iron lungs were taken from hospitals by the regime, just prior to the outbreak of a polio epidemic, because they had been donated by the Fundación. The furnishings in the hospitals, children's homes, temporary shelters and home schools were regarded as too luxurious for the underprivileged and with the gifts of art Evita had given, all were looted or auctioned to friends of the new regime. Military vans took goods from the warehouses to disperse among the governments' friends and what was left was destroyed. One of the commissions set up to destroy the Fundación conceded:

> In spite of the exhaustive investigation carried out, it has not been possible to prove anything which would be penalised by law, because all technical and legal proceedings have at all times fallen within routine administrative norms, but neither can we doubt that some section heads were compromised as many details lead us to this conclusion, although it is impossible to prove it since we lack indispensable elements so we can take no legal action against them.

While the commission admits that nothing untoward was found, it nonetheless quips that there must surely be something; just nothing that can be proven. However, Adela Caprile, a member of the commission established to liquidate the Fundación, concluded:

> It was not a fraud. Evita cannot be accused of having kept one *peso* in her pocket. I would like to be able to say as much of all the ones who collaborated with me in the dissolution of the organisation.[219]

219 Ortiz, op. cit., 291, .

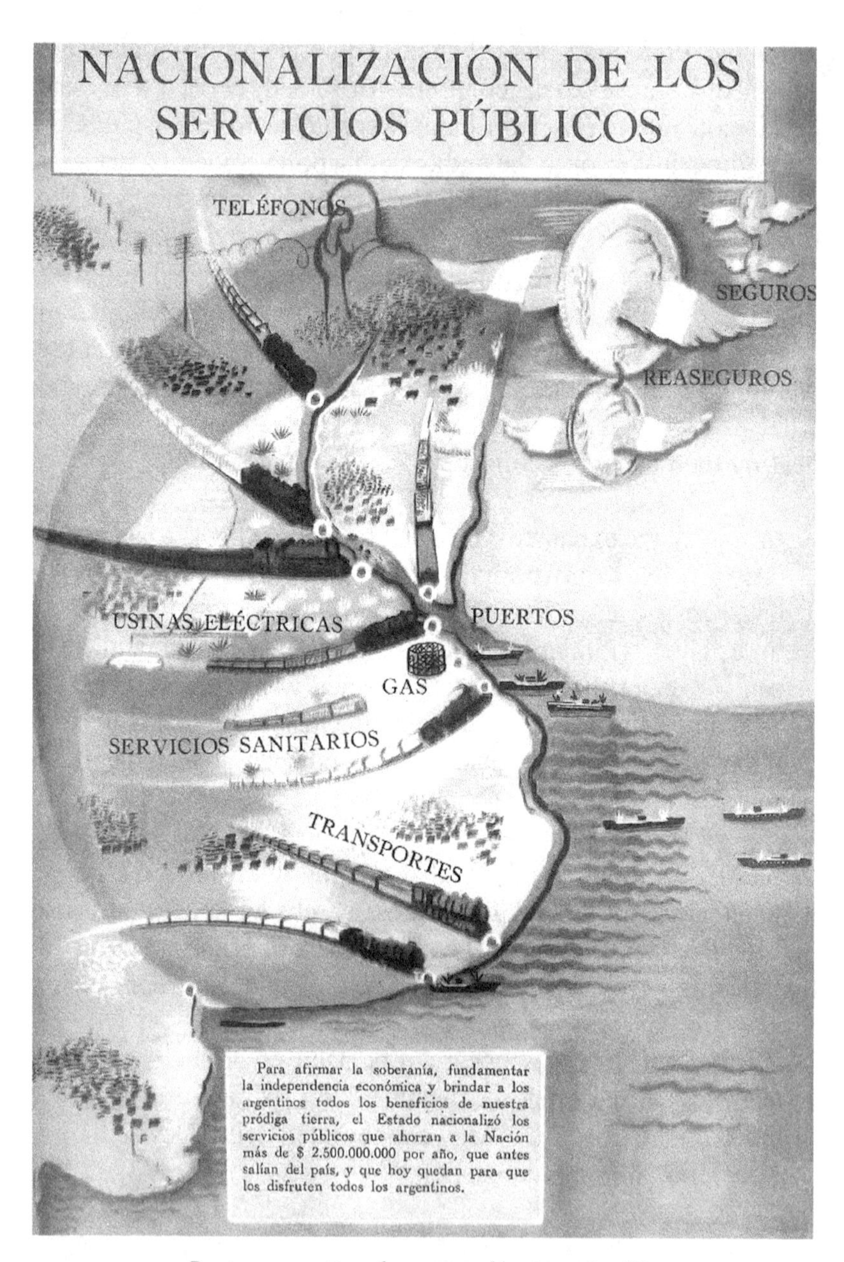

Poster promoting the nationalisation of public services under Perón's first five-year plan.

The Struggle Against International Finance

> *In the capitalist system the currency is an end and not a means, and its absolute value subordinates everything, including man. Perón*

The role of the state in regulating and controlling currency and credit is the prerequisite of national sovereignty. A state cannot freely pursue a policy whilst it is indebted to international finance, and in the post-war world to the policy dictates of the International Monetary Fund. Hence, Argentina did not join the IMF until after Perón was ousted. Few understand or have the courage to acknowledge the role of banks in creating credit and dictating social, political and economic policies.[220] A world war had just been fought on that very issue, as the main Axis states, Germany, Italy and Japan, had assumed control over the banking sector and relegated money to that of the servant of the people, not their master..[221] The First New Zealand Labour Government had undertaken something similar on a smaller scale when it nationalised the Reserve Bank in 1935, and issued Reserve Bank state credit at 1% interest to fund its iconic state housing project; that one measure securing work for 75% of the unemployed.[222]

The Perónist Government nationalised the banking sector as an essential premise for both national sovereignty and social justice. Dr. Sampay reiterated the issue after Perón's ouster:

> The modern way with which a country develops the economy, is no longer with outright annexation of territory, as was the method during the eighteenth and nineteenth centuries, but handling your own credit and currency. Indeed, the development of a country is through its investment policy. Whoever gives the orders on credit and the expansion or contraction of the money supply, controls the development of the country.

220 K. R. Bolton, *The Baking Swindle* (London: Black House Publishing, 2013).

221 Ibid., 103-120.

222 Ibid., 96-100.

Arturo Jauretche On Bank Nationalisation

Arturo Jauretche writing, after the ouster of Perón, on the nationalisation of banks, showed the extent of the knowledge that Perónists had on this most fundamental issue: credit and currency creation by the State, without which talk of both national sovereignty and social justice is meaningless. His essay is worth quoting at length:

> I will go into a topic that is fundamental to the implementation of a national policy : the nationalisation of banks . Preventing nationalisation has been one of the fundamental objectives of the accession to power of the traitors . Not only have they repealed provisions tended to make it effective , but it is still creating destructive conditions .
>
> And one of the most effective ways is to discredit the instruments of State banks. We are now in a smear campaign [against State banking], equal to that of 1955. It is the question of who handles credit and directs and manages the economy far more effectively than the government, with all its instruments.
>
> Whoever handles credit controls more than the issue of currency. By controlling credit trade export and import is also controlled. The control of credit can encourage certain forms of production and weaken others; determine what is to be produced and what not, what can and what cannot get to market facilities, and consequently sales and consumption is also controlled.
>
> The control of credit creates currency for payment and purchasing power. The control of credit decides what is produced in the country and what is not produced, who produces it, how it is produced, how it sells, where it is exported and under what conditions: it determines the conditions over all of the world .

The secret of prosperity or decline, development or backwardness, is held in banks. Laws and business organisations are just the anatomy of economic society. But money is the physiology of a society's commerce. Money is the blood circulating within it, and the price of money, its abundance or scarcity, is determined by the banking system.

Not the Banks' Money

The Banks' money is not the Banks'. It's the whole society that deposits its money there, and from there comes loans. Banks create money through credit, because credit is converted from deposits at a multiplicity of times, and the abundance or shortage of hard cash in circulation, is a reflection of the number of times a bank multiplies its lending. So, if the creation of money is a state function, it must be carefully monitored to suit the needs of the market, otherwise we fall into the tyranny of money, and what is called inflation.

The *Sepoy*[223] and Private Banking

The destruction of the nationalisation of banks was and is a primary object of the *sepoys*: to return to the previous system, placing banks outside the State. The owners of the private banks are not the depositors, but a financial coterie that controls the capital stock, collects the savings of depositors and directs interest back to itself. So when the financial coterie is linked to certain industries, the type of industrial development that is in the interests of the nation is not taken into account, but rather the interests of the financial coterie.

When the bank is foreign owned or is linked to exports or imports, its policy is to benefit exporters and importers ,

223 A reference to those who serve imperialists, from the 'sepoy' Indian servants of the British Raj.

in an economy that has already been made available to the buyer and seller of interests abroad.

This is elementary, but it is objected that the private bank is best run and makes better investments. What determined the best investment is a concept that is relative, because a business can be very good for the merchant and inconvenient for the community.

It is also said that the funds are better managed. But in the short experience since 1955,[224] several privately funded banks have shown that ethics is far below the official bank they are trying to discredit. It is also said that in the hypothetical case, if banks are official, it is the nation that pays for the consequences. But so far this century the country has only paid the consequences of bad private banking business, as in the Mobilizer Institute case during the 'Infamous Decade', in which uncollectible liabilities of private banks were transferred to the community, which took charge of its bad businesses and its connections with the oligarchy and financial interests.[225]

In addition, a nationalised bank is able to control a crisis , graduating their claims, managing its resources.

Private banks can create a crisis deliberately , with a number of banks combing to agree, or they can drift into panic and every man for himself.[226]

Jauretche addresses the primary points on how the private international banking system works, how it is connected with global industries, how the creation and control of bank credit impacts on the economic development of a state, and the

224 That is, since Perón's ouster.

225 The reader might note that current spate of State bailouts of private banks during the present global 'credit crisis'.

226 Arturo Jauretche, '*On the Nationalisation of Banks*', 9 February 1960.

arguments against State involvement in banking that are still being used today by those who want a free reign for plutocracy. The situation has only become worse, with the global debt crisis, the control of industries in the hands of the international banks and the privatisation of state industries and sale of state assets, utilities and resources throughout the world by nations that are swamped in debt to international finance.

One of the most important factors raised by Jauretche is his description of the way banks lend out much more credit than the amount of actual money they have from depositors' savings. Jauretche states: 'Banks create money through credit, because credit is converted from deposits **at a multiplicity of times**, and the abundance or shortage of hard cash in circulation, is a **reflection of the number of times a bank multiplies its lending'.** This is called 'fractional reserve banking' and has been the method of credit creation for centuries, allowing private banks to create credit that is only backed – when at all – by a fraction of the amount of actual reserves the banks have on hand. Every time a deposit is made by a bank's customer, the bank is able to create and lend out credit at many more times than the amount deposited. Most importantly, the bank then charges interest on that credit. Therefore the borrower must pay back in real wealth – created with his own labour – not only the principal of the loan that has been created out of thin air by a mere ledger (or computer) entry, but also added interest. This is not only how your local private bank operates, but how the entire international banking system runs. When the nation becomes so indebted that it cannot even keep up interest payments on loans, it must either take out further loans to pay off the interest on previous loans, or it must start selling off state assets and resources.

The American scholar Dr. Carroll Quigley succinctly defined fractional reserve banking, when describing the establishment of the Bank of England, in his historical *magnum opus* that he used as a textbook for his Harvard University lectures:

> It early became clear that gold need be held on hand only to a fraction of the certificates likely to be presented for payment... In effect the creation of paper claims greater than the reserves available means that bankers were creating money out of nothing. The same thing could be done in another way. Deposit bankers discovered that orders and cheques drawn against deposits by depositors and given to a third person were often not cashed by the latter but were deposited in their own accounts. **Accordingly it was necessary for the bankers to keep on hand in actual money no more than a fraction of deposits likely to be drawn upon and cashed, the rest could be used for loans, and if these loans were made by creating a deposit (account) for the borrower, who in turn would draw cheques upon it rather than withdraw money, such 'created deposits' or loans could also be covered adequately by retaining reserves to only a fraction of their value. Such created deposits were also a creation of money out of nothing**... William Patterson however, on obtaining the Charter of the Bank of England in 1694, said: 'the bank hath benefit of interest on all moneys which it creates out of nothing'.[227] [Emphasis added].

Justicialists were among the few who fully understood the international financial system and took steps to oppose it. The banking system is the fundamental issue, yet how many books on Perón say anything about the banking system other than at most to allude to its having been nationalised? The treatment accorded to this is akin to the way orthodox academe writes mountainous screeds about the Third Reich, but says nothing as to how Germany achieved economic recovery within a few years during the Great Depression, other than to allude to 'rearmament', which explains nothing. Books on New Zealand history site the iconic state housing project, yet say nothing about how it was financed by state credit.

227 Carroll Quigley, *Tragedy and Hope* (New York: Macmillan Co., 1966), 48.

The Marshall Plan and the Closing of Export Markets

> Economic and political reasons converged on the U.S. State Department's decision to retaliate against the attitude of independence that our country had kept during the war. Following the launch of the Marshall Plan, the United States banned the use of foreign currency borrowing to European countries to import Argentine products. A refusal to provide arms to Argentina and the restriction of industrial imports for Argentine agricultural exports in Europe were added. In early 1950, the Argentine foreign trade situation was critical.[228]

Perón had inherited a legacy of colonialism in which Argentina had been reduced to being a *de facto* colony particularly of Britain. This had stunted Argentina's development, and kept her as an agricultural exporter dependent on Britain, with the control of its infrastructure by outsiders. Argentina had very little of her own when Perón assumed the presidency. What he faced was a Herculean effort to establish Argentina as a modern state while transcending the socio-economic divides of developing capitalist states. Perón was able to build on some previous structures such as commodity boards, but for the most part had to establish entirely new organisations and industries.

The foundations of social justice and political sovereignty were achieved primarily by trying to break Argentina free of the international banking system by instituting the state control of credit and currency, and by the use of barter in trade. Perón would not allow Argentina to be subjected to the policies of the IMF in return for loans. He laid the basis for a modern nation. What he was up against from interests both within Argentina and outside, ensured that it would be a colossal struggle. A world war had just been fought around the question of whether nations would be permitted to determine their own destinies, or whether they

228 Perón, 'Retaliation against the attitude of independence', *Democracy* magazine, 1951.

would be forced to subject themselves to plutocracy. Plutocracy won. Perón emerged precisely when the 'third position' of social justice and national sovereignty had been defeated by war and was being excoriated as the ultimate evil as it still is.

The problems encountered by Perón in his second term, and his ouster three years later by a military coup, in alliance with politicised elements of the Church, are often blamed on deficiencies in Perón's policies and personnel. Yet despite the tremendous obstacles that Perón was working through, the failures and the reversals, few leaders in history have achieved as much in as short a time, against so many obstacles, as Perón. In his own time, Roosevelt's much-lauded 'New Deal' was a failure. The USA and Britain could not emerge from the Great Depression without recourse to war production; the irony being that this was the measure by which Germany is still widely thought to have achieved its recovery. Furthermore, the democracies could not overcome their gaping social divisions without appealing to unity in times of war. Perón achieved this social unity in times of peace. His legacy was lasting, Argentina's modern infrastructure having been established primarily by Perón, despite the religious zeal of destruction that was unleashed by the cynically named 'liberating revolution' of 1955.

In 1948 the USA excluded Argentine exports from the Marshall Plan, a plan to ensure that half of Europe would remain reliant on the USA. Argentina's agricultural exports were therefore denied a European market. Joseph Page states of the importance of this that 'the Marshall Plan drove a final nail into the coffin that bore Perón's ambitions to transform Argentina into an industrial power'.[229] While Argentina was kept out of the European market, she was replaced by Canada.

What Perón had said about the character of the IMF and U.S. post-war policy, is confirmed by Argentine economists, Dr.

229 Joseph Page, *Perón: a Biography*, (New York: Random House, 1983), 173.

Mario Rapoport[230] and Dr. Claudius Spiguel.[231] In a paper on the Marshall Plan, and U.S. post-war policy on Argentina, Rapoport and Spiguel state that the U.S. aimed for a 'one world' regime based on free trade.[232] The Marshall Plan for rebuilding war-torn Europe aimed to secure U.S. economic hegemony over Europe, on the condition that recipient states of U.S. loans pursued economic liberalisation. Although the USA would have been pleased for the Soviet bloc to enter into this arrangement, the USSR was not about to dismantle its centralised economic structure, and become subordinated to the USA.

Additionally, the nationalist – autarchic - economy of Perón's Argentina was considered anathema to the USA. Indeed, in 1941, when drafting the 'Atlantic Charter' as the blueprint for the post-war world, President Franklin D. Roosevelt reminded Britain's Prime Minister Winston Churchill, that the war against the Axis was being fought for free trade, and that the imperial trade preferences of the British Empire, or any other empire (let alone the autarchic economy of any other state) would not be permitted in the post-war new world order.[233] The post-war world order would be dominated by the USA, and the economic policy would be what is today called 'globalisation'.

Argentina required technological imports from the USA to pursue industrialisation and modernisation, and to eventually become self-sufficient. One cannot have political independence without economic independence: that was the rationale of Argentina's state credit, investment and banking policies, and barter trade.

230 Director of the Institute of Historical, Economic, Social and International Studies; Senior Researcher at CONICET, and Consulting Professor at the University of Buenos Aires.

231 Institute of Historical Research, Economic, Social and International Studies, and Professor at the University of Buenos Aires.

232 Mario Rapoport and Claudius Spiguel, 'Argentina and the Marshall Plan: Promises and Realities', *Revista Brasileira de Política Internacional,* Vol.52, No.1 Brasília, Jan. / June 2009.

233 Roosevelt's son records this in *Elliott Roosevelt, As He Saw It* (New York: Duell, Sloan and Pearce, 1946) 35. On the 'Atlantic Charter' and its aim of destroying autarchic and imperial economies, see K. R. Bolton, *Babel Inc.* (London: Black House Publishing, 2013), 54-56.

The USA was not about to accept barter agreements, as this goes against the processes of international finance, and Argentina could only pay with agricultural exports. The USA ensured that export markets were increasingly denied to Argentina, claiming that Argentine produce was too high on the world market, while the USA ensured that its own agricultural exports would be sold at high cost, and that they could only be purchased with U.S. dollars. In other words, the reconstruction of Europe via the Marshall Plan, in the face of a hyped up 'Soviet threat', was a scam by the USA to ensure its own domination and profits.

Rapoport and Spiguel write that Argentina's promises of participation in the Plan were used by Washington diplomacy as a weapon of pressure to force the low selling price of Argentine wheat. However, a major objective of the USA was to pressure Argentina into relinquishing her economic policies and open up again to predatory trade and financial practices. The USA 'also sought to liberalize the conditions for the transfer of profits of U.S. companies and restrict or eliminate the role of IAPI (Argentine agency for foreign trade)'. Argentina was willing to sell her agricultural exports at lower prices in exchange for essential imports from the USA, and to change her foreign exchange restrictions.[234]

The U.S. aim was one of 'Achieving and maintaining universal peace … linked to an expansion of international trade without restrictions, to put an end to national barriers and prevailing bilateralism from pre-war'. 'Such objectives that guided U.S. foreign policy since the Depression, required urgently unrestricted access to foreign markets - essential for a massive export economy whose industrial and unchallenged supremacy appeared now to overcome the spectre of a recession…'[235]

Argentina and other states in Latin America, such as Brazil, having not entered the Second World War as part of a zealous

234 Mario Rapoport and Claudius Spiguel, op. cit.

235 Ibid.

crusade to make the world safe for free trade and U.S. export markets, were anachronisms in the post-war world: they were erecting precisely the types of autarchic states that the USA had just fought to destroy among the Axis states, Germany, Italy and Japan, and even to destroy the empires of their wartime allies. The post-war world was one where world trade would be 'regulated and oiled by supranational institutions and a financial centre based in the Treasury of the United States was conceived: that is, the *"Pax Americana"*'.[236] The U.S. diplomatic and economic offensive targeted what was called 'narrow and selfish nationalism', 'especially to all aspects that contradicted the strategy of an "open" world led by the United States: statism, bilateralism, creation of the Argentine Institute for the Promotion of Trade (IAPI), not incorporating the IMF and the World Bank, restrictions on business expansion and U.S. finance capital within Argentina'.[237] Up to mid-1949 Washington 'deployed selective economic pressure' against the ' "autarkic nationalism" by the team of Miguel Miranda, the industrialist who chaired the Central Bank and the IAPI'. Certain officials regarded as 'moderates', were cultivated by the USA, including Foreign Minister Juan Atilio Bramuglia, and General Sosa Molina, Minister of War.

Britain owed Argentina over £150,000,000 (approximately $U.S. 450,000,000) from agricultural exports shipped during the Second World War. This debt mainly existed as Argentine Central Bank reserves that, because of the 1933 Roca-Runciman Treaty between Argentina and Britain, were deposited with the Bank of England. The reserves could not be used by Argentina because the treaty allowed the Bank of England to hold the funds in trust. Britain could not release the reserves because she had indebted herself to the USA to fund her war with Germany through the Lend-Lease agreement.[238] While Argentina's need for U.S. made capital goods increased, there were ongoing limits

236 Ibid.

237 Ibid.

238 David Rock, *Argentina, 1516–1982* (University of California Press, 1987).

on the Argentine Central Bank's availability of hard currency. Argentina's pound Sterling surpluses earned after 1946, worth over $200,000,000, were made convertible to dollars by a treaty negotiated by Central Bank President Miranda; but after a year, British Prime Minister Clement Attlee suspended the provision, with promptings from the USA. Rapoport and Spiguel state that 'on August 20, 1947, a decisive event would deepen the economic difficulties of Argentina: the inconvertibility of the pound, enacted by the United Kingdom with U.S. support. A certain measure for acute difficulties in the balance of payments [brought] Britain on the brink of having to appeal to their gold reserves while the small remnant of the great loan that Washington had given them was about to evaporate'.[239] The only option was for Perón to accept the transfer of over 24,000 km of British-owned railways (over half the total in Argentina) in exchange for the debt, in March 1948, which would then have to be upgraded from the disrepair allowed by the British owners, and the lack of a standard track gauge for the whole rail system. 'Indeed, from that time Argentina could no longer use the currency from trade with Britain, as she had done from the beginning of Miranda-Eady Treaty, to pay for imports from the United States'.[240]

> This threatened the development of the industrialization plan whose progress depended on the acquisition of machinery, supplies and fuel abroad. Even if there were a surplus in inconvertible currencies (European) supply from the old continent and Britain itself, [Argentina] was restricted by the difficulties of these economies and the consequent scarcity and higher prices for goods required.[241]

Diplomatic quarters in the U.S. suggested that Argentina be enabled to import equipment and materials from the USA if she would sell wheat at 'world market prices', and Argentina would be able to participate in the Marshall Plan. However, a

239 Rapoport and Spiguel, op. cit.

240 Ibid.

241 Ibid.

committee of the U.S. Congress objected to any agreement with Argentina because it would 'strengthen the role of the state IAPI as exporter and importer'.[242] The Marshall Plan was intended to destroy any concept of autarchic economies in the world, and the IAPI was a significant bugbear to the internationalists.

> The Report of the Argentine Central Bank, 1947 clearly summed up the situation: 'Two-thirds of Argentina's exports go to countries with [which we have a bilateral] agreement, while the bulk of our purchases must be made in the United States, because of the slowness with which the conversion of European countries operates. Strong demand for products of any kind that supports that market has caused further increases in prices of their products and determined the reintroduction of rationing systems by the U.S. authorities.

Argentina sought 'through its foreign trade policy, to counter the deterioration of terms of trade and to maintain the supply of goods necessary for industrialization'.[243] However the payment of imports with U.S. dollars was only possible if Argentina was an agricultural exporter under the terms of the Marshall Plan, which demanded that Argentina sell her products to Europe at lower prices than the USA, and moreover to abandon its autarchic economic plan, which was the primary reason for pursuing industrialisation in the first place.

An intelligence report by the U.S. State Department in 1948 stated:

> If the government is unable to pay for industrialization with $ freely obtained, on its own, they must pay in concessions and guarantees for U.S. companies. But these concessions to foreign investors involve a change in the nature of Argentina, foreign and domestic policy, as developed by the current government.[244]

242 Ibid.

243 Ibid.

244 Cited by Mario Rapoport and Claudius Spiguel, ibid.

Citing the U.S. State Department Rapoport and Spiguel state that the declared aim of U.S. policy was to 'put Argentina on its knees'. According to Callum MacDonald:

> Washington was hostile to agreed national capital under the first Five-Year Plan preferences. It was particularly opposed to the creation of a base of significant heavy industry in the country. From their point of view, this type of economic development was the basis of nationalism confronting the American objectives in the hemisphere and 'was inextricably linked to the third position in foreign policy'. Argentina was looking to create a control independent of the great powers, something that could not be allowed within the sphere of influence of the United States at the height of the Cold War. In the eyes of Washington, a change in the policy was the preliminary condition for the Argentine alignment with goals North of the country.[245]

Argentine foreign exchange earnings via its exports to the U.S. fell, turning a $100,000,000 surplus into a $300,000,000 deficit. Perón began his second term in June 1952 with serious economic problems, compounded by a severe drought and a $500,000,000 trade deficit.

This combination of pressure from international finance, the USA, and internal factions brought the remarkable state to an end.

245 Callum MacDonald, The U.S., the Cold War and Perón, 1946-1950, in Abel, Christopher and Colin Lewis (eds.), *Latin America. Economic Imperialism and the State* (London: Athlone Press, 1985), 410.

Perón on Banking and Credit

Perón showed himself to be a statesman head and shoulders above almost any other politician in history in recognising the character of the battle against usury, writing:

> Banking reform, its consequent reform of our monetary system and the investment of the credit system are, perhaps, the most essential applications of the visible economic principle.
>
> **In the capitalist system the currency is an end and not a means, and its absolute value subordinates everything, including man.**
>
> All of us remember the days when the entire national economy revolved around the value of the *peso*. The economy - and therefore social welfare - was subordinated to the value of money and this was the first inviolable dogma of the capitalist economy.
>
> We considered this scale of values and decided the value of money should be subordinated to social welfare economics: and unleashed ourselves from the sacred weight of your gold backing.
>
> This is not to deny the value of gold. In a world where it is used as an international currency, we cannot despise gold as a means of international payment, even when we are convinced that it is usually better to have wheat and meat dollars than gold.
>
> **But in the domestic, social economy our doctrine states that the currency is a public service that increases or decreases, is valued or devalued in direct proportion to the wealth produced by the work of the Nation.** [Perón's emphasis].

I wonder if is it possible to put into circulation in 1951, with 13,000 million *pesos* of national income, the same amount of money as in 1945, when income was 16,500 million. More money is needed to serve the economic movement of a developed country.

Money is for us one effective support of real wealth that is created by labour. That is, the value of gold is based on our work as Argentines. It is not valued at weight, as in other currencies based on gold, but by the amount of welfare that can be funded for working men. Neither the dollar nor gold are absolute values, and happily we broke in time with all the dogmas of capitalism and we have no reason to repent. It happens, however, as to those who accept willingly or unwillingly the orders or 'suggestions' of capitalism, that the fate of their currencies is tied to what is minted or printed in the Metropolis, encrypting all the wealth of a country circulating with strong currencies, but without producing anything other than currency trade or speculation. **We despise, perhaps a bit, the value of hard currencies and choose to create instead the currency of work. Maybe this is a little harder than what you earn speculating, but there are fewer variables in the global money game.** [Emphasis added].

Gentlemen: In terms of social economy, it is necessary to establish definitively: **The only currency that applies to us is the real work and production that are born with the job.** [Perón's emphasis].

The appreciation of the Perónist currency will end not in the increase of capital, but in the increase in the purchasing power of wages: Wages have not increased purchasing power according to the extent of the value of gold weight, but to the extent of the work that wages are paid to those producing goods useful to the community.

Perónist supporters in Buenos Aires 1950

> To do all this, Argentina has taken full possession of its currency, making it a simple utility. **Even when to some capitalist mentality this will sound like heresy, we can say flatly that the Argentines do what we want with our currency, subordinating its value to the welfare of our people.**[246] **[Perón's emphasis].**

The answer of the Justicialists was to free the Argentine economy from the international plutocrats by placing their credit and currency on a **work standard**.

246 Juan Perón, *Banking and Credit*, Buenos Aires, ca. 1951.

International Monetary Fund

One of the factors of the Perónist pursuit of a state credit policy was the repudiation of the organisations used by the international bankers to impose their reign over the world. The primary organisation for this purpose remains the International Monetary Fund (IMF). Perón relates that he was promptly approached by the IMF, formed soon after the Second World War, to have Argentina become subjected to the organisation:

> When in 1946 I took over the government, the first visit I received was from the president of the International Monetary Fund who came to invite us to adhere to it. Wisely I replied that I needed time to think. Then I appointed two young technicians to set up a government team to investigate this 'dangerous monster'. The result of this report was clear and precise: in short, the IMF was a putative new imperialism.
>
> The policy of 'currency areas', after the abandonment of the gold standard, has been fruitful in events where business has always been involved. Through various ways of distorting reality, it has formed a long history through the 'sterling area' and the 'dollar area'. Although the pretext was to give indirect support to the currencies of poor countries, really it has been a new way of speculating on the good faith of others.
>
> Shortly after World War II, the loss of much of the gold reserves of the United States seriously threatened the existence of the 'dollar area'. Consequently it was necessary to create the instrument to consolidate the 'dollar area'. The International Monetary Fund was the solution. This would involve most Western countries, committed by contributing to the fund, where it would handle all currencies, which would set not only monetary policy but also the factors that were directly or indirectly linked to the economy of members. In reality it would go much further.

> Here are some of the reasons, besides many others, why the Perónist government of Argentina did not join the International Monetary Fund. For us, the value of our currency was fixed in the country, and we were setting changes according to our needs and conveniences. **For international exchange we resorted to barter: our real currency was our goods.** The permanent reality of international monetary manoeuvring of all types on which the insidious system was created, gave us no recourse but to do so or be robbed with impunity. [Emphasis added].
>
> Time has passed, and almost all countries adhering to the famous International Monetary Fund suffer the consequences. Meanwhile, the United States was responsible, through its companies and capital, for appropriating sources of wealth in all countries where fools or *sepoys* ruled.[247]

As usual, Perón was correct in his assessment. The eminent New Zealand economist and government adviser Dr. William B. Sutch, wrote in the same terms as Perón regarding the character of the IMF:

> The banking interests of the few industrial nations of the non-socialist world control the International Monetary Fund at the level of governments. But even more importantly these interests with their industrial components, working through their supranational groupings, are rapidly getting into a position where they can determine the economic and social development of the non-socialist world and even by their joint action influence the economic development of the socialist world… Their power, of course, could be heavily blunted in a country if the people of that country decided to make their own economic decisions and control the development of their society.[248]

247 Juan Perón, '*Argentina and the International Monetary Fund*'.

248 William B. Sutch, *Takeover New Zealand* (Wellington: A H & A W Reed, 1972), 114.

Perón was one of the few statesmen in the world, from the start of the IMF, who realised the nature of the organisation as a means by which plutocracy would control the economic and social development of all signatory states that become indebted to it. New Zealand did not join the IMF until 1961, and in certain respects its economic and social policies were vaguely similar, although not nearly as bold, as Perón's. Like Argentina, New Zealand was reliant on selling agricultural exports, especially to Britain, and this stunted its economic development.

Sutch stated of the background of the IMF:

> After World War II the international bodies set up to deal with trade and foreign lending were dominated by the USA, whether in control of voting or in doctrine. The doctrine was that of a *laissez faire* international market economy fed by the free flow of capital and goods with, in principle, no hindrance to these flows.[249]

Balance of payments difficulties of a country would be met by IMF loans on condition of 'economic and social, policies agreed by the IMF'.[250] The IMF programme is based on 'austerity', meaning the elimination of social services, and privatisation, or the looting of a nation's resources, utilities and assets by predatory global corporations. Sutch pointed out that New Zealand's economic - and consequently, social - structure had been stunted by joining the IMF in 1961. Perón recognised this would happen to Argentina in 1946. Another crucially important statement made in passing by Perón in regard to the IMF was that 'for international exchange we resorted to barter: our real currency was our goods'.[251] Through barter, as with the issue of state credit, Argentina was bypassing the parasitic international banking system.

---

249 Ibid., 54.

250 Ibid.

251 Perón, *Argentina and the International Monetary Fund*, op. cit.

The Second Perónist Period

Perón was re-elected to a second term in 1951, with 62% of the vote. The day he took office, on 4 June 1952, was the last public appearance of Eva Perón, who had come to be known throughout the world as Evita (Little Eva) due to the affection she inspired among the people. Evita died of cancer the following month, working until the end. Her death had caused an irreplaceable loss. She had been the people's voice with the state, and was the charismatic public face of the tremendous social aid programme that had changed the lives of so many.

On 28 September 1951, while Evita, frail with cancer, was undergoing a blood transfusion, an abortive coup against Perón, was led by General Benjamin Menéndez. When General Berdaguer, in charge of military justice, asked Perón to sign Menéndez's death sentence, Perón replied that his hands will 'never be tainted by a man's blood'.[252] When the CGT assembled at the Plaza de Mayo to denounce the attempted coup, Evita was absent. She had been too ill to be told of the coup, but that evening in a radio address, she asked for prayers to regain her health so that she could continue her work. Despite her ill health, Evita continued to receive about a hundred workers and government ministers every day.[253]

The death of Evita on 26 July 1952, whose popularity had been important in mobilising the zeal of the people, had a deep effect on Perón's morale. This came also at the time of economic crisis, largely the result of losing Britain as the country's primary importer of beef.

While Argentina had become a modern industrial nation under Perón, and great strides had also been made in such areas a steel production, the need for imports such as steel, fuel, and machinery increased due to industrial demand. A harsh winter

252 Ortiz, op. cit., 329.

253 Ibid., 333.

President Juan Perón heads the mourners as they walk behind the coffin of Eva Perón. 13th August 1952

in 1952 was hard upon the people, with a meat shortage and power failures. That year the government adopted its Second Five Year Plan that saw a reversal of some key policies, such as the removal of subsidies on some goods, and a partial ban on meat consumption.[254] However, the primary means was not one of legislation, but of Perón's appeal to sacrifice during a grim period, calling for a reduction in consumption. The state added attention on steel production, and on the manufacturing of tractors and automobiles. Some foreign companies, such as Fiat and Mercedes-Benz established factories.[255] That is not to say however that Perón had compromised with free market economics. The economy recovered with annual growth at 5% between 1953 and 1955, and single digit inflation was maintained. Higher subsidies for agriculture meant an upsurge in that area. Salaries for industrial and agricultural workers were again able to increase.[256]

254 Luis Alberto Romero, A History of Argentina in the Twentieth Century (Pennsylvania State University Press, 2002), 120.

255 Ibid., 121.

256 Eduardo Elena, Dignifying Argentina, Perónism, Citizenship, and Mass Consumption

The 1955 Coup against Perón

In 1955 another coup was attempted and, although this failed, on 3 September Perón declared a state of siege. Navy planes had slaughtered 300 participants at a mass rally at the Plaza de Mayo. The traditional alliance between Perón and the Church was broken when Perón seemed to listen to ill-advice and sought to diminish the Church-State relationship. Catholic processions became political demonstrations, and attempts by Perón to conciliate failed. Perónists and Catholics became increasingly inflamed against one another.

On 16 September another coup took place, again under Navy leadership. The masses of people were willing to rise up to defend the State forcibly, but Perón preferred to stand aside than allow a bloody civil war among his people to ensue. Indeed, a large quantity of weapons that Evita had purchased in 1951 for the arming of the CGT in the event of a coup, had been given to the police by Perón after Evita's death. When the Perónists asked for weapons Perón responded that he did not want a bloodbath. Alicia Ortiz comments that had Evita lived, both Perónists and anti- Perónists agreed that the coup, and the so-called *Revolución Libertadora*, would not have occurred.[257] Now the police joined the Navy to oust Perón. Perón left for Paraguay on 20 September, and then went on to Venezuela, the Dominican Republic and Panama, where he met the third Mrs. Perón, Isabel, before a long exile in Spain.

Perón, in the first interview after his overthrow, stated of the coup and of his refusal to have the people massacred by the military, despite what would have eventually been a successful popular resistance:

> Reporter: Mr. General, in you letter of resignation on September 19 you said that you wanted to avoid losses

(University of Pittsburgh Press, 2011), 231.

257 Ortiz, op. cit., 364.

invaluable to the Nation. Could loyal forces have prolonged the struggle? Did they have chances of success?

Perón: The chances of success were absolute, but this would have been necessary to prolong the fight, killing many people, and destroying what we worked so hard to create. Just think of what would have happened if I had delivered weapons in the arsenals to the workers. I always avoided bloodshed, considering this useless and sterile savagery. Those who arrive with blood, fall with blood.[258]

Of his leadership of Argentina up until 1955, Perón stated, addressing the calumnies that still haunt his memory in regard to his supposed wealth:

My possessions are well known. My salary as president during my first term I donated to the Foundation Eva Perón, the salaries of the second period, returned to the state. I own a house in Buenos Aires that belonged to my wife and it was built before I was first elected. I also have a house in San Vicente, which I bought as a Colonel, before I would even dream of being the constitutional president of my country. I own property besides the estate of my wife which consists of [her] rights as the author of *The Meaning of my Life*, translated and published in many languages around the world, and the legacy that Alberto Dodero made in his will in favour of Eva Perón.

In addition, many gifts that the people and my friends made in quantity to show their appreciation without limits. Neither money nor power ever interested me, but only love for the humble people, whom I served with a loyalty that led me to accomplish what I did. With the property of my wife that I inherited, the Evita Foundation was instituted; a new entity intended to provide shelter for poor students studying

258 Perón interview with Rodolfo Parbst, United Press, Paraguay, 4 October 1955.

Civilian casualties of the coup against Perón 16th September 1955

> in Buenos Aires. Most of the gifts I received were always awarded to poor boys at sports events and students. In my will I bequeath all my goods to the Evita Foundation, to serve the people and the poor. For ten years I have worked tirelessly for the people. If history could repeat itself, I would do the same, because I believe that the people's happiness is worth the sacrifice of a citizen. My honour, my great satisfaction, is the love of the humble and the hatred of the oligarchs' and capitalists' bad law, and also of their henchmen.[259]

Looking on the accomplishments of his regime, Perón stated:

> When I assumed government, people were earning 20 cents a day, labourers earned 15 pesos a month. Workers were murdered in cold blood. In a country that had 45 million cows, people were dying of constitutional weakness. It was a country of fat bulls and weak pawns. Social Welfare was all but unknown, and insignificant pensions covered only public employees and officers of the armed forces.

259 Ibid.

> We instituted pensions for all workers, even for employers. We created old age and disability pensions, banishing from the country the sad spectacle of misery in the midst of plenty. We legalised the existence of the trade union, and promoted the formation of the CGT [which had] six million dues-paying members. We enabled education and instruction absolutely free to all who would like to study, regardless of class, creed or religion, and in only eight years we built 8,000 schools of all types. Large dams with plants increased the Argentine farming heritage. More than 35,000 public works were completed only with the effort of the first five year plan, including the 1,800 kilometer pipeline, Pistarini airport, the Eva Perón oil refinery, which the rebels wanted to bomb, despite costing $400 million and ten years of work, the Rio Turbio coal mining and railroad, more than twenty large power plants, etc.[260]

The 1955 regime fanatically set about trying to obliterate every trace of Perónism and the very name of Perón. It was decreed:

> WHEREAS in its political existence, the Perónist party offends the democratic sentiment of the Argentine people, the interim president of Argentina, in the exercise of legislative power, decrees having the force of law:
>
> Clause 1: prohibited in the entire territory of the nation:
>
> a) The use of Perónist propaganda.
>
> Particularly in violation of this provision are, The use of photographs, or sculptures of Perónist officials or their relatives, the shield and banner, the proper name of the deposed president, his relatives, the terms 'Perónism' shall be deemed 'Perónist', 'PJ', 'third position', the abbreviation 'PP', dates exalted by the deposed regime, marches 'Of the Perónist boys' and 'Captain Evita', 'The reason for my life'[261] and the speeches of the ousted president and his wife.
>
> b) The use of images, symbols and signs 'created or to

260 Perón interview, ibid.

261 Evita's autobiography.

be created', which could be taken by someone with the purposes stated in the preceding paragraph.

c) The reproduction, by any method, of images and articles referred to in the two preceding paragraphs.

Clause 2: Whoever violates this Decree shall be punished:

a) thirty days imprisonment and a fine;

b) absolute disqualification to serve as a public official or politician or business leader;

c) Closing of commercial enterprises.

Sanctions will not be conditional.[262]

At the Chacarita cemetery, a trashcan replaced the bust of Evita over her grave, although flowers continued to be left there. Anything associated with Perónism was destroyed, from Eva Perón Foundation bedspreads to iron lungs in hospitals. Ortiz comments that shortly after 'a polio epidemic broke out and many children died for lack of respiratory assistance'.[263]

In 1971 Evita's body, which had been secretly buried in Milan, was returned to Perón in Madrid. Evita's body had been perfectly preserved when she had died, but on opening the casket, Perón saw that Evita had been mutilated. Evita's sisters, Blanc and Erminda, who went to Madrid to see the body, issued a statement in 1985 'testifying to the gross mistreatment inflicted on our dear sister Evita's remains'. [264] The body had been desecrated by the military when they had taken it from CGT headquarters during the 1955 coup. The statement described the damage:

- Blows of a hammer to the temple, and on the forehead
- A large gash on her cheek and another on her arm
- Her nose almost completely sunken in, the nasal septum fractured
- Her neck practically severed

262 Decree Law 4161, 5 March 1956.

263 Ortiz, op. cit., 366.

264 Cited by Ortiz, ibid., 371.

- A finger cut off
- Her kneecaps, fractured
- Her chest slashed in four places
- The soles of her feet covered with a layer of tar
- The body had been covered with quicklime and occasionally showed burns[265]

It was Isabel, when president, who had Evita's body returned from Madrid to Argentina on 17 November 1974, after Perón's death. The whole matter had been of immense pain to Perón. Dr. Domingo Tellechea repaired the body, and Evita was laid to rest at a residence, until General Videla ousted Isabel Perón in 1976. Soon after her sisters finally laid her to rest at a family vault in the Recoleta cemetery, where a small plaque commemorates her

Aftermath

Although an intense period of anti-Perónist repression followed in the wake of the Aramburu coup, Arturo Frondizi, presidential nominee for the Intransigent Radical Civic Union, a breakaway from the centrist Radical Civic Union, had secretly met Perón and his primary adviser John William Cooke in 1956, in Caracas, Venezuela. Perón instructed his followers to vote for Frondizi, who won the election. Frondizi assumed the presidency in 1958. He nominated Rogelio Frigerio, a prominent businessmen with a progressive social outlook, inspired by Vargas' corporatist 'New State' in Brazil, as Secretary of Socio-Economic Affairs, despite the opposition of the USA and the military, who considered him a radical. However, under Frigerio's advice, Argentina was opened up to foreign capital.

To show post-Perón Argentina's good faith to plutocracy, the state sold to U.S. corporations for $60,000,000 twenty-two power plants that had been constructed under Perón. By 1962 the country was only producing 600,000 tons of steel when it

265 Ibid., 372.

needed 3,000,000. Meat production dropped from a high of 145,000 metric tons under Perón to 87,000 by the end of 1961. The drop in production meant a crippling trade imbalance, with deficits standing at $237,000,000 in 1960, $450,000,000 in 1961 and $640,000,000 in 1962. Credit was tightened due to the trade deficits. Inflation overtook wage increases at leaps and bounds. While wages went up 400% the price of food increased by 750%. Strikes took on the characteristics of local revolts: in Cordoba automobile workers built barricades and fought the army and police.[266]

Frigerio exercised an informal influence with Frondizi, until the president was overthrown in 1962, while attending a Western Hemisphere summit, where he hoped to mediate in the dispute between the USA and Castro's Cuba. While Frondizi was briefly imprisoned, and Frigerio went into exile, the two reunited in 1963 and founded the Integration and Development Movement (MID), although barred from the elections. Throughout 18 years of exile, Perón maintained labour movement support. Although the very name of Perón was banned from Argentine politics, the movement continued underground. Perónist guerrilla movements, particularly the Montoneros, took on a radical Leftist orientation. A division between radical Left and Right elements within Perónism widened, while Perón took the view that both wings contributed to the Justicialist revolution, and would be reconciled when he returned.

While the hard measures imposed on Argentina saw a reduction in inflation and in the trade deficit, real wages had lost 40% of their purchasing power, and inflation returned. Finance minister Martínez de Hoz responded by allowing the banks a free reign while guaranteeing that the state would take over bad debts. Adolfo Diz, who had been educated at Chicago University under the free-market dogmas of Professor Milton Friedman, (and was hence one of the 'Chicago Boys'[267]) now ran the Central Bank.

266 See John Gerassi, *The Great Fear in Latin America* (The Macmillan Company, 1965).

267 The name given to economists educated at Chicago University under Professor

General Juan José Valle headed a rebellion in 1956 against General Aramburu's dictatorship.

Revolt of General Juan José Valle

On 9 June 1956 pro-Perónists under the leadership of General Juan José Valle, who had been purged from the army because of his Perónist loyalties, attempted to overthrow the regime of General Pedro Eugenio Aramburu.[268] Although the revolt was widespread it was quickly suppressed. General Valle and other rebels were executed by firing squad on 12 June.

The revolt was undertaken with the name National Recovery Movement. The immediate aims were to release political prisoners, reinstate those who had been purged from military and civilian positions, restore the prerogatives of the trades unions, and proceed with elections in which all parties could contest. The longer-term aims were to restore social justice and sovereignty,[269] General Valle stating:

Friedman, who implemented free market policies across the world.

268 Aramburu was assassinated in 1970 by the Montoneros guerrillas.

269 General Juan José Valle, Proclamation of the National Recovery Movement, 9 June 1956.

> The National Recovery Movement is launched to revolutionary action with clear objectives and a concrete program to restore sovereignty and social justice and return to the people the full enjoyment of their freedom and their rights.[270]

Perón in exile, while having been informed of the plans for the revolt, did not believe that it would succeed, but could do nothing to prevent it. His scepticism was based on his view that the Perónist movement and the rebels had been infiltrated by informers and traitors, ensuring that 'the failure was marked in advance, given that within the ranks of those brave comrades there had infiltrated individuals simulating Perónism who were worms of intrigue and distrust'.[271]

Those who fell during the revolt or who were executed, are honoured by Justicialists:

Fallen 9 to 12 June 1956

9 June in La Plata
Cro. Raúl Ramón Videla
Cro. Carlos Irigoyen
Cro. Rolando Zanetta
10 June in Lanús
Tte. Col.. Albino José Irigoyen
Cap. Jorge Miguel Costales
Cro. Dante Hipolito Lugo
Cro. Norberto Ross
Cro. Osvaldo Alberto Albedro
Cro. Clemente Ross

10 June in Jose Leon Suarez Landfill
Cro. Carlos Alberto Lisazo
Cro. Nicolas Carranza
Cro. Mario Brion

270 General Juan José Valle, ibid.

271 Ramon Landajo, 'Facts About June 1956 in Argentina', quoting Perón.

The 1955 Coup against Perón

Cro. Vicente Rodriguez
Cro. Francisco Garibotti
Cro. Aldo E. Jofre
Cro. Miguel Angel Mauriño (ACA)

11 June in Campo de Mayo
Col.. Eduardo Alcibiades Cortinez
Col.. Ricardo Santiago Ibazeta
Cap. Nestor Dart Cano
Cap. Eloy Luis Caro
Jorge Noriega
Tte. Marcelo Videla Nestor

11 June in La Plata
Tte. Col Oscar Lorenzo Cogorno

11 June Army School of Mechanics in Buenos Aires
Subof. Ser. Miguel A. Paolini
Subof. Ser. Ernesto Gareca
Sgt. Eladio Hugo Quiroga
Cabo. Jose Miguel Rodriguez

11 June in Buenos Aires Penitentiary
Sgt. Ayud. Costas Isauro
Luciano Isaias Rojas
Sgt. Ayud. Luis Pugnetti

12 June in National Prison Buenos Aires
Division Gral Juan José Valle

La Plata
Sub. Tte. Res. Juan Alberto Abadie
Soldiers Conscripto D. Blas Closs
Police Insp. Ofic. Rafael Fernández

Achievements of the Perónist State

There are surely few states in history that have achieved anywhere near as much as what was accomplished in the nine years of Perón's rule. It is no wonder that the Peróns are venerated by most Argentines, generation after generation, despite prolonged attempts to destroy every vestige of their existence, and grossly slander their characters.

The First Five Year Plan was announced on 21 October 1946. The plan extended State intervention over economics, health, education, and outlined its role in foreign affairs and trade, aiming to release Argentina from dependency on the world market; a difficult move, as Argentina was dependent on its agricultural exports. The new direction was towards national investment in establishing an industrial base. Hence, it was Perón who took the first steps towards establishing Argentina as a modern economy, albeit one intended to be sovereign.

During Perón's first three years as president wages increased by 27% for skilled workers, and 37% for unskilled workers. Salaried workers increased to 55% of the workforce. The GDP expanded to 30%. In 1949 the six-day week was introduced for public sector workers, and most companies followed. Additionally, there were an increasing number of religious, national and Perónist holidays, and an annual day off given to members of each sector's trade union. Increased spending power meant the increased availability of luxuries such as radios. The state sponsored sports facilities for the poor, and seaside holidays for children at state hostels.[272]

While the continued dependence of Argentina on meat and grain exports to Europe meant that it remained vulnerable, in 1947 Perón introduced the Argentine *peso* as an international currency which enabled war ravaged states such as France and

272 Jill Hedges, op. cit., 122-123.

Germany to pay in *pesos*, which they could obtain by exporting machinery to Argentina.[273] Argentina also had to contend with trade competition from the USA, and two Argentine grain harvests remained unsold, although the effects were not noticed.[274] The Argentine analyst and author Adrian Salbuchi, comments on the bilateral trade agreements:

> This clearly posed a clear danger to the post-World War II U.S. Dollar Grand Areas, which in 1948 accelerated the implementation of the U.S. Marshall Plan. In addition, when invited to become a member of the International Monetary Fund and the World Bank, Perón simply refused, saying Argentina had no need of the U.S. Dollar denominated bank loans… And Argentina certainly did not… at least then.[275]

Education, particularly trade and technical education, expanded. Increased wages meant that children could stay at school without the pressing need to find work. New schools were established by the state and later by the Eva Perón Foundation. The National Technology University was established in 1949 to provide free higher technical training for skilled workers. There was also heavy state investment in public health care, including increased educational facilities for nurses and other health care workers. The building of new, modern hospitals and health centers throughout the country, provided free services, where previously the majority had little access to health care.[276]

Dr. Ramó Carrillo, Chief of Neurosurgery at the Central Military Hospital, developed the concept of 'social medicine'. Dr. Carrillo was appointed head of the Ministry of Public Health, the first such body in Argentina. Perón and Carrillo retained a cordial relationship until Carrillo had to resign in 1954 due to health

---

273 Adrian Salbuchi, 'Argentina's Juan Perón and the "Third Position"', unpublished article.

274 Jill Hedges, op. cit., 124.

275 Adrian Salbuchi, op. cit.

276 Jill Hedges, op. cit., 125.

Fabrica Militar de Aviones Plant in Cordoba, Argentina 1950

reasons, dying two years later. He worked closely with Eva Perón in her social aid programmes. Carrillo held that the key to social health was a triune of the biological, psychological and social. In an interview, Carrillo's nephew and niece stated of him:

> He said that a man is not only sick in the body, but also sick in his soul and in his mind. If a person does not have decent work, adequate food, housing, it is very difficult for him to live healthily. So Carrillo inaugurates social medicine in Argentina as a result of having studied the experiences that were recorded in Europe and the great social movements of his time. Social medicine works mainly on prevention and this task involves, of course, medicine, but also other fields of knowledge.
>
> The first health plan was part of the First Five-Year Plan, produced in four months, along with hundreds of collaborators from different disciplines and professions, without distinguishing whether they were Perónists or not. Four thousand pages in three volumes made up the program. There was a centralised conception but an operationally decentralised model arose in the regions.

> He changed a philosophy, a culture and a way of thinking about the practice of medicine. For him, a doctor should be able to analyse his patient in the triple dimension referred to by my sister. What predominated before Carrillo was a split look at the sick, both in social reality and its immediate surroundings. So he articulated action by his Ministry with almost all areas of the state. If you had a patient who lived in a house impossible to inhabit, the Ministry of Health immediately sought a decent house for that person. Who can live in a healthy manner in a home with humidity, no heat, no floors, no indoor bathroom? Hence the tasks he implemented were interrelated.
>
> It is not a simple task to summarise Carrillo's most important achievements. First, what is noteworthy is the introduction of what we call social medicine in the field of health. In other planes it is impossible not to mention the eradication of malaria, for example. Also duplication of beds in public hospitals in less than nine years. The frontal attack against venereal diseases and syphilis that virtually disappear. The decrease in mortality from tuberculosis, from 130 to 36 per hundred thousand inhabitants. Eradicated epidemics such as typhus and brucellosis and reduced infant mortality from 90 per thousand to 56 per thousand. Along with this, you cannot fail to mention the state Medical Specialities, a set of more than one hundred monodrugs free for people who had no access to medicines. It is one of the first decisions made by the Ministry.[277]

In eight years, 4,229 health facilities were built providing the foundations of the Argentine health structure to the present day, just as it was the Perón years that built Argentina's modern industrial base. Prior to the Perónist State, Carrillo's studies had determined that Argentina only had 45% of the hospital beds

277 Interview with Augusto and Maria Salome Carrillo by Pedro Pesatti, 2006, http://www.pensamientonacional.com.ar/docs.php?idpg=pesatti/0006_reportaje_a_augusto_y_mar_a_salom__carrillo.html

that were required, and these were unevenly distributed, with some areas not having any. Carrillo wrote that: 'The Free State hospitals or charitable societies were developing in precarious conditions, lack of staff, food, medicines and equipment. Rural areas were totally unprotected ... The hospitals kept the spirit of charity that charities had from the previous century, far beyond the good intentions that the nature of public service should be'.

At indication of the vindictiveness of the post- Perón regimes was that Carrillo's body could not be returned to Argentina until the return of Perón from exile in 1973.

Centres of Justicialist Party cadres were established throughout Argentina to ensure that every local community was provided with the full measure of services, such as classes and training, forums for local political participation, and even low-cost beautician services. These local services were extended still further when Evita established the Women's Perónist Party.[278]

The National Mortgage Bank provided funding for public housing. Argentina was short of 650,000 houses, according to the last census. Mortgages were made available at low interest. The National Housing Authority supervised the construction of single unit houses. Although the *Banco Hipotecario Nacional* had been established in 1886, under Perón its loan portfolio was increased from 100,000 mortgages in 1946 to 500,000 by the time of Perón's ouster.[279] Loans were mostly made over periods of 15-20 years at 4% interest, adjusted by inflation, allowing most households to be owned by their occupants. Such private ownership shows that Justicialism, so far from being a form of antiquated 'socialism', aimed to more widely distribute property. *Banco Hipotecario Nacional* was privatised in 1997, after having had its role in home finance increasingly reduced over several decades. However, because of lack of private investment interest,

278 Jill Hedges, op. cit.

279 Horacio Gaggero and Alicia Garro, Del trabajo a casa: Politica de vivienda del gobierno Perónista 1946-1955 (Buenos Aires: Editorial Biblos, 1996).

The locomotive 'Presidente Perón' on display in Buenos Aires in 1950

the state retained a 40% share. Under the Perónist Kirchner administrations, the bank now operates as the fourth largest mortgage lender, administering a $4,000,000,000 building programme over four years for 100,000 homes, at long term low interest, funded from the ANSES social insurance agency.

Between 1946-1949 a programme of nationalisation was pursued, starting with the purchase of the United River Plate Telephone Company from ITT, while the corporation remained a supplier of equipment for a system that was in urgent need of modernisation. The British owned railway system was nationalised in 1947. Over $100,000,000 were invested to modernise the railways (which had been built by the British on incompatible gauges).

The Port of Buenos Aires was nationalised. The national merchant marine was tripled to 1.2 million tons displacement, reducing the need for over $100,000,000 in shipping fees. The Río Santiago Shipyards at the port of Ensenada, Buenos Aires, were opened. Ship-building expanded by 500%. The Dodero shipping lines were acquired by the state, albeit based on a miscalculation that Argentina's economy would be strengthened by the USA and Europe soon having to devalue, and that Argentine agricultural exports would be in high demand.[280] What transpired instead was a U.S. plan to keep Argentine products out of Europe by subsidies and loans via the Marshall Plan, a programme designed to rebuild Europe in the face of a Soviet threat.

All commodity exports were marketed via a state Argentina Institute for Promotion of Trade (IAPI). The IAPI bought meat and cereals from producers and sold them on the international market, taking the previous monopoly from conglomerates such as Bunge y Born, which had a near monopoly on cereal and flour exports.[281] Profits were used to assist private, state and provincial needs; subsidise consumer prices, and fund social aid projects. The IAPI also planned and prioritised production and acquired raw materials for manufacturers. Argentina's $1,000,000,000 debt to the Bank of England was paid off.

By 1947, Argentina had its own iron and steel industry. One of the largest steel mills in Latin America was constructed at San Nicolas de los Arroyos, Buenos Aires province. Modern technology was introduced for coal mining at Rio Turbio, albeit the only coal mine in Argentina.

The State energy policy was directed by the National Energy Authority, which had been established in 1943. Under the Authority's direction in 1946 departments were set up to oversee the development of gas and solid fuels, power plants and fuel plants. Hydroelectric capacity during Perón's first term went from 45 to 350 megawatts . By 1954 Perón had initiated more than 45 major hydroelectric projects intended to produce 2,000,000,000 kilowatt-hours of energy.

In 1949 a 1,700km natural gas pipeline between Comodoro Rivadavia and Buenos Aires – the longest in the world - was

280 Jill Hedges, op. cit., 127.

281 Ironically, Bunje and Born was restored to power by the supposed 'Perónist' Carlos Menem, in 1989, the corporation providing two ministers of economics from its ranks, followed by a currency crisis.

completed, increasing supply from 300,000 m^3 to 15,000,000 m^3 daily. Argentina thereby became self-sufficient in natural gas.

Oil requirements remained problematic, however, and with industrial expansion and an expanding home market, cost over one-fifth of the import bill. The *Yacimientos Petrolíferos Fiscales* (YPF), Treasury Petroleum Fields, was established in 1922 by President Hipólito Yrigoyen as the first State run oil company in the world, dealing with exploration, transporting, refining and marketing of oil and gas,with ongoing opposition from oil trusts and most of all by the Rockefeller dynasty's Standard Oil.[282] In 1946 Perón expanded its role with the creation of State Gas, using gas from YPF. YPF oil production rose to more than 23,000,000 barrels by 1953 (82% of Argentina's total oil production). However, despite the massive gains in production, consumption rose until by 1953 60% of the oil needs were imported, obliging Perón to reach deals with foreign oil corporations, including Standard Oil; a major set-back for the Perónist aim of economic self-sufficiency. Pseudo-Perónist President Menem privatised much of the YPF in 1991, but President Cristina Fernández de Kirchner renationalised YPF in 2012.

Regional air carriers were nationalised and merged into the Aerolíneas Argentinas in 1950. The airline was equipped with 36 new DC-3 and DC-4 aeroplanes. An international airport was built with a 22 km freeway into Buenos Aires, and a freeway between Rosario and Santa Fe. An aeronautics industry, with the assistance of German technicians, was among the most innovative in the world, under the direction of Dr. Reymar Horten. Similarly, the locomotive industry, funded by the state development bank from 1948, was advanced by world standards. The innovative flagship of the locomotive industry, 'Presidente Perón', renamed 'Argentina' after 1955, had 'an almost revolutionary thermal efficiency'.[283]

282 Felipe Pigna, Los Mitos de la historia argentina, (Planeta Historia y Sociedad, 2006), 153.

283 Martyn Bane, 'Saving Argentina', http://www.rypn.org/rypn_files/articles/

'For the People of the World'

The Justicialist flag
our banner will be
for the people of the world
the flag of love and peace[284]

Perón stated that Justicialism is the Argentine variant of 'national socialism'. It is by and for Argentines. Nonetheless, Justicialism is part of a broad movement that is universal in scope but national in application. Justicialism has two doctrinal aspects beyond the confines of Argentina that Perón called 'continentalism' and 'universalism'. 'Continentalism' has received a renewed voice today in the concept of geopolitical blocs, or 'vectors', as a challenge to the 'new world order' of superpower hegemony..

One of the most influential ideologues of present day continentalism is Dr. Alexander Dugin, head of the Centre for Conservative Studies at Moscow State University. Dugin's doctrine has been widely influential and is reflected in the speeches and foreign policies of Vladimir Putin.[285] In the aftermath of the Second World War, post-fascist and national socialist movements sought to develop the embryonic continentalism that vied with the petty-statism and national chauvinism within some of these movements before and during the war.

Mosley And Perón

In the latter regard, the British pre-war Fascist leader and philosopher, Sir Oswald Mosley, later noted that Fascism was 'an intensely national creed', and that this nationalism in the aftermath of the Second World War was passé. Mosley rejected Fascism as a post-war creed, while never repudiating his pre-war British Fascist policy, which was based around building an

Articles/050201argentina/default.htm

284 Captain Evita (Capitana Evita), Perónist girl's anthem.

285 K. R. Bolton, *Geopolitics of the Indo-Pacific: Emerging Conflicts, New Alliances* (London: Black House Publishing, 2013), 174-180.

National Party of Europe, Venice Conference attended by, (image left to right), Alvise Loredan: Italy, Oswald Mosley: UK, Adolf von Thadden: Germany, Jean Thiriart: Belgium.

autarchic British Empire. The answer of Mosley and of other former 'fascists' and national socialists for the post-war era was a post-fascism that would replace outmoded national and imperial concepts with the formation of new geopolitical blocs. This not only repudiated the former petty-state nationalism but also the international economic order, based on free trade, that the USA aimed to impose on the world, which had been enunciated as a primary war aim by President Roosevelt in the 'Atlantic Charter',[286] which was being imposed through the Marshall Plan.

Mosley and others advocated firstly the concept of 'Europe-a-Nation', a union of Europe as a 'third force' in world politics, analogous to Perón's 'third position', that would be independent of both the USA and the USSR. Such a union, above all, spiritual and cultural, would ensure that no more intra-European wars were fought at the behest of non-European interests or for narrow national interests. The European Nation would form a self-contained trading bloc, and act jointly on matters of defence and foreign policy. Mosley formed Union Movement in 1948 to

286 F. D. Roosevelt and Winston S. Churchill, '*The Atlantic Charter*', 14 August 1941, http://usinfo.org/docs.democracy/53.htm

advocate a united, syndicalist Europe. Other movements arose throughout Europe with similar ideas. In 1962 delegates from several parties met with Mosley and issued the 'Declaration of Venice' as the basis for a 'National Party of Europe'. Among these was the Belgian national-revolutionary thinker and activist Jean Thiriart. Perón knew both Thiriart and Mosley, and shared their ideas on geopolitical blocs as the means of re-organising the post-war world.

In 1950 Mosley travelled to Argentina to meet those with a like vision. He had the opportunity to meet Perón. He travelled to Argentina on 31 October 1950 under the assumed name of Harry Morley. However, MI5 had already discovered the travel plans from their phone tap on Union Movement headquarters. MI6 and the Foreign Office were informed, and Mosley, on landing in Buenos Aires, was interviewed. He stated that his visit was connected with the sale of his books in Argentina and Chile. While the month-long stay in Argentina was widely reported in the U.S., British and Argentine press, none knew of Mosley's meeting with Perón. [287] Even the Mosley movement's newspaper *Union* only reported that Mosley found much interest in the Spanish and German editions of his book *The Alternative*, and that two major publishing firms had acquired the South American rights of these editions.[288]

The first indication that Mosley had travelled to Argentina came shortly after the overthrow of Perón in 1955. *European Stars and Stripes*, the newspaper of the U.S. army of occupation in Europe, reported that the military junta's investigators had raided the home of Colonel Hans Ulrich Rudel, who had moved to Paraguay when Perón was overthrown. Rudel, the Second World War German air ace, was among the many European refugees whom Perón had taken in after the defeat and occupation of Europe, when vengeance had been unleashed against the political, military

287 Jeffrey Wallder, 'Perón or Death!', *Comrade*, London, Friends of Mosley, May 2013

288 'Mosley Visits Argentina', cited by Wallder, ibid., 5.

and cultural leadership of the Occident.[289] Rudel was among the European war veterans who supported Mosley' post-war vision of a united European. Mosley wrote of these veterans: 'young Germans fresh from the army, and particularly from the SS regiments, were passionately European and supported my advanced European ideals'. Many had become embittered by their persecution although they could not in any way be alleged to have been involved in 'war crimes'. One of these was Rudel, whom Mosley called 'the supreme German hero of the last war'. 'He won every major medal the air force had to give and a special decoration then had to be invented for him. He destroyed five hundred Russian tanks with his own machine, and also a Soviet battleship. After losing a leg, he flew again, was shot down behind Russian lines, and escaped.' However, because of the post-war suppression, his saga of epic heroism could not be published. Mosley brought out Rudel's memoirs, *Stuka Pilot*, through his own publishing company,[290] Euphorion, and the preface was written by Britain's own one-legged air ace, Douglas Bader.

In Rudel, Perón and Mosley had a mutual friend and ally. Rudel served as an adviser to the Perón Government, and was a notable figure at diplomatic receptions and state dinners.[291] It was with Perón's approval that Rudel was granted leave to travel to Europe to promote *Stuka Pilot*.[292]

Did Mosley's 1950 visit help to shape Perón's geopolitical views, not just on Latin American unity, but on how such a bloc would relate to a united Europe? Perón made his first major declaration

289 Perón regarded the Nuremberg Trials against the German leadership as 'a base infamy, an atrocity that History will never forgive'. Cited by Ortiz, op. cit., 123. This was a view shared, but seldom publicised, by eminent legal and military authorities throughout the world. See H. K. Thompson Jr. and Henry Strutz, Doentiz at Nuremberg: A Re-Appraisal – War Crimes and the Military Professional (New York: Amber Publishing Corp., 1976).

290 Oswald Mosley, *My Life* (London: Black House Publishing, 2012), 465.

291 Martin Lee, *The Beast Reawakens* (London: Little Brown and Co., 1997), 111.

292 Jeffrey Wallder, op. cit., 5.

on Continental unity in 1951, shortly after Mosley's visit. Perón's vision was of a philosophical character, well beyond the base economic motives by which such blocs are usually understood in terms of mere trade. Mosley never revealed his meeting with Perón, but they kept in communication, although it is not known whether they ever met again.[293] A letter from Perón, in 1960 from his exile in Spain, addressed to Mosley, reads:

> I see now we have friends in common whom I greatly value, something which makes me reciprocate even more strongly your expressions of solidarity… I offer my best wishes and a warm embrace.[294]

Who those friends were that Mosley and Perón had in common is indicated by Jean Thiriart, himself one of those mutual friends. On a question to Thiriart regarding the relations between a future united Europe and Latin America, he alluded to the close friendship that had existed between Perón, German commando extraordinaire Colonel Otto Skorzeny, and himself in Spain. The three met frequently at Perón's residence or at the Horcher restaurant in Madrid. Thiriart stated:

> Early on, Perón got into contact with me when he learned of my anti-American stance through Skorzeny. I have published letters and interviews with Perón. When it came to discussing the United States, we were definitely on the same wavelength. In Madrid, political pilgrims from all of South America — not just Argentina — came daily to see Perón. There was a continual stream of visitors. He was the symbol of Latin-American dignity.[295]

Colonel Skorzeny, an engineer and representative for Krupp's, met Perón on several occasions in Argentina during the

---

293 Ibid., 6.

294 Perón to Mosley, Malaga, Spain, 20 February 1960, cited by Wallder, ibid.

295 Interview with Thiriart by Gene H. Hogberg, http://home.alphalink.com.au/~radnat/thiriart/interview5.html

1950s,[296] and along with Rudel, assisted with the resettlement of German refugees in Argentina.[297] Both became 'close friends and acquaintances with Mosley'.[298] This had been part of Mosley's search for those of the persecuted generation, who after the Second World War would embrace the pan-European idea. Indeed, Madrid, at around the time Perón settled there, became a centre for a pan-European organisation founded by Rudel and Skorzeny.[299]

While there is no record of the conversation that took place between Mosley and Perón in 1950, the subjects can be deduced from the communications that took place between Thiriart and Perón during the latter's years of exile in Spain. While Mosley considered the USSR to be a greater enemy than the USA towards Europe, Thiriart and Perón both saw the USA as the primary enemy. Indeed, Thiriart talked hopefully of a 'Euro-Soviet Empire'.[300] This was a view also shared by other leading post-fascists, including 'Nazi' veterans such as Rudel,[301] Major General Otto Remer, whose Socialist Reich Party promoted a 'neutralist' line during the Cold War, much to the consternation of the USA, and Dr. Johannes von Leers, who had been Reich propaganda minister Goebbel's chief aide and was prominent in the German refugee community in Argentina that established the newspaper *Der Weg* (The Way).[302]

296 Martin Lee, op. cit., 109.

297 Ibid., 109-111.

298 Stephen Dorril, *Blackshirt: Sir Oswald Mosley and British Fascism* (London: Penguin Books, 2007), 562.

299 Ibid., 591.

300 Interview with Thiriart by Gene H. Hogberg, op. cit. Thiriart saw Marxism as historically a 'spent force'.

301 Martin Lee, op. cit., 115.

302 Ibid., 113.

Thiriart and Perón

Skorzeny introduced Thiriart to Perón and they became 'close collaborators'.[303] Thiriart is a character of particular interest. During the war he trained under Skorzeny[304] in combating extreme Left terrorism – otherwise known as 'The Resistance'. Many others all over Europe supported the Axis, and none more so than the large numbers who volunteered to fight for the national divisions of the Waffen SS. Both of Belgium's ethnic groups, the Walloon's under the *Rexist* leader Leon Degrelle, also an exile in Spain, and the Flemish, supported Germany to a significant extent. Thiriart was jailed for several years in Belgium as a 'collaborator'. Maintaining a low profile for over a decade, supporting a family, and gaining eminence as an optometrist during the early 1960s, Thiriart emerged to establish support groups for the Belgian settlers in the Congo and the French settlers in Algeria, who were faced with indigenous revolts. Soon Thiriart recognised, as had Remer and others, that the USA (aligned with Israel and Zionism) and not the USSR, was the primary enemy of European civilisation. In 1965 his book *Europe: An Empire of 400 Million Men*, was published. A revolutionary pan-European movement, *Jeune Europe*, was organised across the Continent, and started training for guerrilla warfare against the American forces that occupied Europe on the pretext of 'protecting Europe from the Soviet threat'. However, Skorzeny considered guerrilla tactics premature, and *Jeune Europe* was dissolved, although not before the first European volunteer for the Palestinian cause, who had come from the ranks of the Thiriart movement, had died fighting Zionism.[305]

Thiriart considered that Europe would, given no other option, 'unify in a death struggle with the United States'. He suggested that Spanish could become the *lingua franca* of a united Europe. Latin America would become an important factor in an alliance with united Europe, Thiriart stating:

---

303 Ibid., 177-178.

304 'Jean Thiriart : Prophet and Militant', Part I, http://home.alphalink.com.au/~radnat/thiriart/thiriart1.html

305 Ibid.

> The adoption of the Spanish language for the future Europe would immediately allow it to be at the gates if not in the antechamber of the United States. A Europe officially speaking Spanish would immediately be in the suburbs of Los Angeles and Miami! Throughout Latin America, Europe is held in an esteem that it has not enjoyed in the United States especially since the time of Theodore Roosevelt's Big Stick policy… Armed struggle against the United States, armed politico-military struggle (underground activities), has already begun throughout more or less the whole of Latin America even though it has not yet begun here in Europe.[306]

As for Perón, an interview he had with Thiriart in Madrid in 1968 is an informative source on his views on geopolitics. In answer to Thiriart's first question on Perón's book *La Hora de los Pueblos*, Perón stated that the overthrow of his Justicialist Government by 'international forces' shows how difficult it is for a people to remain free. Beyond Argentina, he considered the struggle for the liberation of Latin America as part of a 'global struggle in the continent'. The next step would be for a united Latin America to align with the Third World:

> In this struggle, each country is integral to its neighbours, with whom he must find support. The first priority for these countries is to unite, to integrate. The second point is to achieve effective alliance with the Third World, as we have recommended, my staff and myself, for 25 years! This is the path that should be given to the South American people, not just the leaders, but also to the masses who must be aware of the necessity of the struggle against imperialism. Unify the continent and become free from external influences, ally to the Third World to participate in the global struggle against imperialism; such are the primary objectives.[307]

306 Interview with Thiriart by Gene H. Hogberg, op. cit.

307 Perón to Thiriart, Madrid, 1968.

To Thiriart's question on whether there is a traitor class in Argentina that works with the United States, Perón replied that both the older oligarchy and the quickly growing 'new bourgeoisie' were against 'the people'. Here Perón refers to Justicialism as a form of 'national socialism':

> Justicialism is a form of socialism, national socialism, which responds to the needs and living conditions of Argentina. It is natural that socialism has led to the mass in its name, with its social demands. What it has created is totally different and quite a new system from the old 'democratic' social system of liberalism, which dominated the country shamelessly in the service of imperialism.[308]

The control firstly of the oligarchies throughout Latin America by U.S. interests, and then the use of military coups to establish puppet governments, had overthrown a series of states, the first in line having been Argentina. Thiriart alluded to the move towards European unity having been taken over by U.S. interests and the creation of a bogus 'Europe' around the European Common Market. However, Thiriart commented that the real Europe necessitates 'de-americanisation'. The intention was a 'third force', and indeed Perón regarded American and Soviet imperialism as having amicably agreed to a 'division of the world' between them. This 'third force' could only be created in Latin America by the national resistance movements working simultaneously and in co-operation. While the world had always seen imperialism, Perón stated that according to his theory of 'historical determinism', these empires live in cycles and the current imperialism was on a downward path. Both the USA and Russia were 'rotting from the inside'. National revolutionaries would have to use this cycle of decay against them to 'rush the process of degradation'. This requires a 'sacred union' opposing these forces.

308 Ibid.

Expanding on his theory of 'historical determinism', Perón stated that the process of social evolution has been one of increasing 'integration', 'from the caveman to the present day. The individual family, the tribe, the city, the feudal state, the current nations, it comes to continental integration'. Great geopolitical blocs are the next stage in historical evolution. The small nation-states would not be able to survive and would succumb to such power blocs unless they united with other states with common interests and identity. Europe would have to unite or succumb, as would the Latin America states.

> A united Europe would count a population of nearly 500 million. The South American continent already has more than 250 million. Such blocs would be respected and effectively oppose the enslavement to imperialism which is the lot of a weak and divided country.[309]

Perón concluded by stating that he regularly read Thiriart's journal *La Nation Européenne,* and that he 'fully agrees' with the ideas. However, he stated that Europe must look to alliances beyond the Occident. He regarded an alliance between the future blocs of Europe and Latin America as 'essential'. Of particular note is that Perón identified Latin Americans as 'Europeans, stating:

> Latin America in particular is an essential element to form an alliance with Europe. We Latin Americans are Europeans, not part of the American trend. I personally feel more French, more and more Spanish, German American. The old Jew Disraeli was right when he said: 'The people have no permanent friends or enemies, they have permanent interests', they must associate those interests, even if they are geographically distant, if Europe continues to be the first civilising power in the world.[310]

---

309 Perón to Thiriart, ibid.

310 Perón to Thiriart, Madrid, 1968

We get a clear view of Perón's conception of Latin America as a cultural outpost of Europe, and it is to a future 'European nation' to which a future Latin American bloc should look, as being part of the European cultural organism, from which the USA is quite separate, and indeed, antagonistic. It is an interesting aside, as will be seen, that Argentina continues to promote 'European immigration' as a principle of its constitution.

For Mosley's part, he also alluded to an alliance of a united European bloc with a Latin American bloc as part of a far-reaching 'syndicalist revolution'. Mosley spoke of this syndicalist revolution in public speeches during the 1950s, and it is referred to in an early Union Movement policy statement on syndicalism where – through 'European Socialism' – 'the parasitic financial and industrial boss-class' would be removed, and there would be a uniting of British workers 'with their European comrades, for developing and settling Africa and for achieving the closest co-operation with the syndicalism of South America'.[311] Mosley's Union Movement syndicalist policy document concluded:

> Through European Socialism the full potentialities of three continents can be realised, on the one hand by freeing and encouraging the brilliant individual to use science in transforming resources to produce new forms of wealth: on the other through Syndicalism to share the wealth of continents of those who work in industry. The workers of Europe stand on the threshold of the greatest social advance of their history.[312]

This reference by Union Movement to the emerging syndicalism of Latin America was written several years prior to Perón's removal in 1955, and can only be primarily a reference to Perónist Argentina.

---

311 *A Workers Policy Through Syndicalism* (Union Movement Industrial Council, 1953), 11.

312 Ibid.

Latin American Nation

In 1951 Perón wrote of his vision of a united Latin America:

> The sign of the Southern Cross can be the symbol of triumph of the *numina* of the America of the Southern Hemisphere. Neither Argentina, nor Brazil, nor Chile can, by themselves, dream of the economic unity indispensable to face a destiny of greatness. United, however they form a most formidable unit, astride the two oceans of modern civilisation. Thus, Latin-American unity could be attempted from here, with a multifaceted operative base and unstoppable initial drive.
>
> On this basis, the South American Confederation can be built northward, joining in that union all the peoples of Latin roots. How? It can come easily, if we are really set to do it.
>
> We know that these ideas will not please the imperialists who 'divide and conquer'. United we will be unconquerable; separate, defenceless. If we are not equal to our mission, men and nations will suffer the fate of the mediocre. Fortune will offer us her hand. May God wish we know to take hold of it. Every man and every nation has its hour of destiny. This is the hour of the Latin people.
>
> We Argentines are prepared, ready and waiting. If we throw the first stone, it is because we are blameless.[313]

Perón declared:

> Argentina, alone, is not an economic unit; nor Brazil, or Chile alone. Yet these three countries together form currently the most extraordinary economic unit in the world. No doubt that with this union, other South American countries will come into its orbit.[314]

---

313 Cited in 'Continental Integration: The Perónist Experiment', *Executive Intelligence Review*, 26 September 1986, 60.

314 Cited in Carlos Conde, 'Perón, Vargas, the alliance unfinished', Clarin.com, 19 November 2005, http://edant.clarin.com/suplementos/cultura/2005/11/19/u-01092040.htm

Already in 1946 the press noted that when the new Brazilian ambassador, Dr. Juan Bautista Luzardo, arrived in Buenos Aires, he was greeted at Buenos Aires railway station by a large welcome by Perónistas; while 'General Perón's work and programme of social justice have even won him a certain active support among the proletariat of neighboring countries. Many Bolivian miners are said to be Perónistas, and mysterious leaflets and posters praising Perón's social policy have appeared in Uruguay'.[315]

Latin America was ready for this continental unity, with the election to the presidency in Brazil of Getúlio Vargas in 1950, and of General Carlos Ibáñez del Campo in Chile in 1952. Ibáñez had lived in exile in Buenos Aires and was a close friend of Perón's. A few months after the election of Ibáñez, Perón stated to a Chilean newspaper, before travelling to Chile several days later: 'I believe that Chilean-Argentine unity, a total unity and not halfway, should be complete and immediate. Simple economic unity will not be strong enough… in this situation one must be bold'.[316]

While the governments of Ibáñez are not particularly notable, and their doctrine was imprecise, in Vargas there was very much a kindred spirit. Vargas was inspired by the corporatist 'New State' of Salazar's Portugal, and indeed under Vargas' regime Brazil was also called the 'New State'.

Vargas had assumed leadership of Brazil in 1933, and was re-elected in 1950. He enacted a corporative constitution in 1934 that provided governmental representation based on occupation and location, forty occupational representatives being included in a parliament of 214, despite the opposition of those who wanted to maintain the old system of party politics.[317] In 1953 he named João Goulart Minister of Labour, and the Brazilian General

315 'New Term in Argetnina', *The New York Times*, 4 January 1946.

316 Cited in '*Continental Integration*', op. cit.

317 For a comparative analysis of Perón and Vargas see: Torcuato S. Di Tella, 'Perón Y

Confederation of Workers was organised with the Perónist CGT as the model. Goulart travelled to Argentina and met Perón. Brazilian oil was nationalised in 1953, and the state petroleum corporation was established. Perón said of this: 'Getulio Vargas, genuine representative of the Brazilian people, triumphed against pressures of the North and the dollars of Standard Oil'. [318] Indeed, Argentina had assisted Vargas' presidential campaign with funds, printing and other largesse, and had also provided assistance to Ibáñez in Chile.[319]

However, despite his authoritarian style, Vargas was badly restrained by the predicable capitalist-communist nexus. Shortly after Vargas assumed the presidency, in February 1951, Perón sent his special envoy, Colonel Robert T. Dalton, to see the Brazilian leader, to extend the alliance between Perónism and Getulism as the basis of Latin American unity. Vargas, however, had to reply that the opposition in Congress was too strong to inaugurate the Continental doctrine, and that Brazil was still reliant on economic relations with the USA. However, Vargas reiterated that accord between the two nations remained his aim. In 1954, with an impending insurrection by the armed forces, Vargas committed suicide. Vargas had intended to remain true to his commitments to Perón, but could not overcome entrenched interests. Brazilian writer Carlos Conde states:

> A secret dossier sent to Buenos Aires in July 1954 from the Embassy Argentina shows that Vargas had no backing to fulfil what he had promised. Its content in encrypted diplomatic language, reads as follows: 'President Getúlio Vargas has sympathy for our country, but their means of expression (political and administrative) are cut by a strong opposition (Parliament, media and ruling classes). The political sense forces him to silence his real thinking and

Vargas: Parallel Lives', Paper presented at the Argentina-Brazil Seminar, Pontifical Catholic University of Rio de Janeiro, 15 and August 16, 1996.

318 Cited in 'Continental Integration', op. cit., 61.

319 Carlos Conde, op. cit.

> frees his ministers. To this we owe the profound alterations of the foreign policy of two cabinets of the same president. It is as if the eyes and ears of Juan Perón in Brazil will say: Getúlio Vargas did not betray him.[320]

When Perón went to Chile in 1953 to secure the support of Ibáñez for Continental unity, he assured the Chilean president of Vargas' backing, but was met by opposing statements by the Brazilian Foreign Minister Joao Neves da Fontoura, who publicly condemned regional pacts. Something of the situation Vargas and Perón were facing from outside interference to prevent Latin American unity can be deduced from a newspaper account of Perón's trip:

> LONDON, Sat — As President Perón of Argentina arrived in Chile yesterday for talks on a possible Latin United States, Argentine officials began to look nervously towards Brazil. At the same time, both Chile and Argentina became further involved with Britain over encroachment into British Falkland Islands territory.
>
> President Perón reached Santiago (Chile) for a six day State visit. He was met at the station by his old friend President Carlos Ibanez Del Campo, of Chile, with whom he will discuss the proposal for economic and political unity.
>
> Jets for rival
>
> A Buenos Aires report says Perón is getting nervous about the British delivery of 70 Meteor jet fighter planes to Argentina's historic rival, Brazil. The British planes, swapped for 15,000 bales of Brazilian cotton, will put Brazil well in the lead in Latin American air power. Argentina has been wasting a lot of her own jet planes— all imported from Britain — in flying crashes.

320 Carlos Conde, ibid.

> Falklands Notes
>
> Britain wanted to hush up the newest incident in Antarctica, but got in first by lodging a Note ahead of a 'very strong Note' which Argentina sent to Britain yesterday. Since then Chile has rejected a Note from Britain. According to the British Notes, a party of Argentinians and Chileans last month erected huts on the airstrip of a British base at Deception Island, in the Falklands, while Chileans laid out a lawn the size of a Soccer-pitch and taped 'Chile' in big white letters in the centre. By the time HMS Snipe arrived to investigate rumours of these activities, all but two of the 'trespassers' — both Argentineans — had left. British sailors knocked down the huts and bundled the trespassers aboard the Snipe, which is taking them to Argentina.[321]

It is evident from the above article that British and other outside interests were meddling in Latin American affairs to prevent Continental unity. Britain held out the prospect of building Brazil into an economic and military power on the Continent, if she would reject Perón's overtures. Hence, Vargas faced pressures from within and without to reject a formal accord with his friend and ally, Perón. He was, like Perón, to succumb to the military that opposed his revolutionary aims.

Joseph Page explains the machinations in preventing the Argentina-Brazil pact that would have formed the basis of Continental unity:

> It would have taken a Herculean effort to overcome the antagonism between Argentina and Brazil, a deeply entrenched reality which first Great Britain and later the United States exploited as the cornerstone of their diplomatic policy towards South America. Nonetheless, Getulio Vargas's surprise election victory in 1950 brought

321 'Perón woos Chile, but fears Brazil', *Sunday Mail*,Brisbane, 22 February 1953, 1.

> to the Brazilian presidency the only politician who could have reached an agreement with the Argentines. Vargas was friendly with Perón, and was open to the idea of continental unity. According to Perón, when Vargas took the presidency again, he promised that they would meet in Rio de Janeiro or Buenos Aires to sign the joint agreement that Perón would later seal with Ibáñez.[322]

On Perón's return from Chile he was visited by the journalist Gerardo Rocha, a friend of Vargas', who said to Perón that he had been asked to explain Vargas' position and apologise.[323]

With Perón's visit to Chile, an agreement was signed on economic unity. In July 1953 Ibáñez went to Argentina and signed a treaty with Perón reducing customs tariffs, increasing bilateral trade, and establishing a joint council on Argentine-Chilean relations.

In October 1953 Perón went to Paraguay and signed an accord, but a planned second trip was cancelled due to the coup staged by Alfredo Stroessner in 1954.

In late 1953 Perón signed economic pacts with Ecuador and Nicaragua.[324] Yet, as in Paraguay and Brazil, these initiatives did not come to fruition because of the pressures on those who opposed a Latin American bloc. The so-called 'strong men' of South America could not overcome entrenched interests within, and plutocratic and imperial interests without. Stroessner, like Vargas, was supportive of Perón, but was unable to resist outside pressures, especially with his early reliance on the USA.

The opposition that Perón's vision of Latin American unity faced from oligarchic interests throughout the continent was being addressed already in 1953 with the formation through the Perónist labour union, the CGT, of a labour movement that

322 Joseph Page, *Perón: A Biography* (Random House, 1983), 277.

323 Carlos Conde, op. cit.

324 'Continental Integration', op. cit., 61.

would extend across Latin America: Agrupación de Trabajadores Latinoamericanos Sindicalistas (ATLAS). The purpose is evident: to extend Justicialism across the continent via a new labour movement committed to the 'third position'.

The movement was relatively successful although short-lived. Founded in Mexico, the main instigators were Argentina's CGT and Mexico's CROM (Confederación Regional Obrera Mexicana), a nationalist labour union that had been established in 1918, which continues to exist. In certain respects CROM was a precursor of Justicialism: in 1919 the movement had reached an accord with the new President, General Álvaro Obregón Salido, rejecting class war in favour of collaboration between capital and labour, and the regime established a Labour Department, enacted new labour laws, and disputes were settled by arbitration.[325] ATLAS repudiated both the pro-U.S. ORIT and the pro-Communist CTAL unions, stating that Latin Americans should build a 'third way' free of outside interference. [326] They were joined in 1954 by Venezuela's Confederación Nacional de Trabajadores. ATLAS was banned in 1955, with the overthrow of Perón.[327]

325 Enrique Krauze, *Mexico: Biography of Power* (Harper Collins, 1998), 389.

326 José Luis Rubio, Las internacionales obreras en América, (Madrid: 1971), 85-86

327 Ibid., 86.

The National State

This treatise, *The National State*, having been written by Perón in Buenos Aires in 1972, during a preliminary visit for his return from exile in 1973, just two years before his death, is therefore one of his final and definitive statements on Justicialist doctrine. The document emphasises that Justicialism is in revolt against both 'anti-national liberal forces' and Marxism that are operating in conjunction as a 'synarchy'. *The National State* is one of the most comprehensive documents explaining Justicialism. The three premises of the Justicialist doctrine are:

- Christianity
- Nationalism
- Revolution

> The National Justicialist Movement, to redeem the country, states in three unshakeable senses that it stands for true Christianity, nationalism and revolution. The Christian faith is its highest spiritual value; nationalism its most legitimate and relevant political expression, and its revolutionary sense shows its fitness to lead beyond the outdated demoliberalism and its logical consequence, Marxism, the false panacea of the 'liberation of peoples'.[328]

Justicialism remained a form of 'National Socialism' in its transience of liberal-democracy and Marxism: 'Justicialism as a vernacular version of National Socialism, with its revolutionary concept breaks the vicious scheme of both liberal capitalism and its Marxist face'.[329]

328 Juan Perón, The Nation State, Buenos Aires, 1972, I: Introduction.

329 Ibid.

The National Justicialist State

1. Preliminary Approach

The Superior Driving School of Policy of the Justicialist National Movement has contemplated formulating the basic tenets on which should settle the new order of our national community, in an attempt to sketch the future National Justicialist State.

Its reality is possible, not only to the extent that the bourgeois State continues its self-decomposition, which we are witnessing, but also to the extent that we are encouraged by the revolutionary resolution of the basic structures and hierarchies of the future National Justicialist Government. This designation: the National Justicialist State, reflects the belief that Justicialismo, for the mental, emotional and ideological configuration, will be the main architect of national greatness.

This belief, this faith, is backed by rich Perónist experience, past and present, and the fact that this movement holds within revolutionary trends suitable for the development of new political, economic and social structures that are bringing the people to a specific Social Justice. That is, the Justicialist National Movement combines the fidelity of national authenticity and the possibility of social revolution in the socialist national framework, for in it the national and social, come together as a national expression and convergence with the social expression in the struggle for liberation.

A functionalised community naturally implies the abolition of capitalism, the removal of a regime that is based on the exploitation of man by man or man for the State in all its nuances, as in the case of communism. There will then be neither exploited nor exploiters; that is, there will be no economic classes. Gone will be the salary, or the regime of man miserably selling his skill and effort.

There will, however, be social groups engaged in production, as other groups have organized as other activities (professional, academic, cultural, etc..), where the *national man* can be made.

'We're going to create the syndicalist state (this does not mean a government union); the old dream of the human community. And then all will be represented in government by their own men. I still maintain political parties because we're in evolution, but the day will come when everything is done by the unions'. (Perón, 1952).

Capitalism and Democracy

During the sixteenth, seventeenth and eighteenth centuries economic forces were growing by unknown magnitude, which triggered a series of dynamics that tended to break delimited frameworks imposed by a single society. There were born gigantic economic powers by the creation of banks, trade with the Levant, the discovery of new continents, new ways of communications, technology and the industrial revolution. However, these economic forces lacked political power and, therefore, affirmation and expansion of the bourgeoisie was still controlled by the old traditional state.

These economic forces were needed then to achieve the political citadel, that is, the State. The French Revolution marked this transition and the legalisation of the capitalist system. The bourgeoisie occupied the state and proclaimed the hypocritical slogans of 'liberty, equality and fraternity'. The truth would be quite different. For the Community was subjected by economic forces and history not only met the new tyranny of money, but also a new slavery, the wage.

Perón traced the social revolution that destroyed the remnants of the Medieval era, 'the Hierarchical State', and brought to power the bourgeois. This bourgeois French Revolution not only dispossessed (and exterminated) the nobility but also the artisans, by eliminating their guilds by 'The Chapelier Law'. The economic structures of the old order were replaced with free trade capitalism. A new serfdom arose: the wage-slave. Demoliberalism reduces the role of the State to becoming nothing more than a referee between the contractual rights of property owners. The higher creative role of the State is eliminated in the name of 'freedom'; freedom to exploit and to covet: 'The State ends up being keeper of the interests of a class'. Political parties merely serve to uphold the system, rather than to provide genuine representation, which is better served by 'intermediate' organisations (the syndicates). Perón proceeds:

> No doubt the old frame of the Hierarchical State was not robust enough to withstand the rapid changes introduced by industrial development with its attendant financial shocks. Hence, it is chimerical to think that keeping the old structures have been enough to stop the rise of the bourgeoisie to political power. Perhaps the persistence of the old forms objecting to the economic domination of one class could have been an effective brake, but only that. However, the fighting continued, and postponed for a moment the triumph of new economic instruments. Finally, they triumphed over the hierarchical state. The owner and bourgeoisie of political power, destroys the intermediate community organizations, in order to facilitate the expansion of new economic forces. The Chapelier Law, successor to the Turgot Law, eliminated guilds, which were professional trades bodies with legal, economic and social functions.
>
> The new bourgeois state proclaimed that *laisser faire, laisser passer* is the law for the indiscriminate accumulation of wealth by the capitalist system, as also for the individualistic appropriation by the employer of the instruments of production. The State ends up being keeper

of the interests of a class, and the community becomes dependent on the owners of money. It is in these moments when the era of democracy was born, and proclaimed political parties as divisive elements of the community, or even better, as atomising elements of national unity.

Note that the new institutional forms and suffrage were declared when citizens had fallen under the control of the holders of economic power.

By census suffrage, voting was reserved only for the bourgeois, who had income or provided taxes. The great mass of the population, now proletarian, could not vote. Later the voting procedure was extended, but after the people had been indoctrinated into the liberal myth, thanks to the new state monopoly exercised over school and media, and all members of the community were culturally and ideologically tamed.

Structured according to economics, in the capitalist system money becomes the exclusive source of supreme power and human evaluation, theologically bound by Protestantism in particular,[330] as an end in itself.

Legalised loan interest, that is, *usury*, the civil code, the consolidation of abusive individualistic and unrestricted property, operate as carriers of the new bourgeois order.

The craftsman of yesteryear becomes perforce an employee after a major social decline. The former craftsmen were now limited to selling their labour to the capitalist, who arbitrarily set the price for their efforts in terms of the supposed law of supply and demand.

330 For the Protestant origins of capitalism, whose Reformation was even more tumultuous to the social order than the Jacobin Revolution, see Max Weber, The Protestant Ethic and the Spirit of Capitalism (1905), http://www.stanford.edu/class/sts175/NewFiles/Weber%27s%20Protestant%20Ethic.pdf

> Capitalism refines and generalises the system of wages throughout the production area, or the exploitation of the poor by the wealthy. This gives birth to new economic and social classes. For one, the holders of the means of production - machinery, art, tools, workshops, that is - the capitalist bourgeoisie; on the other hand, employees or the proletariat to deliver the first fruits of their creative efforts.
>
> Man thus becomes a number, without the union corporation, without professional privileges, without the protection and representation of his Estate. The political party establishes the non-functional structure that serves the bourgeoisie in power.

Perón traced the origins of the political parties as part of a divisive process after the dissolution of the organic social order. He described the character of the organic social order, developing through various social bonds, from family, to social groups, and intermediate functional communities, the syndicates, that hierarchically all combine to form the nation. Each of the organic functional bonds are self-governing and are in turn represented at neighbourhood, local, regional, and national levels, through federations of these individual components. The natural social ordering culminates in the syndical state that that was beginning to be achieved in the provinces of Chaco and La Pampa. This is described as the 'organic state' and as the 'organised community'.

> As an instrument of the bourgeoisie, the political party has no natural function and does not represent organic needs. Indeed, man is not an abstract scheme, a number. On the contrary, man is a spiritual and material entity. He is part of a family, as a structure through his labour, professionally, intellectually, artistically, religiously, and, therefore, is part of a first biological social group (family), and other socio-economic groups and professional organisations, or intermediate communities where their personality develops by creative efforts, and also integrates the first

political community: the town, and is part of a high political community: the Nation. Man develops and spreads and plays in different functional levels. In addition, within each living natural organisation in our country, only the Constitution of 1949 and the provincial constitutions of Chaco and La Pampa, began to recognise this process of differentiation and multiplicity.

Indeed, our movement is the ideal synthesis, without which there will be no possibility of the great Social National Revolution in our country. It is clear that the consciousness of this synthesis emerges in its first stage [of Justicialism], although intuitive, vague and imprecise. But events gradually matured, CAUSING THE REVOLUTIONARY RESOLUTION to liquidate the liberal capitalist state, and create new structures boosted by a State with drivability and control. Those who searched consistently into the thinking of the Head of the Justicialist National Movement, General Juan Perón, have found in his speeches, books and writings, the clear picture of the ideological foundations on which will be based the new national system.

The first contribution of the head of our movement, entitled *An Organized Community*, was the start of other work, with the *Perónist Doctrine* (which shows the embodiment of the ideological guidelines), and his book *Political Leadership* (establishing principles on functional organic state action). These were the first doctrinal and cultural starting points to which an ideological clarification by the Superior Driving School Policy of the Justicialist National Movement, is dedicated exclusively. This ideological clarification undoubtedly includes a continuous updating, taking into account the historical needs of the times, ensuring the transformation of our Community. Will this transformation be violent, or will it be peaceful? This is a circumstance about which we cannot worry. The important thing is to be determined to carry it out. Moreover, much

> depends on the attitude taken by our enemies, who are, of course, in control of the country itself, because in the worst case, there might be no choice but blood and fire for the salvation of the country and the release of the people from the liberal-Marxist bias.

The State is the directing centre or the 'brain' of the numerous organs and cells that comprise the organism. The State co-ordinates the various functions of the social organism. The organic state is, as it suggests, analogous to a living organism. A strong central direction must be maintained, as a Justicialist nation will be again the target of international and local conspiracies of foreign financial subversive forces and their *sepoys.* How true this warning is has been shown time and again by the increasing targeting by the USA and its allies of regimes that break free from international finance, including Libya, Serbia and Iraq. However, the State does not become all-pervasive and stifling, like a communist system, because the 'organised community' is comprised of a multiplicity of self-governing entities.

Theory

> A politically sovereign, economically independent and socially just Argentina, is a state free of occupying forces that distort it. The State is returned to its natural condition and drives the entire national community.
>
> The State is an eminently political body that should lead the entire nation **and can not be an expression of dominance of one class over another.** The various and multiple forces that come from the community, certainly need a specialist state, which can interpret and direct forces from the national assembly, being able to project the historical intention of the National body.
>
> We are aware that to bring order to the economic forces now exerting a final despotism over the people and the country,

it will be necessary, at least in a first stage of the National Revolution, to exercise power through a popular national dictatorship, in the face of the risks from international and local conspiracies of foreign financial subversive forces and their *sepoys.*

Also we cannot escape the need for the presence of a single movement to act as custodian of the revolutionary process, until the national community is organised on the basis of functionality.

The Justicialist National Movement has nothing to do with the type of political party of the liberal system which ignores the structural reality of the nation, and separates man from his natural activities and functions, hierarchies and vocations, creating an undifferentiated sum of individuals, an abstract and empty schema.

The Nation is a dynamic multiplicity of groups and intermediate communities. Remove the distortion caused by individualistic democapitalismo, and the State will have to be a synthesis of all the internal forces of the Social Body, represented in an organic way. The Nation is not a collection of individuals or persons. Neither is it the sum of political parties.

Physiognomy of the Justicialist National State

1. No protection of any interests other than those in the service of the national community, including foreign interests; pacts or alliances that compromise the freedom, security and political happiness of the Argentine people and their intermediate communities.

2. Absolute independence of decisions, both in domestic and in international relations and problems.

Key Features

1. Organic directing control.
2. Organic sovereignty.
3. Full State authority, provided the State satisfactorily performs only its own functions.
4. The legitimate state serves the whole nation, without distinction, respecting honest man in all his attributes, rights and metaphysical transcendence, providing assistance to the private good of individuals, groups and intermediate communities and the national common good.

Strong State

1. To carry out the National Revolution.
2. To contribute to the liberation of all the peoples of Latin America, to avoid outside interference, and eventually to become the great American Nation through the Confederation of all the fraternal peoples of this hemisphere, and where each retain their own characteristics.

State Assets

1. To preserve the social security of the people and the groups that comprise our social totality.
2. To impose the higher interests of the community above the interests of a few.
3. To protect the natural right of property, so that the individual, the social group, the intermediate community, and the National Community have the goods they need to fulfil and fully assert their respective roles. The preserving of private property as a natural right, but a social function without constituting

a power in the state and subjecting the Argentine to exploitation prevailing over the best interests of the national community.

4. To establish Social Justice and thereby realise the national concord and happiness of the people.

5. To promote and encourage the enrichment of work, with the increase of production and material goods as a means to spiritual goods that make the perfection of man.

Although Perón called on 'the peoples of the world' to unite to deal with ecological and other problems, Justicialism never can be legitimately an internationalist creed. It is nothing if not a 'national doctrine' and the nation remains one of its three core premises, as seen previously. Justicialism repudiates the levelling impact of liberalism, Marxism and capitalism, which aim to reduce humanity to a nebulous mass of economic cogs regardless of organic differences.[331] Under Justicialism individual personality is actualised through social duty, not stifled, and identity is developed by recognising one's part as a member of a family, neighbourhood, municipality, profession, culture, and nation. Hence, Justicialism is applied within the context of 'race, history and culture'.

Furthermore, Justicialism recognises the danger of superpower hegemony, of 'bi-polarity', and places itself as a pioneer in the now increasingly influential move towards multi-polarity, championed today in particular by Russia's President Vladimir Putin, and by the late Hugo Chavez of Venezuela, a self-declared 'Perónist'. Hence, Perón was a father not only of the 'Third World' 'non-aligned movement' during the Cold War, but also of today's growing movement for a 'multipolar world':

> The power and authority of the National Justicialist State emerge from its deep representation of real communities

331 See K. R. Bolton, Babel Inc. (London: Black House Publishing, 2013).

> that make up the nation, and which is a synthesis, and the will of the national forces of the Argentine people according to their race, history and culture.
>
> In its general conformation, the National Justicialist Government, the Third Position, strictly guards against the superpowers of bi-polarisation in today's world, as a safeguard against the liberal capitalist state, and the Marxist state. The National Justicialist State expresses and projects the historical intention of being Argentine in the quest to fulfil their destiny.

In the following section of *The National Doctrine*, it is reiterated that Justicialism is the Argentine version of 'National Socialism', and its organised political form is the 'Corporate Nation'. The 'national doctrine' is cognisant of the Argentine race and culture. It is evident that Justicialism does not accept the 'melting-pot' ideals of other Latin American states, which have long been influenced by liberalistic Jacobinism. This race-forming process, which has no evident similiarity to the biological determinism of German National Socialism, has the aim of assuring that 'migratory flows [are] associated with our race'. Interestingly, the principle is embodied in the present-day Argentine Constitution, which refers to assuring migration from European sources.

Statement on the National Justicialist State

> According to the fundamental unchanging principles of the Justicialist National Doctrine, synthesised by the Leader of the Movement, General Juan Perón: A SOVEREIGN NATION POLITICALLY, ECONOMICALLY INDEPENDENT AND SOCIALLY JUST, the Justicialist National Government policy to achieve National happiness and realise the great destiny of the country and people, must ensure:
>
> ECONOMY. An economy in social function, where the supreme interests of the Community are above the interests

of the privileged few, and:

To strengthen areas where the economy is weak

To protect all domestic industry, creating bases and providing the necessary means for its great development, along with access to science and technology;

Mobilise completely the resources of the country for the purpose of reaching as far as possible, *autarchy*; an economically independent nation;

Nationalise the banks and exercise control over the economic and financial policy whose power should be channelled primarily for meeting the needs of the people;

A credit policy to develop Argentine industry and those areas that are lacking the necessary means;

To reaffirm Article 40 of the Constitution of 1949;

Nationalise all those foreign companies that do not cooperate in national greatness and the implementation of Social Justice and which constitute a power within the State;

To ensure State prevalence in large companies involved with water and energy, gas, insurance, communications, transportation, merchant marine, airlines, etc.

UNIONS. Trade organisations to ensure the leading role that corresponds to their fundamental form as social groups of the national community. Also their gradual transformation into federations of enterprises in the same branch of production in such a way that they become intermediate socioeconomic communities and play their role within the nation.

Inside the National Justicialist State workers (producers) always receive remuneration entailing suitable means to acquire a sufficiency of life according to the demands of human dignity, for themselves and their families.

POPULATION. A population policy for:

A greatly populated country, providing the necessary measures to make easier and bearable the formation of large families even in the most remote areas of the country;

Provide all relevant means for improvement of the Argentine;

Attract migratory flows associated with our race, which are sifted and oriented according to the national interest;

The children, as Eva Perón wanted, are the only privileged and subject to special protection by the National Justicialist State, as the most valuable asset of the nation.

CULTURE Ensure free education at all levels;. meaningful university education and national responsibility; universities serving the higher interests of the country, the increase of cultural centers for national and moral training, and also to teach responsibility for Argentines as components of a free and sovereign country, and as the natural leader in Latin America.

HOUSES. Pursuant to the requirements of human dignity every family should have their own home. For these purposes, a Ministry of Housing is needed, which is responsible for solving the serious problem of the provision of low-interest, long-term funding. 'Slums' are an ominous witness to the failure of the capitalist social system and should not exist.

Political Socialisation

'There are currently two philosophies that can give an ideological foundation to social reorganisation: the Christian and the Marxist. The first is driving us toward national socialism, the second to an international Marxist dogma. The future world will be socialist, it is up to the people to say of which type. Justicialism is but a Christian national socialism. Those opposed to it are consciously or unconsciously working for communism'. Perón

1. Situation

To rid the country of international capitalist colonialism, and after the analysis of possibilities, to take action to change the structure of production, distribution and marketing. It is therefore necessary to lay down the premises on which Justicialism advocates the change.

2. Preliminary Approach

When artisan production was small there was ownership of the means of production circumscribed by family activity, resources, tools and the techniques of the producer himself. When industry, surpassing craftsmanship, became a large organisation in the modern sense, property became gigantic and a joint technical effort with many producers, but did not materialise in community-based social-property, because it was appropriated and diverted by the bourgeoisie. Thus, property that was owned by a single-family became individualistic property acquired through the hoarding of capital, not responding to the needs of social groups.

Capitalism, in an ascending process and under financial power and the backing of repressive laws against producers (workers) created a depressing sociological picture. Capitalism seized the means of production and monopolised the means of exploitation of man. Thus a new and unfortunate social class was created, the *proletariat*. Cycles of distribution and marketing followed this path. Today, capitalist society sinks to make way for its sequel: either Marxism, or the National Socialist Revolution formulated by General Perón, whose version here and in Latin America is Justicialismo.

3. Industrial Company

Industry is the result of the effort and hierarchical solidarity of all workers. They perform with their physical and intellectual-technical work and their work is in no sense individualistic in these structures. The Justicialist National Government, through its competent bodies, will study and analyse the issue, trying to give the means of production to workers through the corresponding production groups. Thus, property ceases to be a source of social conflict and a source of pathological power.

4. Land Company

The land is not in good use when subjected to the purposes of consumption, but should be an instrument of social production. Therefore, it cannot legitimately be individualistic property. A Justicialist principle applies: 'the land must be for those who work it'. This is not to divide the estates and smallholdings, but to recognise agricultural economic units, existing or to be created, as legal entities, which own their means of production. So farm workers, whatever their rank, shall, in partnership, have the assets that are essential to produce from the land freely, within the requirements of national planning, and they will have the fruits of their labour.

As can be seen from these above two points (3 and 4) the Justicialist 'third position' is no more state capitalism (Marxism) than it is individualistic capitalism, but aims at converting enterprsises into co-operatives where management and profits are shared. The governing bodies would be the syndicates (syndicalism) undertaking production according to a national economic plan (national-syndicalism).

Justicialism therefore believes in corporatism, which has also been called 'national syndicalism' in Spanish Falangism. Perón usually referred to corporatism as the 'organised community'. Corporatism was often of a Catholic character in attempting to fulfil the aims of Catholic social doctrine in offering an alternative to both capitalism and Marxism. Franquist Spain, Salazar's Portugal, Dollfuss' Austria and Vichy France, were specifically Catholic corporatist states to varying degrees.

Perón's friend Vargas set about establishing Brazil as a corporatist state. Fascist Italy has remained the largest experiment of the corporatist state, and here Perón reiterates his belief in the efficacy of what he had observed in Italy decades previously, and despite the wartime and postwar vilification of all things 'fascist'. As Perón states, previously noted, there was much he did not achieve due to the restrictions of working within the 'demoliberal' system of party parliaments, although he did establish two corporatist provinces, and before his rule Governor Fresco, set about establishing a corporatist system in Buenos Aires Province. General Uriburu had also sought a corporatist state. Unlike Left-wing movements that embrace syndicalism, the nation remains the building bloc.

The New Justicialist Constitution

The new Perónist Constitution guarantees genuine popular representation through all intermediate communities and creates a real Corporate Nation. Above this true representation the Head of State will embody the guiding purpose of the Nation. This implies the abolition of capitalism and the party-system instruments that are a demoliberal deception. A community is not organically made of political parties, nor of a part of the Nation that is competing with others.

The only movement that can transform our country in this sense is the National Justicialist Movement. As this only has the national character, popular representation and skills to create revolutionary change.

Indeed, the Justicialist National Movement is the expression of those political and historical currents that are cause for Argentina culturally, spiritually and even in race, with ties yesterday, today and forever. It is, therefore, the truest expression of the historical Argentina, with its imposed beautiful burden of a great historical mission.

It is for this reason, its authenticity and historical consciousness, that the Perónist Revolutionary National Movement has the ability to transform the socio-economic and cultural structures without resorting to stereotyped patterns. That is, the national and social converge naturally in the Justicialist National Movement.

When this powerful synthesis reaches maturity, victory will be inevitable over Capitalism and Communism. The Perónist revolutionary National State created by our Leader, General Perón, leaves behind a past of miseries and indignities.

The Justicialist conception of man is that of transcendence, based on man as more than a physical being or 'matter in motion', as the dialectical materialists of Marxism would have it; born in the image of God, according to the Christian precept, and achieving self-realisation within a social context. Justicialism therefore rejects the hyper-individualism heralded by capitalism and liberalism, and the levelling 'horizontality' of Marxism, both of which stemmed from the 18th century 'Enlightenment' doctrine that 'untied' man from 'the national spirit' and his rootedness to a locale. The impelling force for human transcendence is that of heroism, or what has been called 'heroic vitalism',[332] the philosophy of *heroic will* as the motivating force in history.

Man

'In the midst of a world whose opposing doctrines, man is immersed in the flat horizontality of materialism, as an end and a supreme goal, our doctrine is to raise up man through the verticality of spiritual goals, so that the man formed by us - between us and the stature that God has assigned to the universal concert - can feel again the optimism of his eternity. Our aim is that no man is isolated, but that he lives fully in the community'.- Perón

Man is a substantial unity of body and soul. Among the visible creatures, he is the only one with the independence and dignity of the person. He is a true microcosm, as the ancients said, a little world that exceeds in value all the inanimate worlds. And being the most perfect of all nature the human person and human destiny cannot be, therefore, only of time but of eternity, constituting, therefore, a transcendent unity. Man is created in the image and likeness of God. But this transcendent unity is by nature a **social being:** born of a family (man and woman) as the first basic social group and the parents provide essential care, without which man could not survive. This develops within

332 See for example Thomas Carlyle, On Heroes, Hero Worship, and the Heroic in History (London, 1841), http://www.gutenberg.org/catalog/world/readfile?fk_files=3342021

> a broader community that was forming along the centuries and, therefore, provides the imprint of a civilisation and a historical culture. It develops into productive, cultural, professional, and other intermediate communities.
>
> Therefore, man is guided and bound by a vital society to live and to achieve the fullness of human embodiment and, therefore, depends on society that gives the means of life, and he is required to contribute to the community everything that he can possibly give and sacrifice for it.
>
> The community is not a herd. To progress to the greatest extent possible, requires that all members, fight to find a place according to their ability and intended function. No obstacles are overcome by cowards. Heroism is the first virtue of man. Living dangerously is to live as a human being, to live quietly, without dynamism and action is merely to survive. Heroic men and strong communities make their people. And only strong people make history, are free and sovereign.
>
> The philosophy of Enlightenment individualism which settled in the political structure of liberalism, conceived man as being untied to the national spirit and the historic space. Abstract man replaced the real man of flesh and blood. Therefore, the Argentine man besides transcendent spiritual values, must be inextricably committed to the national destiny. this is the character of the Justicialist National Movement.

The organic, corporative character of the national community is explained as a syndicalist organisation of federations reaching up in pyramidal manner, through 'intermediate' groups – the syndicates – until reaching an apex in the State. The syndicates and federations of syndicates act as cells and organisms that are self-governing according to the nature of their own functions. Therefore Justicialism rejects the stifling centralisation of

Marxism, but develops a national community that also rejects the social atomisation of 'demoliberalism'. The reference to the German philosopher Hegel, who attracted a following among both the Right and the Left, alludes to the distortion of Hegelian thought by Karl Marx in the service of communism. Hegel formulated the theory of dialectics as the moving force of history. Simply put: thesis + antithesis = synthesis, and within the synthesis is a further thesis, and so on. Hegel's doctrine is metaphysical, but Marx deleted the metaphysics and developed the concept of 'dialectical materialism', expressed as class struggle: nobility (thesis)/bourgeoisie (antithesis) = capitalism (synthesis); bourgeoisie/proletariat = socialism. Fascism had its own dialectic: nationalism + socialism = national socialism; which is the same dialectic as Justicialism.

Those of a more metaphysical inclination might see dialectics in the concept of Yin and Yang, and the Yin-Yang symbol, each side of which contains a 'seed' of its opposite, while the circle is a totality of the interaction of both. Similarly, the 'Tree of Life' of the Hebrew Kabbala comprises opposite spheres on columns united by a 'middle column' whose spheres represent the synthesis of both.

Hegelians of both Left and Right focused on the omnipotence of the State. Here Perón, in keeping with the syndicalist or corporatist character of Justicialism, states that the basis of social organisation is with individuals participating in groups which might be of a social, professional, spiritual, military or artistic character, each component comprising a necessary function of the whole social organism. They might also be of a neighbourhood, municipal or occupational character. These 'intermediate groups' each in turn form federations on local, regional and national levels, culminating in an 'organic synthesis'.

The Community

'The Hegelian path led certain groups to madness as they sought to entirely subordinate individuality to the great organization where, truly, the concept of community was reduced to an empty word: the omnipotence of the state over an infinite amount of zeros. The way to understand the individual or group best is that it performs as part of that community, is in its own hierarchy, aware and conscious of its own participation' - Perón

Humanity is a complete and distinct substance from other substances of the same species. It is a substance that is conscious of being, conscious of its actions and its statements, to appropriate them as its own, and able to say 'I am'. But we have seen that man alone is incomplete, precarious and poor. Man is completed by being a part of society, of the community. So the nature of man is projected through his working life, aiming at the greatest possible perfection of the idea of man. Within the Community this can be achieved. Outside it will be impossible.

The social life that involves living in a community with one's fellow men, is a need that is not from a mere wish, but is a necessary part of human nature that serves as an efficient cause of society, that is, that his nature compels social coexistence. It is clear that society, the community, is an intentional way of life for the individual.

Community is used here not in a general, vague, indefinite sense as a way of life, but rather in the sense of social forms that have defined and specific connotations.

The individual is a member of a family, a workshop, a parish, a club, etc., without which he could not procreate, produce, pray or play. These concrete communities respond to the different needs and requirements of human life. Families clustered in certain territory form a geo-social group, the municipality, which is the political extension of political community, or a family. The municipality is the gathering of many families. Several municipalities are provinces, the grouping of provinces make the nation that is the National Community, of which the State, as the most perfect political society, is the organic synthesis, providing awareness and control to ensure the common good of the people.

For man to live, he needs to produce, hence he also belongs to a production structure: the company, factory, etc..

We present the national community as a pyramid consisting of a company, joined with other companies constituting a federation of related entities with the same activity and nature, each self-governing and responsible within the entire social body: a company , a federation of companies according to their branches or activities, a federation of federations to reach the national federation, that is, the organised community. These intermediate groups that are not automatic or juxtaposed, but dynamic, organic and vital conglomerates have their own purposes in conjunction with the common good.

Hence rulers leading the national community must not only apply statecraft but also political science as architectural science that combines all individual ends toward the ultimate goal, that is the common good of the nation. For us Justicialism, synthesised in political sovereignty, economic independence and social justice, is the foundation of national socialism that puts all goods and all things to social function, that is, for the enjoyment of all and not the privileged few, or in state hands for the enjoyment of technobureaucracy, as with liberalism and Marxism respectively.

The Justicialist National Government, as the control device

and driving overall the national community, harmonises and synthesises the two often conflicting interests of intermediate communities that make up the nation, under the constant sign of national affirmation.

But this image of the organised community could not achieve, nor the nation not give their best for the happiness of the people, if governments only represent fractions and work for their own and foreign interests, bypassing the supreme national interest of the social totality, rejecting social justice as a formal principle of all government action.

National Community
Political Sovereignty
Economic Independence
Social Justice

Justicialism repudiates the 18th century 'Enlightenment' ideas that culminated in the French Revolution, most of which were very far from 'enlightened', with rival factions of Jacobins vying to create their own civic religious cults of 'Nature' or of 'Reason' on the ruins of the Catholic Church, and committing mass slaughter in the Vendee region of France in the process. Interestingly, the French Revolution is claimed as the legacy of both communism and capitalism.[333] That is because both are faithless doctrines that put money at the centre of consciousness, and destroy tradition and organic social bonds such as the family. Both engender class war, and see history as contending economic factions. Both eliminate the nation.

One of the major results of the French Revolution was to abolish the ancient craft guilds,[334] and establish a free market economy. Marxists praise, rather than condemn this, because it made the old 'Estates' into conflicting economic classes. Hence they saw this is a progressive step in the 'dialectic of history'. In the

333 See the Marxist theoretician Jean Jaurès, 'Introduction', Socialist History of the French Revolution, http://www.marxists.org/archive/jaures/1901/history/introduction.htm

334 Le Chapelier *Law, 1791.*

following, Justicialism states that this was a backward, rather than a positive step, and aims to return man to his natural social life. Perón repudiates the notion of 'individual equality' in favour of the social meaning of life.

Freedom

> 'I believe that the old formula of "liberty, equality and fraternity", today has to be changed for freedom, justice and solidarity so as to update the concept of "freedom" away from selfishness and individualism. Otherwise it is a hoax and deceives people into reacting violently. What we want to avoid in the Republic is this delayed but violent reaction, because the destruction of values is not what we recommend for the Republic'. - Perón

The French Revolution led to the historical justification of the famous phrase, 'liberty, equality, fraternity'.

It very soon showed its true reality. State economic groups proclaimed 'freedom' as a valuable justification for their undeniable dominance over lower income groups, especially workers. The hypocrisy of the triple 'slogan' was manifested in anything that workers could require the master to improve in their conditions of life and work, because it went against the individual 'freedom' of the employer.

Julio Guesde[335] famously referring to that 'slogan' – 'liberty, equality, fraternity' - called it the 'freedom of the fox in the henhouse', which interpreted with precise clarity the implementing of this 'freedom' that was proclaimed by the French Revolution, that did not demonstrate the true freedom of workers.

335 Julio Guesde (1845-1922) was a leading French socialist and parliamentarian.

Individual equality is an unreal abstraction that ignores the real man integrated with his various community groups, resulting in being overwhelmed by the infamous, real and concrete forces of economic inequality, and in a levelling misery.

The French Revolution politically and legally enshrined the practice of the capitalist system and methodology of the exploitation of man by man, creating at the same time, its antithesis, the exploitation of man by the state under the impulse of Marxism years later. The class struggle was the answer and this sank forever the third term of the 'slogan', libertarian 'brotherhood', declared by the victorious bourgeoisie in subverting the natural social order.

We affirm that freedom, as a generic term, is an elusive abstraction, a pipe dream that can only serve to cover up vile spoliation, like the worst tyrannies.

There is no real freedom if there is no ethical content of life, an axiom of human dignity. The liberal preaching was a false 'freedom'.

Only after this assessment, we begin to find freedom.

As a first condition of our premise – Justice - Perónists do not support the subjugation of our nation by another nation.

The first freedom for us is that of the Fatherland; the real and true freedom that allows our country a unique historical community, making its own sovereign decisions.

Our Leader says: 'You cannot be a free man in a slave country'.

That same ethical sense of justice leads us to man as a person, that is, with human dignity linked to national aims;

> not universal and abstract liberalism and Marxism, but concrete man whom we see forming a family, producing goods, dreaming and perfecting. Hence it is necessary – mandatory - to provide all the real possibilities for man to perform in his various fields of action and within different social groups.
>
> Without a home, without bread, without school culture, THERE IS NO FREEDOM.
>
> Perón masterfully defines these concepts:
>
> 'Freedom should start from definitely entrenched social security, family and national defence. A freedom without security of life, work, education and decent housing, IS A FALSE FREEDOM. Having the freedom to starve, it is a fallacy that is a matter of deception for those who traffic in making smokescreens to hide their real intentions. Only after men have faith in individual and collective destinies, can material well-being, real justice, and freedom be achieved. This is not to restrict freedom but to precisely secure it for all'.
>
> To these concepts we can only add that we do not recognise the 'freedom'[336] that is used to restrict the freedom and security of the country and the Argentine man or subtract the legitimate fruits of their labour.

In the next section Perón described the evolution of money, from a means of exchange, to an interest bearing commodity (*usury*) that has come to dominant the world, politically, economically, and ultimately spiritually, culturally and socially: 'Those who accumulated money by removing its productive creator circuit, used it for loaning with interest'. As we have seen, the issue of state credit was the means by which plutocracy was defeated;

336 A reference to 'free trade'; the 'freedom' of predatory capitalism.

and the reason for the world war against the Axis, whose primary states, Italy, Germany and Japan, issued state credit and achieved economic revival amidst the world depression.[337] Perón also repudiates the 'social darwinism' of the economic survival of the fittest that is used to justify avarice and parasitism at the expense of social duty. Indeed, self-interest as a human motive is not really part of 'human nature', as modern science shows us that so far from species instinct being dominated by nothing other than individual survival, in a natural social order, whether human or antelope, the dominant motive is the survival of the group, to the point of self-sacrifice. Taking the organic analogy further, we might also see that there are certain types of economic and other activities that are 'parasitic', whether one calls such parasites that damage the cells of an organism a ringworm, a cancer or a banker. If the organism, including the social organism, does not eliminate the parasite it dies.

Ethically, Perón rejected the materialist notion that money is an end in itself, and stated that money is only a means to an end; and moreover a servant, not a master. The satisfaction of the material needs, to live in comfort without struggling, is the first step, and once achieved releases the creative energies of man into higher pursuits. Such freedom from material stress might also release the cultural life of an entire nation, as it did during the Medieval era, when working hours were far less than today. During the 1960s the existential philosophers and psychologists such as Abraham Maslow developed the concept of self-actualisation, stating that once the 'primary drives' are satisfied the individual is free to actualize his life creatively. However, these theorists focused on the individual as an end, divorced from social meaning, and the result was the anarchic self-destruction and egotism of the '60s Generation'. Justicialism and kindred doctrines, free man from material need and enable him to self-actualise as a social being.

337 K.R. Bolton, *The Banking Swindle*, op. cit., 103-121.

Capital and Capitalism

'Neither money nor property, nor capital, none of the economic goods, can become an end of the human task. They are nothing but means used by man towards their destiny'.- Perón

When man was spurred by his selfishness and ambition, he forgot the instrumental character of economic goods and there appeared the exploitation of man by man and of man by the state. This distortion is called Capitalism, whether liberal individualist, or whether state or collectivist communism.

It is necessary to review the true nature of economic goods and return them to their nature as instrumental means, placing them at the service of man.

Money appeared when business needs and transactions became more complex. Increased trade, the movement of large quantities of goods and products and relationships with other people increased. The method of barter exchange of goods or products was made outdated.

So then came the coin, money, recognised by all as representing the value of things to facilitate market exchange.

But soon the greed and ambition of some groups determined their hoarding and, forgetting its character as an instrumental means, money became a business itself. Those who accumulated money by removing its productive creator circuit, used it for loaning with interest.

The interest is perceived as a plus. But where does that plus or interest come from? Of course, from the work of others. This is one of the systems on which capitalism is based.

Parasites are enriched at the expense of others' work, eventually acquiring the means of production, consolidating their dominant status, subjugating and subordinating both political and economic structures, for the social demands of their class interests.

This monopoly of surplus value, which is specified by plundering by the individualistic ownership of the instruments of production, is another pillar where the capitalist system is based.

The French Revolution and the Napoleonic Code institutionalised the system. Then capitalist hoarding was launched to dominate international markets. Now we are in the presence of International Finance, International Banking, which has already proletarianised man within its borders of origin, and tends now to do the same internationally. This is another pillar of capitalism.

It will be said, as a gimmicky argument, that profit and the ability to take advantage of economic circumstances is as old as civilisation itself and that is the natural differentiation of humanity, where the 'fittest' conquer and dominate, and that attitude is a right. We accept that this explanation has some truth, but not the whole truth, in the same or similar manner in which the sexual instinct is in human nature, but that instinct and biological capacity is subject to the requirements of morality, ethics. This instinct, moreover, is sublimated in love, and pursues a legitimate aim: the preservation and continuation of the human race through marriage. However, the sexual instinct in human nature is not legitimate when it can lead to the decay of society by simply unleashing the natural instinct.

Similarly, the natural qualitative differentiation of the human person, his different ways to progress, do not justify or authorise or legitimise the domination, nor the exercising of monopoly by a privilege few to the misery of the many. The seizure of the goods produced by the efforts of everyone to the enjoyment of a few, is totally illegitimate.

But this has happened and the owners of money, the masters of finance, established unnatural structures to build a predominance in society that is unfair and distorted, and not only subverts social peace but human activity itself.

Indeed, economic dominance has been so overwhelming that it has achieved the subjecting of legal, cultural, educational, propaganda, and other means. The capitalist dispossession has been and still is considered by 'public opinion' as legitimate and normal. Furthermore, such economic dominance, with the practice of 'democracy', managed to institutionalise its own laws. At the same time, through the media that is dominated by the lords of money, this social pathology is upheld as a legitimate activity.

Justice, labour, virtue, intelligence, the human condition, man himself, were subordinated to this order.

Our doctrine is not that we must hate money, or the machine, or finance. It would be absurd to abhor anything that is inert and has no life. What is repudiated its the misuse of both machine and money and finance.

Capital is a set of goods created and multiplied by fruitful work, but the basic purpose is to provide for the welfare of the entire community in harmonious individual and community relationship.

The Justicialist Party acknowledges capital as an essential instrument. But Justicialismo fights the trend and the practice of capital to dominate man. This trend has a name: Capitalism; Imperialism is its international economic development.

When we achieve our goal, we will open a new age in the history of Men: where freedom is real.

State Capitalism - Communism

'Karl Marx foresaw in the mid-nineteenth century that capitalism would concentrate in a number of increasingly smaller hands. And the middle class would be absorbed by the so-called proletariat'. - Perón

Such predictions have not been fulfilled in the liberal capitalist world. By contrast, the owners of capital became more frequent and the middle class expanded to absorb important sectors of the working class. All this regardless of monopolies supported by international finance.

The bourgeois minority had been able to conquer political power with fire and sword back in the decades after 1789.[338] They enabled other elements to monopolise gold, and finance which were utilised to attack nations and mount insurrections or cause world wars, exploit hunger, chaos and weaknesses to seize power. This began in November 1917 in Tsarist Russia, where barely an embryonic capitalism had managed to prevail. A minority of super-Jacobins[339] funded by international capitalism,[340] took over the Russian state.

Throughout the years that minority was transformed into a techno-bureaucratic oligarchy based on a capitalism more perfect than ever dreamed by the primitive bourgeois view of the 19th century, subjecting man to a helpless misery of the proletariat, without rights, where unions became mere instruments of state control.

338 The year of the French Revolution.

339 A reference to the Bolsheviks as being heirs to the Jacobin French Revolution.

340 Referring to the funding from international banks that the Bolsheviks and other revolutionists received, referred to previously.

> Between liberal capitalism and state capitalism or Bolshevism, there exists only differences which come from different levels, methods and effectiveness. The difference was more marked in the prewar years, until 1939. Today, however, the failure of the communist system is loosening its original hardness and even trying to introduce liberalised profit and competition. The opposite occurs with the liberal-stage of pre-Marxist capitalism, where the state tends to a greater weight in the economic driving of capitalism.
>
> In both forms of capitalism, whether Marxist or liberal, the state is merely an expression of economic factors and has been placed and is used as an effective custodian thereof. The State is the keeper of the interests of the owners of international finance. The State uses all its power to break the community, and turns it into a simple production anthill without greatness and joyless, where man is a spring, a tool, a number.
>
> The Justicialist National State is quite the opposite: it preserves the safety of people and groups that make up the entire social Argentina, which imposes the supreme interests of the community above the interests of the privileged few.

The Justicialist concept of private property is to distribute it widely, rather than the economic concentration entailed under communism and capitalism. The Justicialist concept is analogous to the Distributist Movement founded in Britain during the 1930s by the famous Catholic writers Hilaire Belloc and G. K. Chesterton, and based on the social doctrine enunciated in the encyclicals of Popes Leo XIII[341] and Pius XI.[342] It is evident that these encyclicals were also a major basis for Justicialism, which shares with the Papal social doctrine opposition to usury,

341 Leo XIII, Rerum Novarum: On Capital and Labour, 1891.

342 Pius XI, Quadragesimo Anno, 1931.

advocacy of widespread property distribution, and revival of the labour syndicates, as an alternative to capitalism and communism. Again, co-operative enterprises with co-management and profit-sharing are the means of expanding property ownership while simultaneously giving it a social function.

Property

'Distributing property at a fair limit, but sufficient to allow it to work, at least, enabling it to be used for the greatness and happiness of the nation. The change of ownership of property is subject to the general interest, and it will become social property'. - Perón

There are several types of property: capital goods and consumer use, movable and immovable property; instruments of production, intellectual property, etc.

The different nature of such goods is necessary to reflect the various relationships that exist between man and the objects that can be owned.

Our doctrinal statement that property is a natural right, but also a social function, facilitates our understanding, leading to the apprehension of this seemingly complex and controversial issue.

The dress that covers, foods that nourish, the book that educates and trains, the roof that shelters, are legitimate and indisputable individual property. In light of the Doctrine of Perón, such property cannot be regarded as an expression of capitalism nor can it be collectivised. Both forms of capitalism make it impossible to exercise the natural right of man to property that dignifies the human person, enabling him to live decently. One [capitalism] absorbs and monopolises, the other [communism] collectivises. Both make it impossible for proper human living.

Therefore, the Perónist National Doctrine recreates the concept of private property, allowing the man and the family to live decently, in the light of nature; that property provides a homestead, not profit.

It was a distortion of natural structures when individual and family property was being absorbed by capitalist property, both in agricultural and industrial activity; distortion which is consolidated with the advent of mechanisation and the industrial revolution.

The concentration of production required machinery, raw materials and men working and churning. This ended the concept of individual and family property sustained in the craft workshop. It assumes the new individualistic concept of property founded in the capitalist 'blackmail' that stated: 'I have my machines, you, the workers bring your intelligence, your physical exertion, knowledge, developed over millennia, and you bring everything inherent to work. Without you no production is possible. But I will pay you a salary to survive and not starve. Know also that I am the only owner of the factory and its production tools. And if you do not like my proposal, go to another factory'.

We note that the new emerging capitalist property is activated by the effort of all hierarchical technical producers. However, this property and its use is far from being social, it is individualistic and enjoyed by the capitalist. This is the basis of business and industrial organisation today. It is based on capitalist robbery.

So capitalism has made the modern enterprise of individual property an organisation that must necessarily be shared by all producers, technicians and workers.

But it is not only capitalism that denies the community social ownership but also Marxism, and this is logical, because it is the last division of the capitalist system. Property is denied to the producers, and belongs to the state as the last great pattern. In communist society, the factory and surplus belongs to the state, so the Soviet worker remains an employee of the state.

The Justicialist National Movement will end the company that is owned by the capitalist, and the business community will serve man, family, Nation. Similarly we say that the land must be owned by the worker. We also contend that the factories and businesses will also belong to those who work and they will be integrated to produce a caring community and organised on the basis of the deepest social justice possible.

As for state-ownership, Justicialism considers this legitimate when it ensures national defense, economic independence, taking custody of the mainsprings of the national economy such as the foundation industries, foreign trade production, banking, mineral resources and anything that involves absorbing interests and the domain of foreign interests.

National Justicialismo says private property is a natural right of man; as against the Marxist concept of collectivisation, and against capitalism, with its unrestricted abuse. [The Justicialist State] protects private property, but as an orderly social function, not only to avoid becoming a source of power and profit, and as a means of speculation among Argentines, but so that all members of the national community can enjoy and exercise in a concrete way that natural law. Every Argentine should have his own property, which is all that is necessary and required for human dignity and freedom to live a decent life.

In the following section Perónism returns 'work' to more than an economic grind, in which one works to eke out an existence by selling one's labour as a 'wage slave'. When work serves a social function, then the worker, whether menial or intellectual, serves something higher than economics. He is fulfilling a social role as part of a national organism, by performing those roles that come naturally to him by brain, brawn, character or combinations thereof. In return he receives a part of the profits of the collective labour of the enterprise at which he works, to secure sufficient sustenance for himself and his family. Work as a higher calling than economic drudgery returns to the ancient and Medieval concepts of work that were upheld by the corporations of ancient Rome and the guilds of Medieval Europe, which established an ethical and even a spiritual basis for work; where work was craft and one's 'calling' in life. We see something of this below where Perónism alludes to the 'spiritual energies' of the worker. Work is also part of a cultural heritage, the worker being a link in a chain that adds to the work that has been achieved by prior generations and leaves a legacy for those after him. It is this work legacy that builds a nation, and a people.

Work

> 'For work and virtue, man exalts and dignifies. In Justicialismo are the values we hold most dear. Sweep all that is parasitic and exploitative way'. - Perón
>
> For the Justicialist Party it is work that enhances dignity and man's own national and ennobling activity. His physical and intellectual effort raises him as creator and raises possibilities for material and moral improvement. One's work contributes to the enhancement of the Fatherland and through this, one's highest destiny.
>
> The driver guides the domestic destination with the development of government policies, the official who loyally serves the interests of the nation, the researcher who draws to life the nature of its mysteries, the doctor who cures, the teacher who educates; the miner who roots

into the bowels of the earth for its treasures; the artisan modelling matter, the worker driving a tractor, planting a grove or producing at the factory, is dignified in his creative quest. This is our concept of work. We reject the purely economic connotations assigned to this noble human activity by liberal capitalism and Marxism.

Our concept of the dignity of our work involves simultaneously protest against the exploitation of man by man, or by the state that constrains the producers to be stripped of their spiritual energies.

For us, work is mandatory and confers dignity. The country is a legacy of bygone work efforts and linked in this continuity and vision. Preserving this legacy is sacred and counsels us to eliminate all parasites.

In the revolutionary momentum of Justicialismo the parasite, the saboteur and the individualistic ownership of the means of production disappear, as also all legal fictions that upheld them. They disappear merely as capitalists, but not as human beings, as they can integrate into the production company in the role determined by their technical specialities. That is, they will not work as capitalists, but as those who provide labour.

For National Justicialismo the worker is not synonymous with a manual laborer. For us, the worker is anyone who makes a positive contribution, physically or intellectually, to the benefit of the community.

The Justicialist State will have professional hierarchies because they are qualities of work. Divisions will disappear among those who work. There will then be no capitalist exploitation.

For National Justicialismo, work is also a LAW. Man has

the right to life, then you have the right to work, as this is the means to sustain life. The Justicialist National State will not only work for everyone, but everyone will work under the banner of social justice.

The State is undivided by class or party factions, but through its syndicates organises according to functions that contribute to the social organism, like each individual cell of the body contributes to the whole organism, otherwise it is said to be diseased. This is why it is often called the 'organic state' or the corporate state (*corpus* as in a body), and what Justicialism usually calls the 'organised community'. The aim is not to eliminate differences that reflect talents and personalities, under the dead weight of Marxism, where the ideal is for everyone to become part of a proletariat, but to utilise those differences as social functions, and to have them represented in syndical bodies, and other 'intermediate groups', such as neighbourhood committees.

Political Sovereignty

'No one will argue about the benefits of Economic Independence, Social Justice and the Sovereignty of the Nation'.- Perón

Political Sovereignty is the power of self-determination of the Community, exercised through its specialised body, the State. It is the substantial form that makes the existence of the state, without which there would be no State. It is the essential quality that rejects any other power over it, whether power from inside or outside.

Perónist Doctrine affirms the principle of political sovereignty as the basis for the unconditional freedom of the nation and the Argentine people, and as the outward appearance of national uniqueness that cannot be limited by other powers.

Political Sovereignty

Political sovereignty is a power that excludes all other power, it is the expression of the total National Will, that is, the Homeland, an eternal entity and continuation of a totalising unity that links the past, present and future. So Justicialism believes that political sovereignty does not belong to groups that factionalise national unity, be it from social classes or political parties. Social classes are pathological expressions of typical economic differences in the capitalist system. Political parties, are apart from everything; they are surface structures without organic or natural foundations within the social context. Nobody is born within them. They are a sum of undifferentiated individuals considered as abstract and unrealistic schemes. The nation is not short of political parties, but of a dynamic multiplicity of intermediate groups responding to different natures and functions. Intermediate communities project the legitimate representative of the national will in a total community context. 'The political party is a purely bourgeois establishment and has its origins in the French Revolution', states General Perón. He adds: 'Man can no longer be regarded as an isolated entity, but as an element of the whole'. 'This explains why the old political organisations are being replaced by more natural organisations'.

For National Justicialismo, sovereignty is absolute and totally indivisible. It is part of the national totality and no social or political faction can undermine it. We reject, therefore, the system powers spewing out of parties, who have sovereignty outside the will of the people. Both Marxism, in all its shades, like liberalism, is rejected by the Justicialist National Doctrine, because either with the class or with the party, national unity is factionalised and the ideal of a united country, free and sovereign, is destroyed.

Financial Independence

Economic Independence is another of the fundamental bases of the Justicialist National Doctrine. It is a typical characteristic of imperialism to expand control over sovereign states. Independence implies the harnessing of all national assets for the enjoyment of the people and the greatness of the nation. Perónist economic mobilisation of all national energies for the country to emerge free from any foreign or domestic capitalist influence, is the great task of the National State, having the provision of our economic and financial power to meet the needs of our people and to realise the welfare of the Argentine man in harmonious material and spiritual renewal.

Social Justice

Political self-determination and economic independence are possible through the implementation of Social Justice as an ethic and a caring practice according to the philosophy of of Justicialismo. Social justice was a particular political event during the ten years of Perónist government. It has been said that previous governments to Perónism capitalised[343] the country. However, that supposed capitalisation was not used to free the nation and implement social justice. On the contrary, the country was more a colony dependent on imperialism and the people were left in a state of underconsumption, in poverty, cultural backwardness and with a spectrum of diseases, living in distressing and depressing misery

One of the tenets that stands out for its importance in relation to everything else: Social Justice. The values and functions of a just society derive not from economic wealth but from

343 'Capitalised' and 'capitalisation' is here referring to the encouragement of economic enterprises, although prior to Perónism Argentina remained an agricultural exporter without an industrial base other than the rudimentary capital investments from the USA and Britain.

work, being the only frame of reference of the Justicialist hierarchies. Hence the political, economic, social and cultural functions, from the highest to the humblest, are not based on economic wealth as in the current system, but on intellectual or physical labour as the supreme dignity of man serving Homeland and People.

This is revolutionary and this implies the validity of removing the capitalist structures, and all those fictions that capitalism has mounted to cover the exploitation of man.

The validity of the Social Justice of which we dream for our country is to not only bring the mere redistribution of wealth for the benefit of all Argentines, but a new relationship between the worker and the machine, inseparable from his creative power and, therefore, a moral transformation; a new scale of values, an end to the axiom of man clouded by selfishness, the profit motive and the rule of capitalism.

The following section reiterates Justicialism as being based on Christianity, and the historical, racial, social and cultural factors that go to form the Argentine people. Justicialism is referred to as 'National Christian Socialism'.

Justicialism And Latin America

'In the year 2000 we shall find states or subjects'. - Perón

The philosophy of National Justicialism, is the result of a synthesis of elements closely linked to the great basic ideas that inform and describe authentic Christian thought; historical, social, racial and cultural patterns that characterise or define the national identity of the Argentine people.

The formulation for Argentina was through the doctrine of our Leader, General Perón, over 25 years ago. As he has defined it, it is deeply nationalistic and tends to the establishment of an originally formulated National Christian Socialism.

It should be particularly noted that nationalism is inherent in Justicialismo, not in the sense of the simple exaltation of territorial sovereignty and borders, but to raise the idea of nationhood in a much broader field that links all Latin American people, inheritors of the same tradition, of the same language, the same religion and the same inalienable cultural heritage.

The spiritual history of the Latin America unit had an actual underlying national unity, before territorial divisions were forced on it by Anglo-Saxon imperialism. Past political confrontations emerge revitalised today, distracting the Latin American people's awareness of General Perón's alternative.

The changes in the field of international relations, which have become extremely accelerated, in the structural, technical, economic and political worlds, and that of military power, clearly indicate that the Latin American peoples are at a crossroads that they need to not only understand but to face, as their destiny is at stake as a free and independent people.

Now what characterises the socio-economic reality of our Latin American continent, is political subjugation and economic dependence, and the reign of social injustice.

No single effort can yield positive results. The past experience of Perónist government in our time had partial success, but it was truncated at the continental level. The united action during the adverse international situation dominated by the superpowers that emerged from World War II, the lack of information and awareness of the destiny of the Latin American brother peoples and governments, enabled outsiders composed of the oligarchies and Marxists to operate on the home front.

The year 2000 will find us together in a joint action of peoples and governments. This will be based on respecting and incorporating those values that define the national character of the Latin American hemisphere: the Reconquista of Political Sovereignty, Recovery of Independence, Creating Economic and Social Justice.

The liberation struggle that all Latin American peoples wage today should be marked by integration of all into one nation. The Latin American Federation must already be created not only for the Argentine people but also for all fraternal peoples who think as a common unit of destiny in relation to the rest of the world. This will not based on current economics and politics, but will be a revolution for the common integration under the liberating doctrine of Justicialism. This must operate as a formal principle of Latin American unity, whose people were divided and exploited by Anglo-Saxon imperialism. Even today the release of Slavic or Asian doctrines, both forms of imperialism, converge to a single objective: the domination

> of our peoples. Everything is given for our Doctrine of true liberation to achieve this new unit of Latin American peoples.

Hence, Perón ends with a call for a broader nationalism, a Latin American Nation formed by a shared culture and religion, vis-à-vis non-Latin powers and influences. This Latin American Nation was a vision that he worked for during his first years of presidency, particularly with Brazil and Chile.

Social and National Synthesis

As we have seen from the previous treatise, *The National Doctrine*, after Perón was ousted in 1955 he developed the Justicialist doctrine further still, and maintained that it was a form of 'national socialism', that rejected both capitalism and Marxism, and during the Cold War, remained neutral. Perón was thus one of the fathers of the non-aligned movement. He also specifically rejects 'internationalism', so that when he later wrote of the need for worldwide co-operation on ecological matters, for example, this should not be confused with a sudden endorsement of the internationalism of the United Nations variety. Perón wrote in 1955:

> For us, the justicialists, the world today finds itself divided between capitalists and communists in conflict: we are neither one nor the other. We aspire ideologically to stand outside of that conflict between global interests. This doesn't imply in any way that we are in the internationalist camp, dodging the issue.
>
> We believe that capitalism as well as communism are systems already overtaken by the times. We consider capitalism to be the exploitation of man by capital and communism as the exploitation of the individual by the state. Both 'insectify' the individual by means of different systems.

> We believe more; we think that the abuses of capitalism are the cause and that communism is the effect. Without capitalism, communism would have no reason to exist; we equally believe that, with the extinction of the cause, there will be the beginning of the end for the effect.[344]

Perón talked of one single class of Argentines, which was in fact the creation not so much of a 'class' but of a 'people', economics ultimately serving the spiritual factors that go to form a 'people'. It is here evident that while Perón referred to the Latin American 'race' on numerous occasions, he was not referring to 'race' in a zoological sense but in the formation of an Argentine *ethnos* welded together by a common heritage and destiny. He said of this:

> In Argentina there should not be more than one single class of men: men who work together for the welfare of the nation, without any discrimination whatever. They are good Argentines, no matter what their origin, their race or their religion may be, if they work every day for the greatness of the Nation, and they are bad Argentines, no matter what they say or how much they shout, if they are not laying a new stone every day towards the construction of the building of the happiness and grandeur of our Nation.
>
> That is the only discrimination which Argentina should make among its inhabitants: those who are doing constructive work and those who are not; those who are benefactors to the country and those who are not. For this reason in this freest land of the free, as long as I am President of the Republic, no one will be persecuted by anyone else.[345]

344 Juan Perón, La fuerza es el derecho de las bestias - Force is the Right of the Beasts (Montevideo: Ediciones Cicerón, 1958), 18.

345 Juan Perón, *Perónist Doctrine* (Buenos Aires, 1952), 'One Single Class of Men'.

Eva Duarte Perón in her autobiography writes of social justice being achieved within the nation, which is a natural bond, and the way those who had condemned capitalism often did so with 'doctrines very remote from everything Argentine'.[346]

> 'Their formula for the solution of social injustice was a common system – the same for all countries and for all peoples. I could not believe that, even to destroy so great an evil, it should be necessary to attack and annihilate anything as natural and as great as the nation'.[347]

Eva early in her life came to accept that revolution was necessary, but not 'international revolution', 'created by men foreign to our ways and thoughts'. Whether this was a reference to the disproportionate number of Jewish immigrants in Marxism, and their conspicuous role in the bloody events of 1919 can only be conjectured. Her ideas were simple but profound, not understanding the complexity of economic theories but believing in a 'patriotic solution', 'as national as the very people they are meant to save'. Taking the vision of the nation and of faith out of the lives of the people would only increase misfortune and suffering. 'I thought it would be like taking the sky out of a landscape'. [348] She was talking as someone who had been a trade union leader, as we have seen, and would have been acquainted with all the Marxist rhetoric of the time.

Dr. Arturo Jauretche, founder of FORJA, one of the movements that combined with Perónism, returned to the Justicialist form of 'national socialism' when commenting on the Perónist victory in 1973. Although he had misgivings about the term as sounding as though it was a foreign import linked to Hitlerism, he nonetheless maintained that it was more descriptive of Justicialism than merely calling it 'socialism'.

346 Eva Duarte Perón, *Evita by Evita* (London: Proteus Publishing, 1978), 15-16. Original title: La Razon De Mi Vida, Buenos Aires, 1953.

347 Eva Duarte Perón, ibid., 16.

348 Eva Duarte Perón, ibid.

Jauretche recounted the antecedents of this 'national socialism' as a 'third position' from the time of the FORJA movement:

> At the time of FORJA, when we talked at the street corners, we were sometimes asked, 'Are you fascists?'. 'No', we answered. 'Are you liberal?'. 'No'. 'So are you communists,' they told us. There were apparently only three options. But our choices were not ones that came from the outside. We were pigeonholed with imported options without accepting the possibility of an original creation. [349]

During the 1930s when FORJA was formed, a universal but national synthesis was appearing in politics throughout the world that has since been identified generically as 'fascism'. We have considered this dialectical process previously, which began during the 19th century. The possibilities were as varied as there were nations and peoples each with their own legacies. The commonality between the different doctrines was that they all sought to establish a 'third position', by synthesising the national and the social; concepts that had been divorced from one another by capitalism and Marxism, while the new movement recognised that the nation is necessarily a social totality encompassing all classes other than the parasitic. Therefore, when 'national syndicalism', or *Falangism*, as it is called, arose in Spain its adherents did not ask whether it was a copy of Italian Fascism, but had independently forged a doctrine that was inspired by the historical circumstances of Spain.

Although Sir Oswald Mosley's British Union of Fascists adopted the Italian name for the new doctrine, the British variation had already been formulated by Mosley when he was a minister in the Labour Government, devising policies that would meet the economic crisis faced by Britain. While Germany called its doctrine National Socialism, Justicialism developed its national-social synthesis along entirely Argentine patterns. Jauretche continued:

349 Arturo M. Jauretche, 'Reflections on the Victory', *Quiz* Journal, No. 3, July 1973.

> We were no more than an attempt to think for ourselves from praxis. An alternative of developing, even with the use of the universal elements - filtered through reality - our own ideology. Perón handled that way of thinking and gave the original creation we had wanted but without success.[350]

It is notable that Jauretche refers to the proto-Justicialist doctrine of FORJA as being developed within the context of 'universal elements', recognising that the emerging Argentine 'nation socialist' doctrine was part of the universal move towards social-national synthesis, whether it was called national-syndicalism, national socialism, fascism, or corporatism, etc. Jauretche next refers to the specifically Argentine phenomenon of FORJA-Justicialist 'national socialism', while alluding to the 'third position' of Justicialism as a rejection of subordination to the super-powers. However, he explains that this 'third position', which was later denigrated by the super-powers with the phrase 'Third World', was itself based not merely on a rejection of Cold War alignment, but was the consequence of the Justicialist doctrine that had been developing prior to the Cold War:

> Moreover, 'National Socialism', in its true sense, had its origins in our country. Is not the concept of Third World development the 'third position' proposed by Perón? When the world was divided into two, when they faced the slogans of Moscow on the one hand and, on the other, the slogans of London or New York, the Argentina of Perón produced an attitude of independence that was, outwardly, the prosecution of a doctrine which, internally, was based on social justice. A doctrine inspired earlier. A doctrine which was the result of a method of pragmatism, rather than building a mind-set.[351]

Perón provided the 'pragmatic' application necessary to turn the FORJA ideology into a practical political programme,

350 ibid.

351 Ibid.

'looking at the needs of the country and its possibilities', cleared of 'ideological blinders', and not based on an abstract world of ideas and systems'.

Jauretche wrote that the whole culture of Argentina until recently had been dominated by outside influences. This also affected the political vocabulary: 'Can we rid ourselves of the choice between "right" and "left"?,: that is the question'.[352] FORJA, radical nationalism and elements of Nacionalismo such as the ALN, rejected the 'Left/Right' dichotomy as a superficial division of the organic totality that forms a genuine nation. Returning to the term of 'national socialism', while focusing on youth as the basis of an ever- developing doctrine, Jauretche wrote:

> I have no objection to national socialism, pointing out the danger that it obscures socialism. I think our youth know how to sufficiently build national socialism as a real version of Justicialism, always updated, by its pragmatic attitude. And leave behind the old who cling to what has been accomplished. We cannot stay to watch the navel of yesterday and did not see the umbilical cord that appears, as every day there comes a new Argentina through youth. We cannot convert the 1973 revolution to a mere bureaucratic restoration.[353]

The ongoing development of Justicialism was also aided by a transformation of the Argentine intelligentsia. Where formerly they had been dominated by foreign ideas and cultures, and had been hostile to Justicialism, in the intervening years between Perón's ouster in 1955 and his return in 1973, the intelligentsia had become nationally-orientated and had formed an important element in the survival and development of Perónism:

> We can detect a difference with what happened 30 years ago: the position of the intelligentsia. The intelligentsia that

352 Ibid.

353 Ibid.

> time belonged, almost 'in totum', to colonial Argentina. They were a determining factor in Perón's downfall. But now there is another intelligentsia: it is national. These new generations have nothing in common with the intellectual backwardness of the past. Among them is this revolution.[354]

Jauretche again reminded his readers that Justicialism must remain pragmatic and realistic, and not become a dogma. The purpose of the new intelligentsia was to maintain 'reality', its purpose being 'to build a country, not to fight intellectual battles'. The aim was not an 'ideal society' but a 'better society' based on 'the will of the majority'. 'Justicialism, or PJ, or national socialism, understood as the common name of a way of thinking and acting in accordance with the here and now, prevents young people from those dangers' of becoming fixated with ideological systems. Jauretche counselled the 'old Perónist' not to be afraid of the youth: 'you win with the new, not the old', while being proud to have been the founders of the doctrine.[355]

Perón, just prior to his death, reiterated the Justicialist doctrine of the 'third position' and 'national socialism', in an interview. Nothing had been compromised over the decades, despite the attempted twists and turns of self-styled Justicialists who could not go beyond the old dogmas of 'left' and 'right', while some even resorted to market economics.

> Solanas: General, today Justicialism has the explicit aim in government of implementing National Socialism. As the word socialist has also been used to describe anti-revolutionary or reformist projects, or social democrats like those in Europe, and even social-imperialists, what would socialism be for the Partido Justicialismo?
>
> Perón: Well, actually, the determination of the term socialist in today's world is very difficult, because it includes a

354 Ibid.

355 Ibid.

tremendous range from, say, a dogmatic international movement to democratic. Within that there are thousands of shades and one can observe on five continents different systems, all based on socialism.

Now, there are monarchies with socialist governments, but also the other extreme socialist Marxist movements. Between the extreme left and the extreme right all have socialism. Our Movement in this direction is much more simple, with undoubtedly a socialist base. Why? Because it is based on social justice.

Solanas: What of Capitalism?

Perón: Capitalism was born in the French Revolution. In these two centuries, from the French Revolution to now, it cannot be denied, that there has been a system that advanced the world in an extraordinary way. Especially in the scientific and technical aspects … but at the cost of tremendous sacrifice of the people. So people think today, that same progress may perhaps be slower, but can be done without sacrificing the people. The Partido Justicialismo keeps fighting for progress, maybe not as fast as it has been these past two centuries, but fairer.

We want that sacrifice to disappear, and that the same work is done without sacrifice, only effort. Now that's socialist, because these forms of coexistence emphasise the social aspect. I mean, man is part of the community, but the community is also part of man. For us the Perónist government is one that serves the people. It serves no other interest than that of the people, and does what the people want. And within those forms, the Perónist will fight for the greatness of the community in which he lives. Justicialismo aims for the relationship of the individual with the collective. That is our revolutionary process, and doing so is one of the forms of socialism.

> Solanas: And while this would be the Justicialist socialist project, is it an autonomous Argentine socialism for the Argentines, General?
>
> Perón: Naturally, because each community has its own idiosyncrasies and their own intrinsic values that must be respected. No two communities are the same. They have different characteristics that are influenced by geographical location, race... countless circumstances that bear upon the formation of that community.
>
> Therefore we want one thing for Argentines by Argentines. Man can become independent only in an organised community. Where everyone does his work, they are also performing within the community. … what we have called the ORGANISED COMMUNITY. For the organised community is precisely that, where man can work while all the men of the community are working together.[356]

Perón's final words were on corporatism as the basis of Justicialist social organisation, or what he called the 'organised community', as we have previously seen. He had not compromised with the 'demoliberal' party system, although Justicialism has yet to transcend that system and introduce the corporate state, also called 'national syndicalism', especially in the Spanish-founded states.

National Syndicalism

Perón recalled of his observations of Italy and Germany:

> Italian Fascism led popular organisations to an effective participation in national life, which had always been denied to the people. Before Mussolini's rise to power, the nation was on one hand and the worker on the other, and the latter had no involvement in the former. Exactly the

356 Interview with Perón by Pino Solanas and Octavio Getino, Crisis Magazine, 1974.

> same phenomenon happened in Germany, meaning, an organised state for a perfectly ordered community, as well as for a perfectly ordered population: a community where the state was the tool of the nation, whose representation was, under my view, effective. I thought that this should be the future political form, meaning, the true people's democracy, true social democracy.[357]

That 'effective popular participation in national life by the people', was achieved through the establishment under Italian Fascism of a Corporate State.

Sir Oswald Mosley, in developing his British variation of Fascism before the Second World War, explained corporatism in detail in many British Union of Fascist publications, writing in the BUF manifesto, *The Greater Britain* (1932):

> It envisages, as its name implies, a nation organised as the human body. Every part fulfils its function as a member of the whole, performing its separate task, and yet, by performing it, contributing to the welfare of the whole. The whole body is greatly directed by the central driving brain of government without which no body and system of society can operate.[358]

While corporatism was the basis of Medieval social order, this derived from Classical antiquity. Justicialism incorporated the Classical Greek and Roman models into its doctrine, through Perón, and others such as Dr. Arturo E. Sampay,[359] who synthesised Aristotle with Thomas Aquinas; the corporatism of both the Classical and the medieval worlds. Aristotle wrote of the Classical conception of the organic state:

---

357 Felipe Pigna, Los mitos de la historia argentina 4 (Buenos Aires: Editorial Planeta, 2008), 28.

358 Oswald Mosley, *My Life* (London: Black House Publishing 2012[1968]), 353.

359 Sampay was the leading constitutional authority of Perónism, and drafter of the seminal 1949 Constitution.

> Further, the state is by nature clearly prior to the family and to the individual, since the whole is of necessity prior to the part; for example, if the whole body be destroyed, there will be no foot or hand, except in an equivocal sense, as we might speak of a stone hand; for when destroyed the hand will be no better than that. But things are defined by their working and power; and we ought not to say that they are the same when they no longer have their proper quality, but only that they have the same name. The proof that the state is a creation of nature and prior to the individual is that the individual, when isolated, is not self-sufficing; and therefore he is like a part in relation to the whole.[360]

The Catholic Church was the heir to the Classical legacy, and Thomas Aquinas wrote of the organic conception of society: 'As the part and the whole are in a certain sense identical, so that which belongs to the whole in a sense belongs to the part'.[361] Pope Leo XIII's encyclical *Rerum* Novarum, written in 1891, laid down the Church's alternative to capitalism and socialism, advocating a state based on corporatism and social justice, with a 'Christian constitution of the State', in the interests of the 'commonweal'. [362] Leo referred to the organic character of the state:

> Just as the symmetry of the human frame is the result of the suitable arrangement of the different parts of the body, so in a State is it ordained by nature that these two classes should dwell in harmony and agreement, so as to maintain the balance of the body politic. Each needs the other: capital cannot do without labour, nor labour without capital.[363]

360 Aristotle, Politics, Part II, http://classics.mit.edu/Aristotle/politics.mb.txt

361 Aquinas, Thomas, Summa theologiae, IIa-IIae, q. lxi, are. l, ad 2m.

362 Pope Leo XIII, Rerum Novarum: Rights and Duties of Capital and Labour, (Vatican City: 1891), 1-2, http://www.vatican.va/holy_father/leo_xiii/encyclicals/documents/hf_l-xiii_enc_15051891_rerum-novarum_en.html

363 Leo, ibid., 19.

In 1931 Pope Pius XI returned to the issues that had been addressed by Leo, issuing the encyclical *The Social Order: Quadragesimo Anno*, condemning the Free Trade 'Manchester Liberals' as false, while also condemning the socialist 'intellectuals' for their manipulation of the workers. [364] Pius reiterated the corporatist character of the Catholic state:

> It is obvious that, as in the case of ownership, so in the case of work, especially work hired out to others, there is a social aspect also to be considered in addition to the personal or individual aspect. For man's productive effort cannot yield its fruits unless a truly social and organic body exists, unless a social and juridical order watches over the exercise of work, unless the various occupations, being interdependent, cooperate with and mutually complete one another, and, what is still more important, unless mind, material things, and work combine and form as it were a single whole.[365]

Pius refers to the syndicates and corporations then being formed, obviously referring to Fascist Italy and probably moreso, Salazar's Portugal, the latter organised as a specifically Catholic social state:

> The associations, or corporations, are composed of delegates from the two syndicates (that is, of workers and employers) respectively of the same industry or profession and, as true and proper organs and institutions of the State, they direct the syndicates and coordinate their activities in matters of common interest toward one and the same end.[366]

364 Pius XI, The Social Order: Quadragesimo Anno, 1931, 54-55, http://www.vatican.va/holy_father/pius_xi/encyclicals/documents/hf_p-xi_enc_19310515_quadragesimo-anno_en.html

365 Pius, ibid., 69.

366 Pius, ibid., 93.

These corporatist concepts had a far-reaching impact, with Corporatism as the up-and-coming doctrine that was replacing both communism and capitalism throughout the world prior to the Second World War. In 1937 Vargas, president of Brazil, who would support Perón's efforts to form a Latin American bloc, established Brazil as a corporatist 'New State' on the Portuguese model.

The Corporatist model had found an early audience in Latin America; unsurprisingly, given the Catholic support for Corporatism. Corporatist thinking influenced Latin American nationalism for reasons similar to its impact on Spain, where it was called 'national syndicalism', also known as *Falangism.*[367] Here it developed into a radical movement under the charismatic young leader Jose Antonio Primo de Rivera, who was murdered by Spain's Republican state in 1936. Jose Antonio described the national-syndicalist state:

> What is meant by 'doing away with the contrast between capital and labour'? Work is a function of man just as property is an attribute of man. But property does not mean the same thing as capital; capital is an economic means and as such it should be put into the service of the whole economy and not used for the personal prosperity of one individual, or for giant accumulations of capital.[368]

The similarities between Falangism and Justicialismo are apparent, as is the influence of Catholic social doctrine on both When the Civil War erupted in Spain in 1936 between the Republican State with its broad alliance of Leftists and the rebellious military under Franco with its Rightist allies, the Argentine Nacionalistas were strongly pro-Franco.[369] The

367 Falange Espanol was founded by Jose Antonio Primo de Rivera in 1933.

368 Jose Antonio Primo de Rivera, cited by Ettore Vernier, '*A History of the Spanish Falangists*, n.d.

369 Ronald H. Dolkart, 'The Right in the Décade Infame 1930-1943', in *The Argentine Right*, op. cit., 77-78.

Corporatist doctrine was adopted, for example, by the Argentine Civic League, declaring:

> The State should not be structured as an expression of political parties and their representatives as it is today. It should represent all organised and incorporated elements. This should be consecrated by the will of the nation as expressed in elections pending a census and registering all social groups, conforming to the function that they fulfil in the economic, spiritual, professional, and occupational life of Argentina.
>
> The national economy, constituted by the totality of production and commerce, has to have as its primordial end the well being of the collective and the power of the nation. The State thus made out of all the organised social forces, will be an authentic expression of them and shall coordinate and rationalise the country's production, as well as its distribution and overall economic activity.
>
> Through the intermediary work of respective organised social groups - unions, syndicates, corporations, professions - the State will coordinate and regulate the interests of owners and workers, in equal parity of conditions. The State will ensure fairness in the collective contracts that they reach, mediate the issues that sustain conflict, in effect; it will institute a labour court, thereby avoiding the so-called 'class conflict'.[370]

Soon after his re-election Perón stated to trades union leaders in November 1951:

> Until the present I have maintained traditional political forms because we are in a process of evolution. We are now progressing towards a *Syndicalist State*, the ancient

370 Argentine Civic League, *Combat*, No. 3, 1937.

> aspiration of the human community in which all will be represented in the Legislature and in the Administration by their own people'.[371]

The syndicalist constitution was implemented in Chaco following a Constituent Assembly. Chaco, 450 miles northwest of Buenos Aires, became the Presidente Perón Province in December 1951, and Argentina's 18th province. Half of the members of the Legislature were voted in by the old party electoral system of 200,000 voters, while the other half were voted for by a trades union electorate of 30,000 through vocational franchise.[372] That year Perón stated:

> Agricultural and pastoral farming production should be totally in the hands of the actual producers, and this will only be achieved when the Co-operative organisations cover the whole country and protect production from the land itself to the consumer, Argentine or foreign, replacing the State in the commercialisation process, which should now be realised.[373]

While the Perónist administration had undertaken progressive steps towards economic sovereignty, and hence political sovereignty, by establishing or invigorating state marketing boards, this was a preliminary phase towards syndicalisation, although time was against Perón for the implementation of the programme. However, by 1952, the Perónist administration had succeeded in creating 2000 agricultural Co-operatives, with over 750,000 members. These received state credit loans and the preferential distribution of farm machinery.[374]

---

371 Quoted by Frank Owen in *Perón: His Rise and Fall* (London: The Cressnet Press, 1957), 213.

372 Frank Owen, ibid. Owen, an antagonistic biographer, cites the numerical discrepancy between the party electorate and the trades union electorate presumably as a quip.

373 Perón quoted by Frank Owen, ibid., 214.

374 Frank Owen, ibid., 214.

Eva Duarte de Perón, wrote of syndicalism in 1951:

> The working class forces have triumphed, thanks to the humble, good men and the workers who saw in Perón not only the social reformer, but also the patriot, the man who brought security to the nation, the man who would fight so that when he retired the country would be bigger, happier, and more prosperous than when he found it. These men made the triumph of Perón possible. This is why we Argentines may enjoy our social justice, and our economic independence which grows greater every day, thanks to the patriotic effort and extraordinary vision of General Perón.
>
> General Perón has defeated both capitalism and communism. He has defeated capitalism by suppressing oligarchy, by fighting the economic forces, and the trusts. *La Prensa,*[375] that capitalistic cancer, was not suppressed by Perón, but by the paperboys and the working force. But could the paperboys, the most humble workers of the country, have confronted the powerful paper, through a strike against a business that had so much support, especially from the outside, if there had been no justice, no government which would let them discuss freely and on an equal basis with their bosses. Before, the poor paperboys would have been machine gunned, drowning their hopes forever.
>
> Perón has also defeated internal capitalism, through social economy, putting capital at the service of the economy, and not vice versa, which only gave the workers the right to die of hunger. The law of the funnel, as it is called, the wide part for the capitalists and the narrow part for the people.
>
> General Perón took communism away from the masses, replacing it with syndicalism, for justice and greater well-being, about which I would like to say a few words.

375 Reference to a major anti-Perónist newspaper serving oligarchic interests.

> Syndicalism supports justice and Perón, but this does not mean that syndicalism participates in political action. It is simply a doctrine of social justice, and its creator, Perón, is now above all politics, because the Argentine syndicates (trade unions), by forming syndicalism, that is, by placing themselves within the doctrine of justice, are authentically representing their members; that which before was discussed with guns is no longer discussed; conquests are defended, which is very different. Syndicalism and the Argentine syndicates, within the doctrine of social justice, support Perón politically; they do not support parties or party candidates, because there will never be another Perón, despite his imitators, whose works are always disastrous. The working classes, by supporting Perón, support the leader of the Argentine workers and not the leader of any political party.[376]

Eva Perón pointed out the nature of the embryonic syndicalist state: Perónism sought to embody the nation as a totality, and not only one section of it divided against another. The class nature of both capitalism and communism was overcome by integrating the trades unions into the decision-making process. Thereby the syndicates performed a higher function than as class war battalions reacting against the rulership of capitalism. When capital was put at the service of the nation, rather than controlling the nation, the combative nature of the labour movement was transformed into an organ of the Argentine nation.

Just how viable and genuine this embryonic syndicalist state was is indicated by the enduring popularity of Perónism in the Chaco province.[377]

376 Eva Duarte de Perón, Historia del Perónismo (Buenos Aires: Presidencia de la Nación, 1951).

377 The Perónist, Deolindo Bittel, who had been elected deputy governor on the Perónist ticket in 1953, served as Governor during the 1960s and 1970s, despite each term being prematurely ended by military intervention. In 1962 he was elected Governor as part of a Perónist sweep of the governorship of ten of fourteen provinces, after the lifting the electoral ban on Perónists. However he was prevented by the military from taking office. He won again in alliance with his former opponents of the Conservative

The 'Organised Community'

The Perónist conception of the corporate state is usually called the 'organised community', although the terms 'syndicalist state' and 'corporate nation' have been used. Perón wrote a book on the subject, describing the Justicialist doctrine of the community and the state. He wrote that tremendous economic progress has resulted in materialism, and had reduced 'the intimate perspective of man'; that is to say, it has detached the individual from any sense of community. There is not 'the same degree of personality in the shadow ... next to the thunderous power of the machine'. There was no gradual transition into the machine age, but a 'violent shock' and 'radical changes of modern life' to the 'collective spirit'.[378] This material progress has not brought any corresponding improvement in the view of man's worth.[379]

Justicialism sees problems as ultimately spiritual, and never forsook its Christian ethos. From the time of the Renaissance the European spirit had been undermined by rationalism and science, and eventually replaced by the 'American spirit', a product of the 18th century Enlightenment philosophers. Man has been 'placed before God'. The result, fermenting among the intelligentsia of Europe, was to have 'replaced the worship of God by the worship of humanity'.

Following this 'Age of Enlightenment' was Darwin's theory of evolution. This further undermined the bond between man and the spiritual, making him a mere biological object, like capitalism and Marxism see man as an economic object. 'And below the scientific world, the question arises as to whether the

---

Party, was sworn in as Governor in 1963, and was re-elected in 1965. He again became Governor in 1973, when Perón assumed Office, but again his term was shortened by the military coup against Isabel Perón in 1976. He ran the Perónist Party when it was pushed underground following the military coup. He entered the Senate for Chaco Province, withdrawing in 1987 to become Mayor of the provincial capital, Resistencia, and returned to the Senate in 1989 dying shortly before the end of his term in 1997.

378 Perón, *The Organised Community: A Philosophical Sketch* (Buenos Aires: 1974 edition), II.

379 Perón, ibid., III.

human soul can digest the replacing of traditional worship with the purely scientific' . 'Elevated to such a general explanation, man, society and the state, are forced to suddenly invent a new scale of values, a new morality.... discarding all metaphysical reasoning..'[380]

The ancient Socratic and Platonic ideas of community, inherited by the Church, had been replaced by Hobbesian[381] self-interest which was augmented by politicised notions of Darwinian evolution.[382] This provided a pseudo-scientific justification for free trade and its accompanying materialism and egotism in the so-called 'struggle for the survival of the fittest'. Perón commented on this:

> Something is wrong in nature if it is possible to conceive, as Hobbes in *Leviathan, bominis Homo lupus,* the state of man against man, all against all, where manhood can relate the exploits of the raptor. Hobbes belongs to that moment when the lights of Socratic evangelical hope begin to fade before the cold glare of Reason, which in turn will soon embrace materialism. When Marx says that economic relations depend on the social structure and class division and therefore the history of humanity is only the history of class struggles, we begin to make out clearly, in its effects, the picture of *Leviathan.*[383]

380 Perón, ibid., VI.

381 Thomas Hobbes (1588-1679) wrote Leviathan or The Matter, Forme and Power of a Common Wealth Ecclesiasticall and Civil, published in 1651. Hobbes described man as 'matter in motion' and therefore predates Marxism by two centuries. He stated that innate human brutality can only be checked by foregoing rights, and that the primary motive for accepting such an order is fear of death in a state of naturalistic anarchy. In order to avert a deadly free-for-all humans must legally contract to be governed.

382 'Social Darwinism', or Darwinian evolution applied to economics, whereby only the economically strongest survive, whether they are businessmen or labourers. While this economic 'survival of the fittest' was openly propounded as the doctrine of the Free Trade school that dominated English economics during the 19th century, it remains the doctrine of today's Free Trade capitalism, although dressed in other garb, with terms such as 'economic efficiency'.

383 Perón, op. cit., IX.

Here we see that Perón recognised what other philosophers such as Oswald Spengler, had pointed out; that Marxism and capitalism are both the same in their world outlook because they both arose from the same Age where economic thinking was dominant. What arose was a combative division between group interests within what was once the same community; what Marx heralded as 'class struggle'. Perón challenged the efficacy of this 'struggle', and asserted to the contrary that more could have been achieved had there been a social bond rather than conflict:

> There is no possibility of virtue, not even a trace of individual dignity, where the necessity of the struggle that is essentially open dissociation of the natural elements of the community is proclaimed. Yes, there are different interests and different needs, which can gradually diminish, persuading those who can give, do give, or stimulate the progress of the stragglers. But that operation - in which society is busy with painful events over a century – had no need to scream and grunt of the threat, much less blood, to yield the desired results. Love between men would have gotten better results in less time, and if it was found that doors were closed by selfishness, this was because there was not intense moral education to dispel these defects, but it was as planting grudges.[384]

Returning to the classical idea, Perón cites Aristotle, who contended that man is a social being, and that this sociality is reflected in politics: 'Man is to be in an ordered social coexistence, the greater good is not achieved consequently in individual human life, but in the super-individual state agency, ethics culminates in politics'.[385] Hence Justicialism does not aim to quash the individual, as in Marxism, but to reorganise the social polity so that in pursuing individual objectives, the individual also fulfils a greater social function. That is the aim of the corporative, organic, state.

384 Perón, ibid.

385 Aristotle cited by Perón, ibid., X.

'[Herbert] Spencer says that the ultimate sense of ethics consists in correcting selfishness. It is this 'selfishness that forged the class struggle and inspired the anathemas of materialism', resulting in 'an overestimation of one's own interests'. Selfishness is the denial of values.[386]

Citing Hegel, whose dialectics had been misappropriated by Marxism, Perón stated: 'Hegel ... said the spirit, *which exists by itself,* which can only come to *be* fully *itself* to the extent that *I* was raised to *us* or, in his words, the *self of humanity*'.[387] The dissolution of the organic polity was rendered by 'the sparks of a political-economic revolution, with the erection of industrialism and capitalism, generated by Progress in the bowels of the Liberal Revolution, which led to the expansion of individual values...'[388] On the other hand, the adaptation of Hegelianism by Marx produced a reaction that made the State omnipotent to the detriment of the individual: 'Hegel's path led certain groups to madness as they entirely subordinate individuality to the ideal organisation, automatically the concept of humanity was reduced to an empty word: *the omnipotence of the state over an infinite amount of zeros*'.[389] The search for a 'third position' is implicit. What the post-capitalist era requires is not the stifling edifice of the Marxist state, but a balance between the individual and the community, where both are in organic service to each other, quoting the German philosopher Fichte that '*man is not a free personality until he learns to respect others*'. The 'free personality', states Perón, cannot achieve 'accentuation' through social 'isolation'.[390]

Drawing on the ancient Hindu *Vedas*, on Aristotle, Plato, and on the Thomist doctrine of Catholicism, Perón returned to the search for an alternative to the conflict between spirit and matter.

386 Ibid., X.

387 Perón citing Hegel, ibid., XI.

388 Perón,ibid., XII.

389 Ibid., XIV.

390 Ibid.

A duality has arisen which throughout history is in conflict for domination:

> We have gone from the communion of matter and spirit to the full rule of soul, its dissociation and its final cancellation. Indeed, despite the ebb and flow of theories, man, composed of soul, remains the same. What has changed is the meaning of his existence, subject to higher currents.[391]

The soul had been sidelined by science and material progress. Man has become, as Perón often used the term' 'insectified'; that is, a nebulous mass without consciousness, and man feels small and insignificant amongst the forces of technical progress. The result is a 'demoralised society'. The choices offered have been 'two major adulterations: one being amoral individualism, predisposed to the subversive, to selfishness, to return to lower states of evolution of the species; another lies in the interpretation of life trying to depersonalise man in the atomiser of collectivism'.[392]

Man has lost faith in his purpose and meaning. Universal 'disappointment' in life is the result What is required of humanity is a 'return to the combative attitude of faith in his mission, individually, in family and collectively'. Moral and ethical values have not kept pace with technical progress, and hence there is confusion and lack of certainty.[393] The legitimacy of Perón's view that life has lost meaning despite the technical achievements and material comforts of many is reflected ever more by the feelings of general discontent with life, with the rates of suicide, drug addiction, alcoholism, and anti-depressant medication, with general unhappiness being more prevalent in the affluent countries. Once the material needs are satisfied, man innately wants a higher meaning to life that cannot be found in

391 Ibid., XVI.

392 JuIbid., XVII.

393 Ibid., XIX.

President Juan and Eva Perón on the balcony of Casa Rosada Government House in 1950

the pursuit of ever more material possessions. The more selfish individuals become, paradoxically the more they lack as sense of self. As one sees in one of the classes that epitomise modern 'success', movie and music 'stars', here are the greatest number of drug addicts, neurotics, alcoholics and divorcees. As Aristotle stated long ago, man finds purpose in community and social duty, not in egotism and hedonism.

The 'organised community' returns meaning to the individual life, when the individual starts thinking of 'we' rather than 'I'. . Returning to the Greek ideal:

> You could create a world in which ideals and practices are representations of values which were likely to occur with some familiarity. Plato said: *Good is order, harmony, proportion, hence the supreme virtue is justice* As such we noticed the first rule of antiquity converted into political

> *discipline*. Socrates had tried to define man, whom Aristotle would emphasise is a strict political vocation, that is, in the language of the time, a sense of order in the common life. The Platonist idea that man and the community to which he belongs are an irresistible mutual integration seems to us fundamental. The Greek city [was] carried in its essence to the empire of Rome...[394]

Perón now makes it plain that what he is referring to as the 'organised community' is his concept of the corporative, 'organic state':

> ... political society as a body governed by the immutable laws of harmony: heart, digestive system, muscles, will, brain, are in the simile of Plato bodies happily taken by their functions and purposes of collective biology: *A State of Justice, where each class exercises their functions in the service of all.,* The whole, with a central proposition of law, as a law of harmony, the human body, predominated over singularities[395] on the Greek political horizon, which is also the first political horizon of our civilization.[396]

The inequalities of classical civilisation were tempered by the rise of Christianity, in producing as new synthesis of the organic state of the pagan world with the Christian ethos of humility. 'The Greek idea needed a new contemplation of human unity to be completed from a higher viewpoint. That contribution was reserved for Christianity', with man as the 'image of God', and particularly the Thomistic doctrine which states that man serves the community.[397]

The democratic revolutions that overthrew the monarchies failed to provide humanity with a spiritual basis for its new-found

394 Ibid., XX.

395 The Greek City-States.

396 Perón, *The Organised Community*, op. cit., XX.

397 Ibid.

'freedom'. Man was left half human, half beast, a type of 'centaur'; and has been left as a slave to material appetites. What is now required is to 'recover the meaning of life. 'Our community, to which we aspire, is one where freedom and responsibility are cause and effect in that there is joy to be founded on dignity. A community where the individual actually has something to offer to the general good'.[398]

Man needs liberating from his half bestial, centaur existence, by returning to the Classical ideal of harmony. Perón suggested another historical era might unfold, where 'we think of man in the "I" and the *us,* [and] that our choice should be the subject of deep meditation'.[399] The aim would be to 'restore harmony between material progress and spiritual values and provide again man with an accurate view of their reality. We are collectivist, but the basis of that collectivism is individualistic, and its root is a supreme faith in the treasure that man, by the fact of its existence, represents'. The question is 'to try to resolve whether to accentuate the life of the community ... or if it will be only prudent for individual freedom to reign alone, blind to the interests and common needs, provided with an unstoppable material ambition'.

> What our philosophy tries to restore is harmony ... overall, a sense of fullness of life ... Our freedom is coexistence of freedom that comes from an ethics for the general good which is always alive, present, imperative. This community that pursues spiritual and material ends, yearning to improve and be fairer, kinder and happier, will welcome the future man from his high tower with the noble conviction of Spinoza: *'We feel, we experience that we are eternal'.*[400]

Perón returned to the 'organised community' in 1971, speaking at Madrid during a filmed lecture. Here he focuses on Justicialism

398 Ibid., XXI.

399 Ibid.,

400 Ibid., XX.

being a 'national', Argentine, 'socialism'; that each people, being of different 'race' and having different 'idiosyncrasies', must find their own path to nationhood founded on social justice.

> Each community has its own idiosyncrasies and their own intrinsic values, which must be respected. No two communities are the same: there are different characteristics that are influenced by the geographical location, race, and finally, a number of circumstances that bear upon the formation of that community.[401]

Justicialism can only be established on the basis of the 'intrinsic conditions' of a community:

> And this is a fundamental thing that, if a socialist movement in Argentina is made, it must be a movement made by the Argentines for the Argentines. Why? Because you cannot make socialism the same for the 'peasant' in the Asian area as for a man of the Argentine pampas. The two are farmers, but are diametrically opposed in all their psychic and physical manifestations. And the medium is different, and the activity is also different. Consequently, what we want is one thing for the Argentine, by Argentines.[402]

The premise of Justicialism in the socio-economic and ultimately ethical and moral realms is that a parasitic class does not function, where 'types may exist even when they do not produce what they consume. ... Now, to produce, man must be given the conditions of dignity, happiness and peace of mind, so you can produce without sacrifice; that's what we want'.[403] The 'organised community' exists only when man sacrifices selfishness for the common interest. Individualism is 'devoid of social meaning', and has thrown man in bestial struggle against man, and nation against

401 Perón, 'Doctrinal and Policy Update', Part I, Madrid, June, July, October, 1971, appended to *The Organised Community*, Buenos Aires, 1974.

402 Ibid.

403 Ibid.

nation. 'The Perónist states that the organised community is the starting point. And it is also the point of arrival of Justicialismo'.[404]

In practise the 'organised community' means not only representation through syndical organisations ascending from factory floor to legislative assembly, but assuring that every interest is heard at every level. In local government, this means the creation of 'neighbourhood committees' to provide input to municipalities from the most localised unit of a community. In *The Organised Community* Perón wrote of this that,

> the sense of community comes from below and not from above, which should not be an order imposed by the State, but is an order imposed from the base itself. This confirms our view how these natural bodies of the community arise from the bottom up, and are free in their functions as contributing factors in the state apparatus.[405]

Like the syndical organisation of labour and the professions, neighbourhood communities are self-governing. Perón stated that 'neighbourhood committees are the sectors of the organised population designating their representatives to defend their own interests to the municipal government. In other words, they are the natural and logical entities which contribute to the government'.[406]

---

404 Ibid.

405 Ibid., Chapter XVII, paragraph 9.

406 Perón, First Neighbourhood Commissions Congress, Buenos Aires, 1954.

'International Synarchy'

Perón explained to the historian Felix Luna, an anti-Perónist who served as a bureaucrat in the post-1955 regime:

> There are two historical lines in the country with reference to the men of government: the Hispanic line and the Anglo-Saxon line. All who presided over the country on behalf of the Anglo-Saxon line, are Masons, from Posadas. Only three who were not Masons: Juan Manuel de Rosas, Juan Hipólito Yrigoyen and Perón ...

Perón used the term 'international synarchy' to embrace the concept of what would today be described by orthodox academe as 'conspiracy theory'. The 'international synarchy' he referred to is a convergence of seemingly contradictory forces that are united in their opposition to the 'third position'. What these various forces have in common is an animosity towards the concept of national self-determination, and the aim of creating a world state.

During an interview in 1971 Perón described 'the great international synarchy [that] is manipulated from the United Nations, where communism, capitalism, Judaism, the Catholic Church and Masonry are found'.[407] In his prologue for Enrique Pavón Pereyra's book *Coloquios con Perón*, Perón wrote that the 'Great Internationals' such as 'Communist Imperialism and Capitalist Imperialism' form tactical alliances 'with other Internationals, such as Vaticanism, Masonry and Judaism'.[408] In December 1972 Perón told a group of priests that this 'synarchy' had been responsible for ending 'Argentine sovereignty'.[409] That year he stated:

> *The problem is to free the country and to remain free.*

407 Juan Perón in Primera Plana, July 1971, quoted by Leonardo Sankman, 'The Right and Civilian Regimes', in *The Argentine Right*, op. cit., 136.

408 Quoted by Leonardo Sankman, ibid., 137.

409 Leonardo Sankman, ibid., 137.

That is, we must confront the international Synarchy of communism, capitalism, Freemasonry, Judaism and the Catholic Church, operated from the United Nations. All of these forces act on the world through thousands of agencies.[410]

Having already considered the role of international finance, we shall now consider the other components of this 'international synarchy': Masonry, 'Vaticanism', Communism, and Judaism/Zionism.

Freemasonry

Freemasonry had historically been in the forefront of conspiratorial accusations, especially since the time of the French Revolution. Interestingly, in his comments to Professor Luna, Perón identified the English line of Freemasonry as the enemy of Argentina, whereas usually it is the Occidental line of Freemasonry, headed by the Grand Orient de France, which is held – especially by Catholic theorists – to be the fomenter of subversion and revolutions, while the English version (including the American) is regarded as a harmless benevolent society.

Indeed, Freemasonry was a major subversive element in Argentina as it was throughout South and Central America and southern, central and eastern Europe; particularly through the Grand Orient and Scottish Rite forms of Masonry which have historically been active in political agitation. Professor Orlando Ruben Sconza, historian and sociologist from the University of Buenos Aires, enthuses of Masonry: 'There was an intellectual element that had a strong presence in countries like France, the United States, Spain or the South American region…'[411]

---

410 Juan Perón, *Reason Journal*, Buenos Aires, 4 July 1972.

411 Adrian Royo Coldiz, 'Freemasonry in Argentina', The Argentine Independent, 14 October 2009, http://www.argentinaindependent.com/feature/freemasonry-in-argentina/

Angel Jorge Clavero, current Grand Master of the Argentine Lodge, states:

> Our institution advocates strongly for the values being pursued since the years of the French Revolution. We shape men and teach them how to think for themselves through symbology, in hopes that they will become better members of our society. If they become better citizens, the quality of our country's political reality improves…something that we may be needing right now.[412]

Clavero places Argentine Masonry within the realm of Jacobin-type Grand Orient Masonry. However, as noted above, Perón focused on Anglophone Masonry, generally regarded as apolitical, as a vehicle that had maintained Argentina's subjugation to Britain. Given the historical links between Masonry and the 'English Establishment', this should not be surprising. Indeed, the well-known metaphysician, Rudolf Steiner, founder of Anthroposophy and the Waldorf education system, stated of English (that is, United Grand Lodge) Masonry that it was just as politicised and subversive as Grand Orient Masonry, and that the British government was subverted by secret societies. In particular, foreign affairs was controlled by an 'inner committee'.[413]

Steiner, in tracing the origins of Grand Orient Masonry to the United Grand Lodge, stated:

> But everywhere in a different way, in many places outside the actual British realm, Freemasonry pursues exclusively or mainly political interests. Such political interests in the most palpable sense are pursued by the 'Grand-Orient de France', but also by other 'Grand Orients'. One might now say: what has that to do with the English? But view

412 Adrian Royo Coldiz, ibid.

413 Rudolf Steiner, '*The Karma of Untruthfulness*', 'Rudolf Steiner Archive, GA 173', 18 December 1916, http://www.rsarchive.org/Lectures/GA/index.php?ga=GA0173

> this in conjunction with the fact that the first High-degree Lodge in Paris was founded from England, not France! Not French people but Britons founded it; they only wove the French into their Lodge.[414]

After listing the Lodges that were founded under the auspices of the United Grand Lodge, from Spain to Russia, Steiner stated that 'these Lodges were founded as the external instruments for certain occult-political impulses'. These impulses included the 'fury of the Jacobins', (who launched a Reign of Terror over France in the name of 'Liberty, Equality, Fraternity')...'[415]Steiner alluded to the disingenuousness of United Grand Lodge Masonry in being able to say:

> [L]ook at our Lodges, they are very respectable – and we are not concerned with the others'. But if one can see through the historical connections and the driving forces in an interplay of mutual opposition to one another, then it is indeed high British politics that is concealed behind it.[416]

Steiner warned:

> If one wants as a person of modern times to see clearly in order to meet the world openly and understand it, then one should not let oneself be blinded by democratic logic, which is justified only in its own sphere, or by phrases concerning democratic progress etc. One would have also to point to the interposing of something that reveals itself in the attempt to give rulership to the few through the means available within the Lodges – namely, ritual and its suggestive effect.[417]

414 Rudolf Steiner, 'T*he Karma of Untruthfulness, Part II*', GA 174, 8 January 1917, http://www.rsarchive.org/GA/index.php?ga=GA0174

415 Ibid.

416 Ibid.

417 Steiner, ibid.

One might be reminded here of what Argentine Grand Master Clavero recently stated about Masonry 'shaping men… through symbology', and of Argentine Masonry's embrace of Jacobin doctrines, which puts Argentine Masonry into the subversive political realm.

Steiner was speaking with a wide, first-hand knowledge of these societies. As for Argentina and the United Grand Lodge-derived Masonry, that Perón contended was active in keeping Argentines subordinate to Britain, a leading Mason who had lived 38 years in Argentina, returning to the USA in 1955 stated that Perón had driven Masonry underground. However, what is also notable is that by 1957, after Perón's ouster, Masonry was again flourishing. Dr. Fred Aden, who had been Grand Master of the Columbia Masonic Lodge in Buenos Aires, speaking at a luncheon of Masons, calling themselves the Lodi High Twelve Club, stated that there were now (1957) 27 English-speaking 'Blue Lodges' chartered by the United Grand Lodge of England, and one English-speaking Lodge chartered by the Grand Orient of Argentina.

> They, as similar Lodges throughout the world, provide strong fraternal bonds for Americans and Englishmen as well as all Masons. Dr. Aden said that Perón confiscated the headquarters of Argentine Masonry when he was in power. However, where property had been conveyed to individuals this could not be done. Masonic meetings were not publicised although they were held.[418]

It seems evident that Masonry provided an underground network for English and Americans in Argentina during the Perón years. The strictures placed on Masonry by the Justicialist State were removed under the post-1955 military regime that was nonetheless repressive in most other ways.

418 'Struggle of Masons Under Perón Told', *Lodi News-Sentinel*, California, 9 July 1957.

Does Masonic (and Marxist) subversion of the Justicialist Party explain the catastrophic breach between Perón and the Catholic Church? The Perónist regime had from the start enjoyed the support of the Church, and Catholics had been counselled by their hierarchy to vote for Perón. Yet in 1955 Perón suddenly embarked on a course that reversed the role of Catholicism in Argentina.

CGT Secretary General Eduardo Vuletich announced the strictures against the Church in a speech from the balcony of Government House on 1 May 1955. He stated that the labour unions, through their legislators, would push for the removal of religious instruction in schools and the separation of Church and State. The proposals included the legalisation of divorce and prostitution; removal of compulsory teaching of religion in public schools; ending of State grants to Catholic schools; the secularisation of hitherto religious holidays; real estate taxes levied on Church properties and banning of demonstrations, processions and outdoors religious gatherings that do not have the permission of the police. A motion by Vuletich that the 1949 Constitution should be amended separating Church and State would be put to Congress.

The measures against the Church are typically Masonic and had been enacted wherever Masons had been involved in revolutions in Catholic countries, such as the Portuguese Republic prior to Salazar and that of Mexico under Calles, which resulted in a very bloody civil war.

Following Perón's ouster General Pedro Aramburu was appointed interim President. An Argentine book on Freemasonry gives an insight into the relationship of Masonry with the post- Perón regime, already indicated by the statement of Dr. Aden:

> On April 8, 1959 the interim ex-president, Pedro Aramburu, was bid good-bye in a secret meeting, by the Rotarian, Ramos Mejía, before taking a trip to Europe. Presiding

> at the table, as a guest of honor, was Sir Drysdale, Grand Master of Argentinean Masonry. At his right sat the ex-president dressed in his 33 degree Masonic apron.[419]

Aramburu had been made an honorary member of Rotary International, stating:

> I know the high purposes that this institution pursues and so was delighted to be invited. I hope that institutions like Rotary will multiply in this country, because from them comes a spiritual force so extraordinary that they support, and are a strong guarantee of democracy and liberty.[420]

Rotary is widely considered to be a front for Freemasonry in Latin America. Certainly, we might at least consider Rotary as having been a convenient front in Argentina during the Perón regime. Certain Rotarian principles at least are identical with those of Masonry, the Argentine Rotarian, Dr. Forno, stating in 1944 that 'morality without dogma forms the conscience of Rotary'.[421] This is exactly the premise of Masonry, especially in Catholic states where the primary objective is to destroy the Catholic basis of a nation behind the façade of high moral purpose. On 11 April 1944, Julián J. Lastra of the Rotary Club of Neuquén stated:

> On the summit of the mountain of the centuries there is a new cross of Rotary, but it is a cross without a victim. Our moral Rotarian code is without dogmatic principles, but it is empirical and like the Gospel of the sacred scripture. With our good neighbor policy and our word of honor, we will achieve peace between men and harmony among nations.

419 Anibal A. Rottjer, *Masonry in Argentina and the World* (Buenos Aires: Editorial Nuevo Orden, 4th ed., 1973), 189.

420 Ibid.

421 Ibid.

This is the same theory of the Rotarian founder Harris, who said, forgetting about the coming of Jesus Christ and His Gospel, 'the firm cement on which permanent world peace will be built, excluding all other, is Rotary'.[422] Again the formulae is exactly Masonic, and the reader might note that Lastra refers to Rotary as being an alternative religion, with a direct snipe against Christianity, in referring to 'the cross without a victim'. The Latin American Rotarians are apparently committed to the secular-humanist dogmas of Freemasonry. The agenda was frankly stated even by a leading U.S. Rotarian:

> In 1926 the Rotarians sent a telegram to the 'executioner' of the Catholic Church in Mexico, President Plutarco Calles. After congratulating him, they wrote: 'we are willing to cooperate with your government to the extent we are able'. Upon speaking about the Mexican religious question the New York Mason, Robert A. Grennfield, declared: 'Masonry makes use of YMCA (Protestant) and also Rotary to combat Catholicism'.[423]

Latin American Catholic authorities regard the conflict with Rotary and Masonry as the same.[424] The Bishop of Palencia stated:

> Rotary makes a profession of absolute secularism, of universal religious indifference, and attempts to present morality to individuals and societies by means of a naturalist, rationalist and even atheist doctrine. Therefore, our beloved faithful, good Catholics may not enter Rotarian clubs.[425]

422 El Rotario Argentino, Revista Rotaria Internacional, May, 1944, 22, quoted by Anibal A. Rottjer, ibid.

423 Anibal A. Rottjer, ibid., 190.

424 See for example Jose Maria Cardinal Caro y Rodriguez, Archbishop of Santiago, Chile, *The Mystery of Freemasonry Unveiled* (Hawthorne, California: Christian Book Club of America, 1971, 1980 [1957]).

425 Anibal A. Rottjer, op. cit..., 194.

Between Church And Masonry

Masonic manipulation of Perón into a confrontation with the Church was the view expressed by Antonio Plaza, Archbishop of La Plata, who in 1959 called for Perón to be permitted to return to Argentina. Speaking to labour leaders during a series of meetings in La Plata, he stated to a meeting at Cordoba, that Freemasons had been responsible for attacks on churches during the rioting that took place in 1955, leading to the coup against. Perón.[426] A bomb was placed at the Archbishop's Palace, but he was unhurt. The same year 33 Bishops led by Cardinal Antonio Caggiano issued a statement on 20 February expressing concern that Freemasonry and Communism in Latin America were seeking the same aims. Caggiano, head of Catholic Action during the 1930s, had expounded Catholic social doctrine as a 'third position' to communism and capitalism, before mass audiences, among workers, Catholics and Nacionalistas, and was one of the precursors for Perónism. He had been one of the primary individuals liaising with the Vatican after the Second World War, to enable French anti-Communists to find refuge in Argentina at a time when French communists and democrats were running amok killing those who had established the Catholic corporatist state at Vichy under Marshall Petain. Ironically, it was Catholic Action that became one of the main anti-Perónist factions during the 1950s.

While there are indications that Perón was manipulated into taking a line that would antagonise many Catholics, it was Catholic laymen who initiated the confrontation between the Church and the Perónists. As it should by now be clear, Justicialism has been one of the most significant exponents and practitioners of traditional Catholic social doctrine. Since the birth of the Perónist party Catholic priests had blessed proceedings and those of the trades unions.[427] From 1954, these Catholic laymen began expounding a 'new Christendom', and founded the Christian Democratic Party,

426 'Bishop Sanctions Return of Perón; Creates Furor', The Milwaukee Sentinel, 22 October 1959, 34.

427 Frank Owen, Perón: His Rise and Fall, op. cit., 221.

with the expectation of replacing Justicialism.[428] On 10 November Perón, during a broadcast, alleged that some priests and Catholic Action were infiltrating trades unions and student organisations in order to establish their own political influence, and that the Bishops of La Rioja, Santa Fé and Cordoba were involved in anti-State activities. Perón named twenty priests engaged in open attacks on the Government.[429] During that month several priests were arrested for 'fomenting public disturbances', but most were quickly released. The harshest sentences were five days each for Father Bordagaray, and Father Olmos, of Cordoba. Police raided Catholic student clubs at the Universities of Santa Fé and Cordoba, where large quantities of anti-State literature were found, and seven students were arrested. Father Carboni was arrested and sentenced to thirty days for preaching a sermon at his Church in Buenos Aires, against the Government.

The following month the University of Cordoba was purged of anti-Government professors, including priests. A majority of Archbishops signed the pastoral letter of Cardinal Copello protesting the Government's actions, yet stating that 'no priest can take part in the struggles of political parties without compromising the Church… Catholic Action, similarly, should remain outside and above the political parties'.[430] Nonetheless, the cry went up at religious processions, 'Christ or Perón?' On 28 November, an anti-Government demonstration was organised outside Cardinal Copello's residence, and although the action contravened the law, it was not suppressed.

Elements of the Church had already been antagonistic towards the State's assumption of its previous control of charitable activities, State interference in education, the cult of personality around the Peróns, and the Perónist organisation of students. In September 1954 conflict erupted when competing demonstrations

428 Enrique Dussell, A History of the Church in Latin America (Missouri: William B. Eerdmans Publishing, 1981), 155.

429 Frank Owen, op. cit.., 222.

430 Ibid., 223, quoting the pastoral letter.

celebrating the Day of the Student, in Cordoba, were organised by Catholics and the other by the Union of Secondary Students.[431]

In May 1955 Catholic Action organised an anti- Perónist demonstration in Buenos Aires, regardless of the law.[432] In June Mgr. Manuel Tato and Mgr. Ramon Novoa were deported to Rome for instigating riots the previous week during the Corpus Christi procession in Buenos Aires, and police raided the headquarters of Catholic Action. In response the Vatican excommunicated those who had acted against the Church, without naming anyone.[433] Within hours of the news reaching Argentina, the Navy launched its bloody revolt.

Perón responded to escalating conflicts between 'Perónists (or Masonic and Marxist *agents provocateur*), and Catholics by appealing for calm, after Catholic backing for the Navy revolt. He stated that the issue of the Church and State would be resolved during the upcoming general elections. He said in Congress that while justice would be meted out to the rebels with due process, 'I am a Catholic and we have many Catholics with us. We are not attacking religion. Let us try to decide things not with violence but by popular vote'. Perón also stated that communists had taken advantage of the situation to 'set fire to churches', after a State investigation found that 'communists had committed acts of pillage'.[434]

Certainly the *modus operandi* of burning Churches in Buenos Aires, and attacks on Church property in Cordoba, seem more akin to communism than to Justicialism. The abortive Navy coup, which was put down by the Army, resulted in 202 dead and 964 wounded, mostly civilians, as the result of the Navy bombing of streets neighbouring Government House, Perón narrowly escaping death.[435]

---

431 Luis Alberto Romero, A History of Argentina in the Twentieth Century (Pennsylvania State University Press, 2002), 128.

432 Frank Owen, op. cit., 226.

433 'Two Church Leaders Exiled by Argentina', *The Times*, London, 16 June 1955.

434 'Pillage by Communists', *The Times*, London, 18 June 1955.

435 Ibid.

It was after this slaughter of innocents, on 16 June, that several Churches were torched. The following day Perón broadcasted a message of restraint, holding communists responsible for the arson. All priests and Catholic laymen were released from detention. Minister of War General Franklin Lucero, a staunch Catholic, was made Commander-in-Chief of the Armed Forces, and of the police. Police were positioned to prevent demonstrations or attacks against churches.[436] Perón realised that anti-national forces within his own Administration and party had manipulated him. Five Secretaries of State and sixteen Cabinet Ministers resigned. Vuletich, who had avidly promoted the anti-Church measures, resigned his position as secretary general of the labour confederation, as did other anti-Church luminaries, Interior and Justice Minister Angel Borlenghi and Minister of Education Armando San Martin, while Foreign Minister and Minister of Worship, Jerónimo Remorino, retired. The Church was restored to all of its former privileges, while the Communist Party was banned. The Church hierarchy for its part issued a statement repudiating Church involvement in any political party, including the Christian Democrats.[437]

It seemed that both sides had amicably settled the conflict, with Perón taking broad and swift measures to purge the subversive elements in his Government. However, certain political and religious factions, including Catholic Action, did not relent. The Radical Party leader, Dr. Arturo Frondizi, went on the offensive and repudiated any notion of reconciliation. On 31 August 1955 Perón offered to resign 'if it will guarantee peace', but this was rejected by the Perónist Party and the CGT, which called a nationwide strike until Perón withdrew his resignation. Again, despite all the efforts at conciliation and national unity, clashes occurred between rival factions, and a state of siege was declared in Buenos Aires. The following month another coup, again primarily by the Navy, succeeded in ousting Perón. Cardinal Copello appealed for calm, but anti- Perónist mobs went on a

436 Frank Owen, op. cit., 229.

437 Ibid., 223.

rampage of destruction, especially focusing on dragging statues of Perón and Evita through the gutters. With the ouster of Perón, General Lonardi assumed the presidency, to the acclaim of Copello and 'many leading Church dignitaries'.[438]. Five hundred heavily armed members of the Alianza Libertadora Nacionalista made a last stand in their headquarters and only surrendered after heavy losses and the shelling of their building.[439]

In 1963, a faction of Christian Democracy, 'Social Christianity', 'became open to Perónism', through a new group, 'Human Economy'. During the 1960s divisions widened between priests as many now became pro-Perón.[440]

On the matter of Perón's excommunication from the Church, Father Pedro Badanelli, a doctor of law, who had supported Justicialism from the start, challenged its legitimacy according to Canon Law. Badanelli contended that the ill-defined excommunication of Perónists, prompted by the expulsions of Mgr. Tato and Mgr. Novoa 'could never be a reason' under Canonical law. They had no immunity from performing actions against the State. Badanelli also contended that a body could not be excommunicated, rather than specified individuals. Therefore since Perón was not named, he was not lawfully excommunicated. In cases involving excommunication of heads of state, under Canon Law 227,[441] this must be undertaken by the Pope, and not by a Church body, and no such excommunication of Perón by Pius XII was given. The 'excommunication' decree was issued by the Consistorial Congregation against anyone who had acted against 'the rights of the Church' and of Mgr. Tao (Novoa was not mentioned). Perón was therefore not lawfully

438 Ibid., 241.

439 Ibid., 243.

440 Enrique Dussell,op. cit..

441 Canon Law 227: 'The decrees of the Council have no definite binding force, unless they shall have been confirmed by the Roman Pontiff and promulgated by his orders'. Rev. S. Woywod, The New Canon Law: A Commentary and Summary of the New Code of Canon Law (York: Joseph F. Wagner Inc., 1918), 'The Canon Law', Chapter 38, Section 158,

excommunicated.[442] Nor was a 'vitandi excommunication' obliging all Catholics to break off all communication with Perón, decreed.[443]

Father Badanelli had worked on developing an Argentine Catholic Church not subjected to the Vatican, and with the return of Perón from exile, he resumed this work in 1973, founding the Católica Apostólica Argentina.

442 Father Pedro Badanelli, Perón Not Excommunicated: A Legal Challenge to the Global Episcopate (Buenos Aires: Editorial Tartessos, 1959).

443 'Vatican Ban on Argentine Government', *The Times*, London, 16 June 1955.

Communism

Despite Perón's deeply held opposition to communism, he sought diplomatic relations with the USSR as soon as he attained the presidency. There is nothing inconsistent about this. Many German anti-communist nationalists and conservatives between the world wars sought diplomacy with Stalin's Russia, as a common front against plutocracy, seeing that Stalinism was pursuing a national course, away from Marxism and internationalism.[444] Nor did his establishing of diplomatic relations with the USSR perturb even the anti-communists among the Nacionalista military. Perón opened trade relations with the USSR in 1946. Comments at the time referred to demands for relations with the Soviet Union coming not just from communists, but also from 'even Nationalists who represent the extreme Right'.

> Some Argentine Nationalists argue that it is merely continuity of foreign policy for Argentina to be friendly with any great power which is a rival of the United States. Among the names of those who have sponsored a proposal to create an Argentine-Russian Cultural Institute in Buenos Aires there appear several well-known Nationalists who have in the past been notorious anti-Communists. These Nationalists do not wish Argentina to be in Russia's sphere of influence, but merely desire their country to be more independent of the United States. The Nationalists deplored Argentina's declaration of war on Germany and Japan, but have been staunch supporters of General Perón since last October when Perón was overthrown and restored to power. The Nationalists rallied to Perón's side as soon as they realised that the pro-United States elements were against him.[445]

444 K. R. Bolton, *Stalin: The Enduring Legacy* (London: Black House Publishing, 2012). The USSR for its part cultivated contacts with German nationalists, who joined organisations promoting Soviet-German relations. See K. R. Bolton, 'Junger and National Bolshevism', in *Junger: Thoughts and Perspectives,* Vol. 11, ed. Troy Southgate (London: Black Front Press, 2012), 17-18.

445 'New Term in Argentina, Improved Relations with Russia', *The Times*, London, 4

In 1970 Perón wrote to his old friend and comrade,[446] Father Pedro Badanelli on communism, the letter being published as an introduction to Badanelli's book *Communism or Justicialism?*[447] Badanelli regarded the letter as particularly valuable.[448]

My dear friend:

I answer your kind letter of 30 August that I received by hand.

I toured this beautiful land and I have stayed in Sevilla, Málaga, Torremolinos, etc.[449] And as you say, with justifiable pride, the best of Spain, Andalucía, is to my liking. There I spent the best days of my exile, between the simple and good people who know how to sweeten life and make merry without the useless tricks that people today seem to covet. The Andalusians have treated me in a way that will force my gratitude for the rest of my life.

As you say in your book *Communism or PJ*, with prophetic truth, which is being fulfilled: communism is advancing everywhere with devilish speed. I, who am a man of the past century, have lived this history that many do not seem to want to understand. When the twentieth century began, Communism was just an idea, doctrinally presented in the book *Das Kapital*, by Karl Marx. Two or three German ideologues developed it and three or four prominent agitators expanded it.

Now, I have been able to observe the panorama of the world with greater confidence and experience, I have

June 1946.

446 Perónto Badanelli, Madrid, 17 September 1970.

447 Pedro Badanelli, *Communism or Justicialism?* (Buenos Aires: Metal Workers Union of Argentina, 1975). The first edition was published in 1951.

448 Ibid., 'Prologue'.

449 Badanelli was born in Spain.

come to appreciate the causes and consequences that are overwhelming the world, and have come to the conclusion that if all goes well, in not many years there will be a communist world which cannot be avoided because the clash of ideologies cannot but lead to the imminent catastrophe, which everyone seems to want to avoid, but for which no one does anything that is intelligent and rational.

International capitalism and oligarchies; organised to exploit man, do not look at the consequences. International communism, also organised in the last analysis to do the same as international capitalism (insectify man), does not hit down and replace its bitter enemy. The victim of both capitalism and communism is the people.

We avoided this situation in Argentina, but we have paid a heavy price in blood and sacrifice. Now, facing the grim picture that comes up with the misunderstanding and selfishness of all, we can see clearly what many, blinded by passion and interest, do not see. The desperate people beset by poverty and exploitation, are considered incapable of freeing their fate against international forces that dominate the satraps who rule them. With reason and justice, they turn to the only force that is also internationally organised, communism. I myself do not know if, in such circumstances, I would think differently and take a different path. Only heroes or saints could do otherwise but only men form peoples.

What is happening in Cuba is, as you say, by way of example. But what happens there is the same thing that is happening in each of the proletarian households of our country and the world today. Nobody believes in fallacious Yankee propaganda or in the words of the capitalist world that condemn communism, because to live the misery and injustice that is felt, the words sound like mockery. That is really, really, the determinant of the spread of communism in space and its intensification in time.

Justicialism reached out in our country, but interests, hatreds and passions, prevented it from being understood. If Justicialism had been listened to and imitated there was still time to overcome the great evils that awaited us. Today, the reality of the facts has surpassed them all, and only a miracle can save us. The ill-fated 'liberating revolution' rolled violently against our patriotic endeavour and prepared the advent of the current chaos preparing the way for the triumph of communism.

Communism has, from nothing, come to dominate three quarters of the world. I cannot delude myself that they are going to stop now with the Yankee robot brain and soul of merchants.

I see the very serious situation, and especially in our country where there is no outlet within existing procedures that carry us all with the only expedient way for the People: communism. Facing the international conspiracy of capitalism is the international communist conspiracy. That is currently the terrible dilemma of the Argentine people in their own homeland [where Justicialism is] banned, persecuted, exploited and mocked.

We will continue to work hard but I'm afraid we will not arrive on time. Latin America is intensely shaken by the conflict that poisons the world and the wave of pollution that was imposed on Cuba by the misunderstanding and Yankee knavery seems to spread like wildfire over all Latin American peoples. The Church, in Argentina, Venezuela, Cuba, Dominican Republic, Colombia, etc., worked in favour of communism and seems now to be realising the fact of the disastrous policy of Pope Pius XII.

Faced with this bleak picture that the world has shown in Argentina we see a group who believes the problem can be solved by handing the country over to the greed of

> capitalist exploitation, which is the origin and cause of the communist success. They do not think you need to address the causes and effects. The people will win with the sickle and hammer if you cannot win with national attributes, but they will win. I always told our oligarchs and capitalists, the choice was between the triumph of Justicialism or of Communism. They seem to have chosen the latter.
>
> The armed forces seem to dominate in Argentina, using if necessary military methods: violent repression and persecution. They know of nothing better to succeed. The U.S. FBI handling information and intelligence in Argentina will only extend the mistakes that were made famous in the world and have led to failure in noisy writhing today. The undignified, discredited Government, with no hint of authority, with intrigue and fraud, assists undaunted the thefts by both civilians and military; ideal for the chaos that reigns and the Cataclysm that is fast approaching. The Church, clinging to their interests and passions has thrown back the true Christian doctrine and selfishly ignores its fundamental mission to be of service, is another member of the coven adjuvant. Only the people with that fabulous insight that has always characterized them maintained firmly, a truth that others do not want to see. So it expires.

While we might now say that Perón and others who were concerned about the victory of communism, have been wrong, with the implosion of the USSR and the integration of China into the global economy, what really has occurred is something far worse: the triumph of doctrinal communism under the banner of plutocracy, which, as Perón knew, used communism, and financed the Bolshevik Revolution.[450] While the Soviet bloc had been rejecting Marxist dogma since Stalin defeated Trotsky for the rulership of the USSR in 1928, the USA pursued a Bolshevik

450 Juan Perón, *Fundamentals of Partido Justicialism National Doctrine,* 'VIII: Supranational Power', op. cit.

formula of world revolution, with the same core aim of Marxism,[451] the reduction of man to a mere economic automaton at the behest of economic demands; what Perón called the 'insectifying' of humanity. The USA continues to push socialism and communism under the slogans of 'human rights' and 'democracy' in their so-called 'colour revolutions' across the world. Communism has moved over the world in the name of capitalism and under the auspices of the USA. Perón saw 'demoliberalism' and communism as fundamentally capitalist, referring to the latter as 'state capitalism'. In particular, Perón insisted that the 'third position' was the means of eliminating communism, by dealing with the cause – capitalism.

The first edition of *Communism or Justicialism?* was published in 1951 when communism seemed in ascent, and again in 1971 when Chile was being wracked with chaos through the inauguration of the Marxist regime of Salvador Allende. Badanelli analysed communism psychologically, inspired by the 1920s American writer Lothrop Stoddard, who saw Marxism as a form of psychosis. I have treated this subject in detail in *The Psychotic Left*.[452] Father Badanelli's analysis was also influenced by the German conservative historian-philosopher Oswald Spengler, who saw Bolshevism as the leader of a coloured world revolt.

Badanelli regarded the Marxist rampage in Chile as 'the most serious problem that has happened in America since it was discovered'. Marxism was not a problem to be rooted out with military measures but by a higher ideology.[453] This ideological conflict also had a foundation in race, that between the 'East and West', with Bolshevism representing the Mongol challenge to Western Civilisation. Badanelli referred to 'Mongolian communism'. He considered the conflict not so much as matter of class or politics but a difference in psychology. It feeds off genuine

451 K. R. Bolton, *Stalin: The Enduring Legacy*, op. cit.

452 K. R. Bolton, *The Psychotic Left: From Jacobin France to the Occupy Movement* (London: Black House Publishing, 2013).

453 Badanelli, *Communism or Justicialism?*, op. cit, 24.

misery but its cure is worse than the disease. 'Thus the Bolshevik Revolution was something harsh and sour, and convulsive, bloody and brutal, ugly, painful...'[454] In this psychological and ultimately spiritual struggle, Badanelli cast Russia as part of Asia against European, which culturally and spiritually includes the Americas. 'Russia is not Europe, Russia is Asia, and not in the abstract, but specifically Mongol, Kalmic, morphologically and psychologically that of Tartary'.[455] Badanelli quotes the head of the Communist International, Zionoviev, from 1920: 'Russia tends to reach to Asia not only because she is also Asian, but because eight hundred million Asians are necessary to fight imperialism and Western capitalism'; and Lenin's statement: 'let us return to Asia: We will come to the end of the West by the East'.

There is much about Badanelli's depiction of Communism and Soviet Russia that is Spenglerian, the great historian-philosopher Oswald Spengler[456] having described the USSR in *The Hour of Decision*, as leading the 'coloured world revolution' against Western Civilisation', in a racial-cultural-spiritual conflict with the socio-economic doctrine of Bolshevism as a rallying cry.[457] The American historian Lothrop Stoddard also wrote in similar vein in his book *The Revolt Against Civilisation*,[458] and it is notable that Badanelli mentions Stoddard in regard to Russian population expansion.[459] He likewise refers to the 'global colour revolution'.[460] Badanelli writes:

> For all these reasons and repeated threats, it is extraordinarily childish to still believe that Bolshevism is but a social theory, a simple interpretation of economic

454 Ibid., 29.

455 Ibid., 31.

456 Indeed, Badanelli does allude to Spengler on page 149 of *Communism or Justicialism*.

457 Oswald Spengler, *The Hour of Decision* (New York: Alfred A. Knopf, 1933), 'The Colored World-Revolution', 204-230.

458 Lothrop Stoddard, *The Revolt Against Civilisation* (London: Chapman and Hall, 1922).

459 Badanelli, *Communism or Justicialism?,* op. cit., 36.

460 Ibid., 38.

> life and history. The reality is more serious, much more serious, because Bolshevism is nothing less than a 'virus' cultivated and packaged in Russia, and now, also, in communist China, with a view to the 'exportation' and annihilating subjugation of the West. It is simply an anti-Western and anti-human revolt, par excellence, enclosed within the primitivism of the Mongolian soul. For by Oriental we have to understand that Mongolian ... Moscow ... is all that is in direct opposition to our Western culture.[461]

Interestingly Spengler refers to the Latin American revolts as being led by 'white men' such as Bolivar, Miranda, San Martin and, in Argentina, Rosas, who opposed the Jacobin doctrines that were being imported from France[462] with Masonic backing. Perón's rejection of the French rationalist and Jacobin doctrines and his fight against Freemasonry is rooted in the birth of nations among Latin Americans. Perón, moreover, sought Argentina's cultural roots in Italy and Spain and sought, as we have seen, to rebuild the Classical ideal of humanity among the Argentines.

For Badanelli the seminal event of civilised humanity was the Second World War in which Western states insanely supported Russia against Germany, 'precisely the one nation in the world to have done, once and for all, with the universal nightmare of Russia'.[463] This view of the Second World War, as we have seen, is one that Perón also unapologetically maintained.

The conflict was between two doctrines of 'cosmic' proportions, Justicialism and Bolshevism, the latter being 'atavistic'[464] (the theme of Stoddard's analysis of Bolshevism), while Justicialism stands for human ascent and the joy of living.[465] Against this Bolshevik virus each nation must formulate its own defence,

461 Ibid., 33.

462 Oswald Spengler, *The Hour of Decision,* op. cit., 215.

463 Badanelli, *Communism or Justicialism?*, op. cit., 37.

464 That is, the unleashing of the primitive in man.

465 Badanelli, op. cit.., 39.

and for Argentina it is Justicialism, just as for Germany, it was Hitler's National Socialism.[466]

The first part of *Communism or Justicialism?* Takes up the theme of Stoddard, that communism is a disease that is used by unbalanced types to overthrow the restraints demanded by civilised society and to atavistically return man to a state of savagery and 'sadism'. Hence, using the biological analogy: 'Russian Bolshevism... is truly a "psychological microbe", the process of incubation, gestation, and development, follows the same parabola as that of any pathological bacteria'.[467] Like any such virus it can spread its infection, and does so by appealing to the genuine grievances of dispossessed social groups. Hence, the 'social incumbents' for the unleashing of Bolshevism were the ruling classes and oligarchs who had lost a sense of proportion and responsibility, although Bolshevism was worse as a 'cure'.[468] The Third International was created to 'infect the world with the Bolshevik virus'.

If Bolshevism mobilised a Mongol mass, it had done so under Jewish prompting, as Badanelli alludes to the importance of Karl Marx's Jewishness in his formulation of communism: 'Karl Marx was a Jew. To forget this would be to overlook the integral factor of not only his personality but of the characteristics that permeated his sense of communism'. [469] This is a difference of worldviews between the Classical world and the Jewish world:

> Everything always has a messianic eminently Jewish etiology, and is therefore anti-Greek. The ideological descendants of Marx are all possessed of the same feelings... that there is a coming world catastrophe, that a new era is preparing to liberate oppressed humanity, and

466 Ibid., 42-44.

467 Ibid.,93. The premise has been further developed, with the study of specific personalities and movements in K. R. Bolton, *The Psychotic Left*, op. cit.

468 Badanelli, *Communism or Justicalism?*,op. cit., 93.

469 Badanelli, ibid., 136.

so on. An apocalyptic faith in the Final Judgement.[470]

We can see here that what Badanelli is attempting to explain is that despite Marx's atheism and rejection of the Jewish religion, he retained the messianic mentality and the sense of an end of history with a final judgement whereafter a new millennium reigns forever, and the historical cycle is broken. The new god is communism. History has come to an end. The same messianic outlook has been taken up by apologists for capitalist globalisation who now refer to 'the end of history', once globalisation has become dominant. Writing in the influential 'neoconservative' (that is to say, 'neoliberal') journal, *The National Interest*, one of the primary intellectual exponents of liberal world hegemony under U.S. auspices, Francis Fukuyama, explained the messianic character of what Perón called 'demoliberalism':

> What we may be witnessing is not just the end of the Cold War, or the passing of a particular period of post-war history, but the end of history as such: that is, the end point of mankind's ideological evolution and the universalization of Western liberal democracy as the final form of human government.[471]

It is this *one-size-fits* all mentality that the USA seeks to impose over every corner of the world, whether by sweets or by bombs, and what 'neo-con' policy makers in the U.S. government audaciously called the 'New American Century'. It is what is behind the wars and well-planned and funded 'spontaneous revolts' against Syria, Iraq, Serbia, the 'Arab Spring', the 'colour revolutions' in the former Soviet bloc, all designed to establish this 'universalization of Western liberal democracy as the final form of human government'. This is what Justicialist national socialism fought from an early stage. As will be seen

---

470 Badanelli, ibid., 138.

471 Francis Fukuyama, 'The End of History?', The National Interest, Summer 1989. This essay was expanded into an influential book, *The End of History and the Last Man* (Free Press, 1992).

below, Badanelli pointed out that, in contrast, Perón was 'anti-messianic'; Justicialism was his formulation of national socialism for Argentina, and as a national doctrine, holds that each people must find its own way to renewal.

Having in the first half of *Communism or Justicialism?* analysed Communism as a virus, Badanelli proceeds in the second half to examine Justicialism as the antidote to that virus, starting with the chapter 'The Argentine Idea'. Badanelli opens by drawing on Spengler and others to state that the European Civilisation, like civilisations preceding it, is in decline.[472] 'No need, says Keyserling, to accept Spengler's hypothesis to recognise that the old culture is in decline. But not only the Western European. All traditional cultures of the world are in decline.'[473] Citing Michael Prawdin[474] that 'Europe no longer has any new ideas to offer the world', Badanelli states that the great new idea for the new era has emerged from Argentina as Justicialism.[475] As a 'New Idea' what is required also to understand and fulfil Justicialism is a 'New Man'. Part of its historical mission is not to defend the West against the East, but to 'correctly connect East with West',[476] Justicialism transcending both Anglo-capitalism and Bolshevism.[477]

Writing of 'Perón: The Man' in a chapter of that title, Badanelli, who had lectured as a professor of both penal law and psychology, opined that Perón was – in contrast to the Bolshevik revolutionaries and theorists who were analysed in the first part of his book – 'a man of exceptional rare merit [with] perfect mental normality, [from the viewpoint of] foolproof clinical

472 The primary contention of Spengler was that all Civilisations go through analogous organic cycles of birth, youth, maturity, senility and death. Western Civilisation is in its declining phase, but has a last historical mission, a type of final bow on the world stage, before leaving, to be replaced by a new, virile culture. See Oswald Spengler, *The Decline of The West* (London: George Allein & Unwin, 1971).

473 Badanelli, *Communism or Justicalism?*,op. cit., 149.

474 Michale Prawdin (1894-1970), Ukrainian historical writer who reached Germany after the 1917 Bolshevik Revolution, studying there and writing in German.

475 Badanelli, *Communism or Justicalism?*,op. cit., 150.

476 Badanelli, ibid., 156.

477 Ibid., 157-158.

examination'.... 'with a wealth of wisdom and experience that comes to make him the "Perfect elder"'.[478] In contrast to the 'world saviour' delusions of Lenin and Marx, Perón's aim was nothing other than to save Argentina. Other than that Justicialism offered an alternative to communism and capitalism for others insofar as they could embrace a national and social synthesis according to their own circumstances. Justicialism was what Badanelli described, in contrast to communism, as 'proposed but not imposed' and 'anti-messianic'.[479]

Badanelli explains in the chapter 'The Doctrine of Justicialism', that it is not sufficient merely to have brought social and economic benefits; Justicialism itself must be understood. A doctrine should serve two purposes: the theory and the practice.[480] This theory and practice, unlike communism, guarantees the freedom of the individual personality to create and self-actualise, but within the context of the national community, and 'long-term collective planning'.[481] Indeed, as we have seen, the basis of Justicialism, drawing from the Aristotelean idea, is that 'man is a social being', and fulfils his individuality within the social context, rather than the transient satisfaction of the ego: the *raison d'etre* of demoliberal existence.

The cynically named 'Liberating Revolution' that had ousted Perón in 1955 had prepared its work by slanders against Perón through the agency of the 'international synarchy', what Badanelli referred to as the work of 'the inevitable international Jewry, British interests, Masonry', 'and no small number of clergy', unleashing the naval bombardment around Government House, and killing hundreds of innocents.[482]

478 Ibid., 166-167.

479 1 Ibid., 74.

480 Badan Ibid., 185.

481 Ibid., 190.

482 Ibid., 223.

'Judaism' And Zionism

The relationship between Justicialism and Jewry and Zionism often seems ambiguous. This is not due to opportunism, but the result of the ambiguous character of Jewry. Perón sought the unity of all Argentines above factions, sects, parties and ethnicities. However, Justicialism was not without a conception of 'race'. Perón stated that the Argentine 'race' is forged through a shared history, culture and destiny, and he rejected the notion of a nebulous mass of economic automatons, heralded by both capitalism and Marxism.

A national-social doctrine such as Justicialism, that demands the subordination of sectional interests to the common national interest, is going to immediately conflict with certain interests whose identity is focused on a dual loyalty. Zionism and elements of Judaism come within the code of dual loyalty, just as much as an agent working for the Communist International or a plutocrat working for some large economic interest. These involve interests other than those of the national community. The corporate state is intended to resolve conflicts, particularly between class interests. However, Zionism and other doctrines identified by Perón as part of the 'international synarchy' cannot, by nature, be incorporated fully into the life of the corporate nation. They exist quite literally as social cancers, insofar as they eat at the *body politik*, conflicting with the organs and cells of the organic state. Zionism requires Jews to subordinate themselves to the interests of Israel, regardless of where they live. The subversive and treasonous character of Zionism and the historical animosity between traditional Catholicism and the anti-Christian nature of orthodox Judaism, as well as the large numbers of Jews present in Marxist organisations, and most conspicuously among the leaders of the Communist cell that resulted in the rioting of 'Tragic Week', resulted in 'anti-Semitic' tendencies among the military, the Nacionalistas and particularly the militants of the Alianza Libertadora Nacionalista (ALN).

Support for neutrality during the Second World War was often coupled with denunciations of Jewish influences. The Alianza de la Juventud Nacionalista, founded during the late 1930s by an ex-military officer, Brigadier General Juan Bautista Molina, which synthesised nationalism with demands for social justice, opposed Jewish influence and demanded neutrality.[483] While Jews were able to enter previously closed positions in the diplomatic service and the army, and assume high positions in the Perónist party, at the same time the opposition to Jewish influence by the ALN was permitted to continue. Such a two-pronged policy would have had the effect of offering the Jewish community a clear-cut choice of serving as patriotic Argentines within the 'organised community', or facing elimination from Argentina as a disloyal element.

After the Second World War, when the Jewish issue in Argentina was raised by a German refugee, Perón replied that given the defeat Hitler had suffered with his 'one hundred million Germans', it would be disastrous for Argentina to 'get bogged down in this problem'. 'The only solution was to let them work within our community'.[484]

Perón granted diplomatic recognition to Israel. The Israeli Minister to Argentina presented his credentials to Perón on 1 August 1949.[485] The following year Israeli Minister Yaacov Tsur praised Perón's recognition of Israel and his efforts to 'fight racial intolerance in Argentina', which was the first Latin American state to open a legation in Israel. Eva Perón was thanked for sending clothes to children in Israel through the Eva Perón Foundation.[486]. However, Jewish organisations opposed Perón, prompting him to support the formation of a Jewish Perónist organisation, the Organizaćion Israelita Argentina

483 Ronald H. Dolkart, 'The Right in the Décade Infame 1930-1943', in *The Argentine Right*, op. cit., 90-91.

484 *Humor magazine*, February 1992, cited by Ortiz, op. cit., 123.

485 'Israeli Minister to Argentina Presents Credentials to President Juan Perón', Jewish Telegraphic Agency (JTA), 2 August 1949.

486 'Israel Minister to Argentina Lauds Perón for His Fight Against Intolerance', JTA, 3 November 1950.

(OIA), in 1947. This was used to undermine the mainstream Jewish organisation, the Delegación de Asociaciones Israelitas Argentinas (DAIA), which was a constituent part of the World Jewish Congress, the primary international body of Organised Jewry.[487] It is notable that 'Jewish Communists' received 'much greater support' than the OIA.[488]

When Perón was ousted in 1955 organised Jewry undertook a purge of pro-Perónist Jews 'from any official position in Jewish social, economic or philanthropic institutions'.[489] Perón's efforts at integrating the Jewish community as part of the Argentine nation had been unsuccessful. Rein comments that 'most historians' state that the majority of Jews remained hostile to Perón. Argentine Jews, because of their position in the oligarchy, were also suspicious of a regime that 'was identified with benefits for the Argentine working class'.[490] Rein states that while this view is 'not mistaken', it is 'exaggerated', and points to individual Jews, especially labour leaders, as Perónists. He also points to the majority of votes among Jewish agricultural communities in Santa Fe and Entre Rios going to Perón in 1951.

On the other hand, Perónist Jewish candidates in the November 1951 election were all defeated, and the bloc votes of the Jewish community put three Jews from the Radical Party into Congress. Only one Jewish Perónist remained in Congress.[491] Despite the cordial relations that Perón attempted to forge with Argentine Jews and with Israel, Israeli ambassador Yaacov Tsur – despite his flattery towards Perón - was to write in his memoirs of the Organizaćion Israelita Argentina (OIA) as 'a handful of Jewish bootlickers', and 'a sycophantic Jewish organization against which the entire Jewish community is united'. I. Schwartzbart of

487 'DAIA', Jewish Virtual Library, http://www.jewishvirtuallibrary.org/jsource/judaica/ejud_0002_0005_0_04812.html

488 'DAIA', Jewish Virtual Library, ibid.

489 Raanan Rein, *Argentine Jews or Jewish Argentines?* (Leiden, The Netherlands: Koninlijke Brill NV, 2010), 164. .

490 Ibid., 133-134.

491 Ibid., 143,

CGT supporters for the Perón-Perón candidacy, outside the Ministry of Public Works in the Avenida 9 de Julio

the World Jewish Congress smeared the OIA as being comprised of criminals and swindlers, merely echoing the opinion of the so-called 'Liberating Revolution' of the 1955 coup.[492] Indeed, the powerful World Jewish Congress had kept up a relentless smear campaign against the OIA, and called OIA fund-raising for a new Jewish hospital in the Entre Rios province, being undertaken by the Eva Perón Foundation, a 'thieving demand of the OIA to defraud [the community of] three million to construct a hospital with the name of the First Lady'. Jews were described as having to practice their faith in secret and the OIA was accused of conducting 'terrorism' against the DAIA.[493]

One might understand now how Perón, after his overthrow, described with hindsight 'Judaism' as part of an 'international synarchy'. He had attempted to bring Argentine Jewry into the

492 Ibid., 145.

493 Cited by Rein, ibid., 145.

national organism, but his efforts had been rejected, because his nationalist and social revolutionary policies coincidentally hit at both the position of many Jews as part of the oligarchy[494], and because such doctrines do not accord with the dual loyalty demanded of Jews by Zionism. Perónist Jews were targeted by the main bodies of Organised Jewry, not only in Argentina but further afield. The DAIA was quick to reach an accord with the post- Perón tyranny, saying little about the disappearance of many Jews under the military regimes.[495]

Jose Ber Gelbard, head of the Confederación General Económica (CGE), a confederation of small and medium-sized businesses, was appointed minister of economics under the interim Perónist administration of Hector Campora in 1972. Gelbard planned and implemented the *Pacto Social*, imposing wage and price freezes, in agreement with both the CGE and CGT.[496] The agreement drew opposition from both liberals and Rightists,[497] the latter with the patronage of Perón's long-time personal aide, Lopez Rega, who was appointed minister of social welfare. The *Pacto Social* was regarded as subversion by Jewish elements of Justicialism, including Gelbard, Julio Bronner, who assumed Gelbard's position as president of the CGE, the influential journalist Jacobo Timerman, and the financier David Graiver. The anti-pact factions regarded these individuals from press and commerce as part of the 'international synarchy'.[498] After Perón's assumption to the presidency in 1973, the Government did not attempt to suppress the criticism, and references to the 'international synarchy' became common.

The CGT charged that the 'international synarchy' was targeting

494 For example 'both Banco Mercantile and Banco Comercial were founded by Jews', 'Argentina', Jewish Virtual Library, http://www.jewishvirtuallibrary.org/jsource/vjw/Argentina.html

495 'DAIA', Jewish Virtual Library, op. cit.

496 Lonardo Senkman, 'The Right and Civilian Regimes 1955-1976', in The Argentine Right, op. cit., 132-133.

497 Ibid., 134.

498 Lonardo Senkman, ibid.

its leaders.[499] It is notable that José Ignacio Rucci, general secretary of the CGT, was killed by the Montoneros terrorists on 25 September 1973. Rucci, a veteran of the 17 October 1945 workers' uprising, was being prepared as Perón's successor. Perón stated of Rucci's murder: 'They killed my son. They cut off my right arm'.[500] Perón went into a state of depression and his health declined. It was a mortal blow to Perónism and to Perón, undertaken by those claiming to be the most avid Perónistas.

As for the 'international synarchy' and the Montoneros, the investor for the Montoneros was David Graiver Jr., head of the Bank of La Plata, through which stolen and extorted Montoneros money was laundered. Graiver paid the Montoneros $130,000 a month interest, the Montoneros having $17,000,000 deposited with his bank. This money was used by Graiver to buy a controlling interest in the American Bank & Trust Co., New York City. This collapsed in 1976 due to Graiver's manipulations, as did the banks he bought in Belgium and Switzerland. The American Bank & Trust Co. case 'caused considerable losses to Argentines', 'involved many Argentine Jews and has been used to stir up anti-Semitic feelings by some elements in and outside the Argentine government', stated the JTA in their obituary for Gelbard, who was suspected of being complicit with Graiver.[501] Graiver was appointed Undersecretary of Social Welfare in the Government of General Alejandro Lanusse in 1970. He became a policy adviser for Gelbard when the latter assumed his ministerial post in the Campora Government in 1972.[502] Gelbard had introduced Perón to Graiver while the former was still in exile in Madrid, and persuaded Perón to trust the banker.[503]

---

499 CGT press communiqué 7 April 1974.

500 Catalina Pantuso, 'The Price of Loyalty', http://www.solesdigital.com.ar/libros/rucci.htm

501 'Jose Gelbard Dead at 60', JTA, 6 October 1977, http://www.jta.org/1977/10/06/archive/jose-gelbard-dead-at-60

502 'Papel Prensa', El Dia, http://www.eldia.com.ar/edis/20100901/informaciongeneral0.htm

503 'Who was David Graiver?', La Nacion, 2 September 2010, http://www.lanacion.com.ar/1300383-quien-fue-david-graiver

Gelbard had been a member of the Radical Party, the traditional party of the Argentine oligarchy, and a member of the Democratic Union, the alliance of communists, oligarchs, and liberals, that had opposed Perón's presidential campaign in 1946. The Argentine correspondent for the Soviet news agency TASS, Isidoro Giblert, stated in a book on the Argentine Communist Party, that Gelbard had also been one of the Party's principal benefactors.[504] Gelbard in his position as economics minister assisted Graiver in acquiring 26% of the shares of the newsprint manufacturer, Civita Editorial Abril Group.

The military regime of General Jorge Rafael Videla, following the ouster of Isabel Perón, did not acquiesce to Jews, Zionists, communists or financiers. Jewish sources claim that of the 9,000 Argentines who 'went missing', among whom were of course many Perónistas, there were approximately 1000 Jews. General Ramón Camps, who brought charges of treason against the Graiver family (David Graiver purportedly dying in an aeroplane crash in 1975, after the collapse of his banks), stated in response to the release of members of the Graiver family from jail in 1982, and the predicable whitewash that followed: 'The Graivers' hands are stained with the blood of good Argentines. The link of Graiver, Jacobo Timerman and Jose Gelbard with the subversion cannot be questioned'.[505] General Camps referred to the *entrismo* of the Graiver-Timerman-Gelbard *troika* into 'economic, political and cultural organisations'.[506] Graiver had funded Timerman's newspaper, *La Opinion*,[507] and funded the creation of the newspaper *La Tarde*, for Hector Timerman, Jacobo's son. According to a military intelligence investigation,

504 Isidoro Gilbert, El oro de Moscú (Buenos Aires: Editorial Planeta, 1994), 232-252. There is nothing unusual about such oligarchal relationships with Communism; e.g. Israel Helphand (Parvus), the German-based arms dealer; Olof Aschberg, the Swedish-based 'Bolshevik banker'; Armand Hammer of Occidental Petroleum, et al

505 Edward Schumacher, 'New Twist in Case of Missing Argentine Financier', *New York Times*, 27 August 1982.

506 Ramón Camps, El poder en la sombras: edl affaire Graiver (Buenos Aires: 1983), 211-214, cited by Leonardo Senkman, *The Right in Agentina*, op. cit., 140.

507 Edward Schumacher, op. cit.

Jacobo Timerman also handled Montoneros funds. As a young migrant to Argentina, Timerman had joined the *Hashomer Hatzair*, a Zionist-Socialist youth organisation, and he remained committed to these doctrines. Due to U.S. and Israeli pressure Timerman was released from jail under the Videla regime, and he was sent to Israel.[508]

After Perón's death the conflict between Perónism and the 'international synarchy' became more pronounced than ever, as Lopez Rega's 'Triple A' (Argentine Anticommunist Alliance) counter-terrorist organisation attempted to weed out the subversives. Some unity among Perónistas and hitherto hostile Nacionalistas was achieved, Acción Nacionalista Argentina being formed as a united front against 'Judaeo-Marxism and International Zionism', in defence of 'the National, Popular and Christian Revolution'.[509]

A nexus had existed between three Jews, Gelbard, Graiver, and Timerman, in association with the Montoneros. This nexus did much to destabilise the Perónist state in the name of a more 'revolutionary' Perónism, only to bring ruin. Not long before the ouster of Isabel Perón, Horacio Calderon, a leader of Perónist Youth, who has since become a scholar in international affairs, wrote a book, *Argentina Judia,* detailing the Jewish issue in Argentina, causing uproar from Organised Jewry.

Calderon was appointed press director of the Buenos Aires National University just after the publication of *Argentina Judia* in 1976, which was seen by Jewish organisations as indicating State approval. The Jewish Telegraphic Agency reported that the book had been launched at a press conference 'attended by church officials, academicians and representatives of the Libyan Embassy', including 'the Rev. Father Raul Sanchez Abelenda,[510]

508 'Jounralist Jacobo Timerman Dead', La Nacion, 12 November 1999, http://www.lanacion.com.ar/160880-murio-el-periodista-jacobo-timerman

509 Leonardo Senkman, *The Right in Agentina*, op. cit., 138.

510 Father Abelenda was a traditionalist priest who had opposed the liberalising tendencies

dean of the philosophy faculty at Buenos Aires University, and Rodolfo Tecera Del Franco, dean of the sociology department'. The JTA report quoted Calderon as focusing on the themes that had been addressed by Perón:

> At the press conference, Calderon stated that the 'visible powers of Judaism are known as international synarchy whose various prongs are Zionist projects, diaspora projects. Jewish-Christian projects divided into capitalist, Communist, Masonic and Vatican internationals'. Regarding the alleged Vatican international, the author declared in his speech that 'it participates actively in synarchic activity and has been established after a prolonged and persistent process of Jewish infiltration in the ranks of the Church'.[511]
>
> Calderon espouses the concept of 'synarchy' developed by the late President Juan D. Perón who viewed all world events as the outcome of a sinister link between capitalism. Communism, Freemasonry and the Church, all controlled in some occult manner by 'international Judaism'.
>
> Calderon declared in his speech that his book places Argentina among the non-aligned countries. 'Thus, we shall stop being satellites of imperialism and particularly obedient instruments of the Kissinger plan (U.S. Secretary of State Henry A. Kissinger) which concentrates the secret powers of Judaism and international synarchy'. [512]

The JTA report noted that Arab organisations had been active

---

to change the Church since the Second Vatican Council. See Father Mauricio María Zárate, In Memoriam: Raul Sanchez Abelenda RP (1929-1996)', 30 April 2009, http://capillavedia.blogspot.co.nz/2009/04/in-memoriam-r-p-raul-sanchez-abelenda.html

511 On the subversion of Jewish ideas into the Church during the Second Vatican Council, see Joseph Roddy, 'How the Jews Changed Catholic Thinking', *Look*, 25 January 1966, http://www.dailycatholic.org/issue/05Jan/jan29agg.htm

512 'Book Charges Jews Have Infiltrated Major World Institutions, Including the Ranks of the Catholic Church', Jewish Telegraphic Agency, 5 January1976.

in publicising the plight of Palestine in the Argentine press, quoting Palestinian leader Yasser Arafat, and Perón in an advertisement: 'The ad noted with satisfaction that during 1975 a street in the city of Rosario was named "Palestine Street" and a square in the resort town of San Clemente Del Tuyu was named "Palestine State"'.

We can see a similar 'international synarchy' at work today with organizations and funds such as USAID, National Endowment for Democracy, Freedom House, Ford Foundation, Rockefeller Foundation, Alliance of Youth Movements, the 'Open Society' network of the globalist oligarch George Soros, and a multitude of others, interlocking and with U.S. State Department connections, funding 'colour revolutions' against states that are hindrances to the internationalist agenda.[513]

---

513 See K. R. Bolton, *Revolution from Above*, op. cit., 213-244.

Third World: Third Position

Beyond a Latin American bloc Perón addressed the 'Third World' as a manifestation of the 'third position'. While the generally perceived notion today is that 'Third world' is synonymous for backward ex-colonial subjects, the concept arose during the Cold War to distinguish non-aligned nations that refused the domination of the USSR or the USA, and the doctrines of capitalism and Marxism. Hence, the 'Third World' states were often governed by doctrines similar to Justicialism, in that they synthesise both nationalism and socialism. The 'Arab socialism' of Egypt's Colonel Nasser, and the 'Third Universal Theory' of Libya's Colonel Muammar Al Kaddhafi, a martyr of the 'international synarchy', are particularly notable 'third position' doctrines. Perón, as one of the fathers of the Third World, from his exile in Madrid addressed the Third World peoples in 1972. He warned of the rampant industrialisation that is destroying the environment in the service of profits, the alienation of humanity from nature, the 'suicidal undertaking of humanity' 'through contamination of the environment and the biosphere, and the squandering of natural resources from unbridled growth'. He warned, like scientists such as the ethologist Konrad Lorenz[514] and the psychologist Carl Jung, that human consciousness is not keeping pace with technical progress:

> Humanity is changing the living conditions so quickly that it fails to adapt to the new conditions. Its action is faster than its grasp of reality and man has not come to understand, among other things, that the vital resources for himself and his descendants derived from nature and not from mental power. Thus, daily life becomes an endless chain of contradictions.[515]

Perón condemned the devastating ecological consequences of the market economy, planned obsolescence and consumerism, stating:

514 Konrad Lorenz, *Civilised Man's Eigth Deadly Sins* (Harcourt Brace Jovanovich Incorporated, 1974).

515 Juan Perón, 'Message to the Peoples and Governments of the World', Madrid, 1972.

> The so-called 'consumer societies' are actually massive wasteful social systems based on spending because spending produces profit. Production is wasted by unnecessary or superfluous goods and, among these, which should be durable, they are intentionally designed to be short-lived because the renewal is profitable. They spend millions in investments to change the look of the items, but not to replace the goods harmful to human health, and even make toxic appeals to new procedures to satisfy human vanity. As an example, cars that should have been replaced by electric motors, or the toxic lead that is added to gasoline.[516]

Perón condemned the exploitation of the resources of the Third World as due to the wastefulness of the Western system 'consuming vast natural resources provided by the Third World'. However, while the 'low-tech' countries' suffer from privation, the capitalist states, with their 'excess consumption', have created populations that 'are not rationally fed or do not enjoy an authentic culture or spiritual life or who are not physically healthy. They struggle in the midst of anxiety and boredom and the misuse of leisure'. Hence, one part of the world is impoverished by under-consumption while the other is morally, culturally and spiritually debased by over-consumption. He foresaw that 'housewives would make their purchases from their homes from television and pay by electronic systems'. He foresaw 'global warming' in the rush towards 'progress':

> Man, blinded by the mirage of technology, has forgotten the truths that are the foundation of his existence. And so, as the moon is reached thanks to cybernetics, new metallurgy, powerful fuel, electronics and a host of great knowledge, the oxygen you breathe is killed, the water we drink and the soil that feeds us, and permanent temperature rises without measuring environmental biological consequences. Now at the height of his folly, he could kill the sea as the last base of support.[517]

516 Ibid.

517 Ibid.

The myriad of ecological problems are created by 'greed and human improvidence, and the characteristics of some social systems, the abuse of technology, the lack of biological relationships and of the natural progression of human population growth'. What is required is a 'mental revolution', especially among leaders in industrialised nations; 'a change in the social and productive structures worldwide, particularly in high-tech countries with market driven economies', and the emergence of ecologically sound societies, even if this requires 'giving up some of the amenities civilisation has given us'.

> Changing social and productive structures in the world implies that profit and waste can no longer be the basic engine of any society, and that social justice should be erected at the base of any system, to increase the production of food and goods needed, and consequently, the priorities of production of goods and services should be altered to a greater or lesser degree depending on the country. In other words: we need new models of production, consumption, organisational and technological development, while giving priority to meeting the basic needs of human beings, to ration natural resource consumption to a minimum and reduce environmental pollution.
>
> We need a new humanity mentally and physically. You cannot build a new society based on full development of the human personality in a world tainted by environmental pollution, exhausted by hunger and thirst and maddened by noise and overcrowding. We must transform the present prison cities into garden cities.
>
> All these problems are inextricably linked with social justice, the political sovereignty and economic independence of the Third World, and detente and international cooperation. Many of these problems must be addressed over ideological differences that separate individuals within their societies or states within the international community.

Finally, I make some recommendations for our Third World countries:

1. We cherish our natural resources tooth and nail from the voracity of the international monopolies that seek to feed a nonsense type of industrialisation and development in high-tech centers with market driven economies. You cannot cause a massive increase in food production in the Third World without the parallel development of industries. So each gram of raw material taken away today equates in Third World countries with kilos of food that will not be produced tomorrow;

2. Halting the exodus of our natural resources will be to no avail if we cling to methods of development advocated by those same monopolies, that mean the denial of the rational use of our resources;

3. In defence of their interests, countries should aim at regional integration and joint action;

4. Do not forget that the basic problem of most Third World countries is the absence of genuine social justice and popular participation in the conduct of public affairs. Without social justice the Third World will not be able to face the agonisingly difficult decades ahead.[518]

Perón here showed just how farsighted a statesman he was, addressing problems that have now been rendered as clichés by demoliberal politicians, and as further methods of control of world resources by those responsible for the problems who are offering bogus solutions, such as the profitable 'carbon trading' market, that has become a new form of international finance.[519] Here also Perón calls for the formation of geopolitical blocs. There is also an appeal to the First World, which is debasing itself in a cycle of decay, engineered by overconsumption and hedonism.

---

518 Juan Perón, ibid.

519 See K. R. Bolton, *Revolution from Above*, op. cit, 201-212.

Libya and the Third Universal Theory

On 24 January 1974 an Argentina mission departed Buenos Aires for Colonel Kaddhafi's Libya. Argentine social welfare minister, José López Rega, who signed wide-raging agreements with Libyan Minister of Information, Abouzeid Durda, led the Argentine delegation. Provisions included:

> Cooperation in science, commercial relations, peaceful use of nuclear energy, cooperation in culture and information, installation in Buenos Aires of a Libyan-Argentine Bank for the filing of investments in Latin America and other countries, participation of Argentina in the Tripoli International Fair.[520]

Cultural centres would be built in the two nations, and a Mosque and Islamic Centre in Buenos Aires. There would be extensive and preferential trade relations, exchanges in resources, youth delegations, scientists and technicians, teachers and university lecturers; participation in sporting, cultural and other festivals; the dissemination of information on the culture, history and politics of the two states; tourism, summer camps such as scouting events; dissemination in Libya and the rest of the Arab world of information about the 'Justicialist Revolution', and information about the 'Libyan Revolution' throughout the Americas; joint construction of industrial plants, and training of specialised personnel.

The agreement included provisions for the extensions of relations between Arab and American states, Peru being mentioned specifically, indicating the commitment that Perón maintained towards Latin American unity, and Kaddhafi's commitment to Arab unity. Hence, both leaders envisaged the Libyan-Argentine alliance as the nucleus for an Arab-American bloc.

520 Mision Argentina En Libia, (Buenos Aires: Secretaría de Prensa y Difusión, 1974).

This special Libyan-Argentine alliance was cemented by doctrinal accord. While Perónism was called the 'third position', Kaddhafi's revolution was doctrinally based on what he similarly called the 'third universal theory'. Both eschewed Marxism and liberal-capitalism. Both were forms of 'national socialism', or in Libya's case 'Arab socialism', both were religiously based and rejected Marxism and capitalism as being materialistic and godless. Both sought to create a 'third world' bloc independent of super-power hegemony. Perón referred to the pact as having an 'extraordinary importance from the political and economic point of view and, above all from the moral point of view'.[521] The preliminary remarks to the document on the agreement referred to 'transcending all possible political and economic boundaries to achieve what is spiritual'. This agreement would be looked at with concern by the 'greedy superpowers', and of the agreement achieving 'independence from the superpowers of the synarchy'. This would be the first step of alignment between states that could 'dispense with the false bipolar alternative'. That is to say, a new bloc could emerge around the Libya-Argentine pact, of states that would no longer feel they must be drawn into either the USA or the USSR.

The 'total understanding' that had been reached indicated that Libya recognised the validity of the 'third position in international politics, which Perón had begun to advocate thirty years previously'. The agreements would provide the basis for the 'third position' between the Arab and Latin American worlds as an 'emancipatory crusade'. The ideological positions between Libya and Argentina had an 'amazing similarity in their configuration of policy', that was cause for 'elation'.[522] The tactic of the superpowers towards those who sought alliances beyond 'bipolarity' was that of 'silence' when 'misrepresentation' did not work. However, the return of Perónism and the Libyan revolution provide an option of social justice beyond capitalism and communism.

521 Juan Perón, February 1974, in Mision, ibid.

522 Mision, ibid., p. 20.

Libya's destiny would be based on a 'national search' based on both 'the tradition of its people, and to the same time its eagerness to transform'. Describing the character of Colonel Muammar Al-Kaddhafi, without him the people's revolution would fail, as he is 'the symbol of the new Libya'. Only 29 when he assumed rulership he 'is the personification of that balance between tradition and change that all revolutions of the Arabic unit recognize under the confessed influence of [the Egyptian statesman] Nasser. The religious basis and rejection of materialism is emphasised as a commonality between the two 'third positions' in 'a world of materialism', 'the Libyan chief recently noting that without religion there is no morality. And without morality there is no Nation'.

Perón had followed the Libyan revolution while still in exile in Madrid, while Colonel Al-Kaddhafi considered General Perón as one of his teachers. Libya's First Minister, Abdusalam Jallud, stated that 'General Perón and his government express the philosophy and the Ideas that Libya holds in the Arabic world'. The 'total agreement' between the two states reflected the 'third position' of both as 'the only road able of destroy the synarchic scheme', and was the 'road map for the people of the Third World to follow', in repudiating the 'financial and political tactics of the superpowers'.

The Third Universal Theory is an Arabic version of the national-socialist synthesis. While Justicialism is set forth in what amounts to a vast corpus of speeches, articles and books that at least equal in scope the celebrated philosophers of Marxism and Liberalism, the Third Universal Theory is primarily explained in *The Green Book*. Like Perón, Kaddhafi was dismissive of party politics as the best means of representation, pointing out that under liberal democracy it is money that counts the votes.[523] The very concept of the political party divides the people.[524] 'Economic classes' are similarly divisive, and parties that emerge 'inevitably'

523 Muammar Al-Kaddhafi, The Green Book, Part I: 'Parliaments'; http://www.mathaba.net/gci/theory/gb1.htm

524 Ibid., 'The Party'.

represent single class interests.[525] Kaddhafi's suggestion for direct representation of the entire nation was through 'popular conferences' and 'people's committees'.[526] Perón's method was through 'intermediary organisations' in what he called the 'organised community', as we have seen, from neighbourhood, factory floor, and upwards. Both the Third Universal Theory and the Perónist Third Position implemented popular representation 'vocationally and functionally'.[527]

Like Perón, Kaddhafi rejected social democracy and Marxism as insufficient. The gains that had been made by social democracy under capitalism amounted to no more than 'wage slavery'. Likewise, Marxism and nationalised enterprises do not directly represent the producers, and they remain wage slaves, albeit to the state rather than to individual owners. Kaddhafi referred to 'natural socialism', or what we have seen under Perónism as the 'organic state'. As in Perónist Argentina, Kaddhafi's Libya provided for profit-sharing, since every individual worker within an enterprise is essential:

> Because production cannot be achieved without the essential role of each of these components, it has to be equally divided amongst them. The preponderance of one of them contravenes the natural rule of equality and becomes an encroachment upon the others' rights. Thus, each must be awarded an equal share, regardless of the number of components in the process of production. If the components are two, each receives half of the production; if three, then one-third.[528]

Therefore, there are no longer 'wage earners', but 'partners'.[529]

525 Ibid., 'Class'.

526 Ibid., 'Popular Conferences and People's Committees'.

527 Ibid.

528 Ibid., Part II: 'The Solution of the Economic Problem', 'Socialism'.

529 Ibid., 'Income'.

Kaddhafi used the term 'producer' rather than 'worker', 'labourer' and 'toiler', because of the advance of science and technology in changing the previous character of work.[530] While Perón continued to use the term 'worker', he nonetheless also recognised the changing role of work, and the Argentine workers became synonymous with 'producer'.

The Third Universal Theory, as with Justicialism, starts from the premise of the human 'social bond', as an innate urge. The 'nation' is the expression of that social bond.[531] Hence, both the Third Universal Theory and the Third Position reject the Marxist notion that the nation is an artificial class construct that must be transcended by international proletarian solidarity. Of course both also reject that capitalist idea of what is today called 'globalisation' which, no less than Marxism, aims to achieve a world order by the obliteration of nations, peoples and cultures in the pursuit of a 'new world order'. Where minority problems exist, it is because 'they are nations whose nationalism has been destroyed and thus torn apart'. 'The social factor is, therefore, a factor of life - a factor of survival. It is the nation's innate momentum for survival'.[532] Here the Arab version of 'national socialism' is evident: the nation is a social unit; something that is lost on capitalism and liberalism which see the nation as a convenient legal construct for the conducting of commerce between individuals, to be ignored or discarded when getting in the way of trade.

The Third Universal Theory and Justicialism have a common outlook in seeing each nation as being based on a religion: Christianity for Justicialism; Islam for Arab nationalism. Religion provides the most effective means of social bonding and unity. 'When the social factor is compatible with the religious factor, harmony prevails and the life of communities becomes stable,

530 Ibid., 'Socialism'.

531 Ibid., Part III: 'The Social Basis of the Third Universal Theory'.

532 Ibid.

strong, and develops soundly'.[533] Kaddhafi, in contrast to Marx, saw 'family, tribe and nation'[534] as the organic components of human social evolution.

When the Perónist delegation arrived in Libya in 1974 it would have been immediately apparent that the two states were guided by the same type of doctrine that, like other examples of the social-national synthesis that had been emerging since the late 19th century, had developed spontaneously and therefore organically as the next stage of human development. As recent history shows, this development has been aborted by not only the wars unleashed by the 'international synarchy', but more pervasively, by the moral corruption that has destroyed traditional nations, peoples and cultures, in the name of 'human rights' and 'democracy'. In such a corrupt world, Kaddhafi maintained the People's Libya for a remarkably long time.

As the Perónists stated, the pact between the two states had the potential to be the nucleus of a bloc that could resist the 'international synarchy'. Among the 'international synarchy', as Perón had defined it, Zionists were quick to express concern. The Jewish Telegraphic Agency reported that the series of pacts between Libya and Argentina could affect relations between Israel and Argentina, quoting the official communiqué on the negotiations that stated, 'above and beyond the economic, financial and cultural results of the mission, its success should be measured by the total accord obtained in the political and ideological fields', and that Argentina had become 'the undisputed bridge country linking the brotherly Arab world with Latin America'. 'The true liberation from the yoke of imperialism starts with the resolute integration of third world peoples'. [535]

Despite the death of Perón soon after, and then the destruction

533 Ibid.

534 Ibid.

535 'Argentina-Libya Pacts cause of concern', Jewish Telegraphic Agency, 11 February 1974.

of the Libyan-Argentine pact with Isabel Perón's ouster in 1976, Kaddhafi nonetheless continued to build alliances with Latin America. The Perónist accord was renewed in 2008 when Cristina Kirchner and a delegation visited Libya and the states signed agreements on investment, agriculture and education. However, when the 'international synarchy' brought destruction upon Libya in 2011, in the name of 'democracy', 'human rights' and the global economy, Kirchner equivocated. A more 'Perónist' response came rather from Hugo Chavez of the Venezuelan Bolivarian Republic, who had maintained the closets relationship with Libya of any Latin American leader, more than one hundred conventions having been signed between the two states. Alone among the Latin American leaders, Chavez declared "viva Libya". [536]

Perónistas, Left and Right

Like the other 'third position' movements the doctrinal rationale of Perónism was – and remains – the synthesising and transcending of the orthodox Left and Right on the premise that the State and the people are part of an organic unity, the nation, and not separate entities in conflict. However, like other forms of the national and social synthesis there remains a division – at times violent - between Left and Right within Perónism. The most tragic of this conflict was the shooting between factions of Left and Right when Perón was due to return from exile in 1973, and the irreplaceable loss with the killing of Perónist labour leader Rucci by the Montoneros.

On the 'Right', the remnant of the Alianza Libertadora Nacionalista (ALN), that had fought a last-ditch stand against the overthrow of Perón in 1955, re-formed. The ALN also provided an important

536 For Latin American reactions to the globalist war against Libya in 2011 see Gabriel Elizondo, 'Latin America's sudden silence on Gaddafi', 26 February 2011, http://blogs.aljazeera.com/blog/americas/latin-americas-sudden-silence-gaddafi
Also, 'South American countries divided over allied bombing of Libya', MercoPress, 23 March 2011, http://en.mercopress.com/2011/03/23/south-american-countries-divided-over-allied-bombings-of-libya http://en.mercopress.com/2011/03/23/south-american-countries-divided-over-allied-bombings-of-libya

component of the Perónist underground. From 1958 through to 1973 the ALN published news-sheets under the title *Alianza*, and opposed the crypto-Marxist faction within Perónism. In 1953 Guillermo Patricio Kelly[537] assumed leadership of the ALN from Juan Queraltó. The ALN paper was published under the name of *Alianza del Perónismo rebelde* (Rebel Alliance of Perónism). *Alianza* newspaper appeared as with the byline of the ALN in February 1972, the movement now being headed by Antonio Fernández. With Perón's return the ALN resumed its traditional role as the militant defender of the Perónist regime, focusing on fighting the subversion of the Left, or what it called 'Marxist sectors of the movement'. In 1973 the ALN welcomed the emergence of the magazine *El Caudillo* and *del Documento Reservado* as 'so far almost the only two valid expressions of the national line drawn by San Martin Rosas, and Perón'.[538]

Those who had been imbued with the spirit of Justicialism as a genuine 'third position' were well aware that Justicialist 'national socialism' was no more Marxist than it was capitalist. Perónists cogently explained the differences between 'national socialism' and 'international socialism' by way of comparisons in an article published shortly before Perón's death.

1. **Justicialism:** It is a philosophy profoundly humanistic and Christian. **International Socialism:** An atheistic doctrine, the enemy of religion, with a doctrine that is materialistic.
2. **Justicialism:** Society is founded on justice and therefore is a creation of permanent value. **International Socialism:** Society is founded on class struggle, and therefore on the permanent destruction of values.
3. **Justicialism:** Not for class, but for national unity. **International Socialism:** It is based on class and therefore the great family of Argentina disintegrates.

537 Kelly however, departed from the ALN and started a journal called *Marchar*. He fell out with the government of Isabel Perón, was arrested and the magazine closed.

538 'Alianza Libertadora Nacionalista', http://www.ruinasdigitales.com/blog/23263/

4. **Justicialism:** Has a humanist conception of work. **International Socialism**: Its design is for slave labour.
5. **Justicialism:** considers the *latifundia*[539] as large, unproductive extensions. **International Socialism**: considers 'estates' as large expanses of a single owner.
6. **Justicialism:** Establishes a fair balance between the individual and the state. **International Socialism:** *Insectifica*,[540] depersonalises the individual for a police state…
7. **Justicialism:** …so there are no exploited. **International Socialism:** …therefore man is exploited by the state.
8. **Justicialism**: Relies on the infallibility of the truth: 'He who has the truth does not need violence, and violence never has the truth'. **International Socialism:** Based on terrorist subversion in the violent elimination of those elements contrary to its views.
9. **Justicialism:** Respect for the concept of private property as a social function. **International Socialism:** denies the concept of private property, promoting the bloody spoil.[541]

Perón's strong, charismatic leadership held the factions together tenuously, and he hoped that despite the conflicts Justicialism as a whole would continue to move forward and eventually the conflicts would be resolved. Therefore, from exile, Perón continued to back both factions.[542] They were operating on different levels, with a radical Left forming a guerrilla movement, while the Perónist Right continued to dominate the trades unions.

---

539 Latifundia: the large private estates of Latin America. The differences in outlook between Justicialism and international socialism are being referred to here: Justicialism opposes the Latifundia because they are unproductive and larger than a private owner requires for his sustenance; international socialism is opposed to private property per se.

540 A frequent saying of Perón's was that communism stands for the 'insectification' of man; that is, dehumanising man to the level of a work drone.

541 'Diferencias: Justicialismo/ Socialismos Internacionalas', Revista El Caudillo, No. 18, 14 March 1974.

542 Celina Andreassi, 'History of Perónism', Part I, op. cit.

It was in this era of severe repression that Perónism became an underground resistance. One of the primary leaders was John William Cooke, a former Perónist legislator, who was named as Justicialist leader within Argentina during Perón's exile. Although elections were held in 1958, the Perónists were barred from participation. However, Cooke negotiated a secret alliance with UCR candidate Arturo Frondizi who, on becoming president, restored the liberties of the labour movement. Frondizi was removed by the military in 1962 after allowing Perónist candidates to successfully run in provincial elections. Of the 14 provinces whose governorships were contested, Perónists carried 10, including the ever-popular Bittel's win in Chaco. The presidency of Arturo Illia during 1963-1969 was marked by labour militancy against the government. He was ousted by a coup led by General Juan Carlos Onganía, who resumed an anti-Perónist stance, and brutally suppressed a student protest at the University of Buenos Aires (known as the 'Night of the long batons').

A faction of the CGT led by a metal worker, Augusto Vandor, sought to negotiate with the government, and pursue what he called 'Perónism without Perón'. This caused a split in the CGT in 1968 and the creation of the CGT de los Argentinos (CGTA), which eschewed negotiations with the state.

In May 1969 the radical CGTA, along with Perónist students, and non-Perónist left-wing elements, rose against the government in the city of Córdoba. After weeks of strikes and protests, a worker was killed, and massive riots erupted. these were violently suppressed. Strikes and riots spread across Argentina, resulting in Onganía's removal by the military. What became known as 'Cordobazo' resulted in a guerrilla movement, primarily of Perónist youth, that was not willing to negotiate with the state, and who opposed the domesticated policy of the CGT under Vandor. What emerged was an uneasy mix of Perónists and Marxists.

Other Perónists opposed the 'Trotskyite and Marxist infiltrators' of the Justicialist movement. Pedro Michelini, editor of *Retorno*, advocated the national-syndicalism of the martyred 1930s Spanish *Falangist* leader Jose Antonio de Rivera, as the basis for a Justicialist revolution, and supported the military in suppressing 'Masonist and stateless liberalism'. Michelini was a respected Perónist, being appointed leader of the Justicialist Party for Buenos Aires province.[543]

Perónist Guerrilla Warfare

Given the repressive character of successive regimes against the Perónistas, Perón approved guerrilla actions. In 1969 he issued a declaration on revolutionary activities, referring to the 'synarchy' of U.S. and Soviet imperialism:

> For a quarter of a century, the Justicialist Revolution in Argentina promoted a popular transformative movement without bloodshed that, responding to its evolution, has given birth to a 'third position' that is equally distant ideologically from the dominant imperialisms and from the system they tried to impose throughout the world. The international synarchy, that harbours the imperialist interests in both zones, has promoted a 'modus vivendi' that in the name of 'coexistence' opposes any other evolution that is not within the ideologies or systems imposed by them. So, the reaction of both imperialisms is characterised by violent domination, whether it is economic, military, or both at the same time, as evidenced in Latin America, in the zone of the Russian satellite states, or more specifically in Santo Domingo and Czechoslovakia.[544]

Perón saw the emerging revolutionary movements as an undeniable force of nature, which 'is nothing but the dynamic development of these suppressed forces'. Where open civil war

543 Leonardo Senkman, 'The Right and Civilian Regimes', in *The Argentine Right*, op. cit., 131.

544 Juan Perón, Anuario, 'Las Base' (1969), 25-26.

from a revolt does not ensue, what emerges is a guerrilla war of small, separate cells, striking at the common enemy.

However, John William Cooke, on the 'Left' of Perónism, refined and cultivated the strategy of guerrilla warfare. Cooke was backed by Castro, and veered increasingly to the Left. He urged Perón to depart from Franco's Spain and settle in Cuba. While Cooke was dedicated to Perónism he laid a course that was to see Perónist guerrilla movements such as the Montoneros becoming increasingly Marxist and Castroite, resulting in a bloody breach with Perón.

In June 1969 Vandor was assassinated in what was called 'Operation Judas', by members of a small cell that would soon become part of the Montoneros, the most notorious of the Perónist guerrilla groups. This Perónist underground was a Leftist faction of the Perónist Youth, called La Tendencia Revolucionaria (Revolutionary Trend) or simply 'La Tendencia'.

On the first anniversary of the 1969 Cordobazo revolt that had been violently suppressed by the military, the Montoneros announced their existence by kidnapping and murdering ex-president (1955-58) General Eugenio Aramburu. The execution was undertaken in the name of the 30 Perónistas who had been executed in the aftermath of the 1956 revolt of Perónist General Juan José Valle.

The Montoneros had been formed by a group of students originally from an ultra-right wing Catholic organisation. The group continually moved Left until it was espousing 'socialist revolution' that seemed little different from Marxism, although continuing in the name of Perón. This ultra-Leftism was to be repudiated by Perón on his return to Argentina in 1973. The Montoneros wanted to continue the revolution and have a show-down with rival elements of Perónism, particularly the trade union leadership. Like the Trotskyites following the 1917 Bolshevik Revolution and the consolidation of the USSR under Stalin, they appear to have embraced a doctrine that was Trotskyism in all but name, but heralded in the name of Perón, and especially of Evita. With Perón's return to Argentina, Justicialism had been victorious over the forces of repression, and the continuation of what Trotskyites call a 'permanent revolution' could only be destructive.

Argentina was heading towards reconciliation, under the regime of General Lanusse, who assumed office in 1971. Perón was permitted to return from exile in 1973, and although not permitted to run in the elections, he chose Hector Campora to act in his place. Campora would then call an election the following year with Perón as the candidate. Cámpora was elected president that year under the slogan 'Government for Cámpora, power for Perón'. In July Campora resigned, declaring an election. Raúl Lastiri, Lopez Rega's son-in-law, stepped in as interim president of the Chamber of Deputies, while electoral preparations were undertaken.

Campora had been aligned with 'La Tendencia' and many were in mid-level positions under his administration.[545] The crowds that had celebrated the Campora victory had Montoneros, Perónist Youth and other Leftists prominently displaying their banners for a 'Socialist Fatherland'. Even now, there were fights breaking out with mainline Perónists, and the labour unions in particular, who answered with their slogan 'For a Perónist Fatherland'. With Rega as Minister of Social Welfare and his son-in-law as president of the Chamber, the extreme Left saw their victories fading. Argentina was already on the verge of civil war when Perón returned.

545 Antonius C.G. M. Robben, *Political Violence and Trauma in Argentina* (University of Pennsylvania Press, 2005), 67.

Perónism and Che Guevara

The Bolivian Marxist guerrilla leader Che Guevara, instrumental in staging the revolt against the Batista regime in Cuba, has been heralded as an icon by the New Left, especially throughout the West and Latin America. His attraction has continued to the present, partly as a fashion icon whose face adorns the clothing and accessories of the ignorant and partly because the capitalist publishing industry has been very kind to him.

Guevara as a youth was apolitical and his family was anti-Perón. He did not participate in any of the great questions of the day during the first Perón era. His sister Ana Maria, states of Guevara's student days that on Perón, 'he did not take sides one way or another. He sort of stayed on the sidelines'.[546] The only comment he made on the Peróns was his surprise at the admiration they had among the people of Chile and Peru, when he was travelling through those countries during the early 1950s.[547] His biographer, Castaneda, finds Guevara's indifference to Perón during these tumultuous years, 'striking'.[548] When Guevara departed from Argentina in 1953, he never returned.[549]

When Perón was ousted by the Navy coup in 1955, the response from Guevara was bland and brief, and he seems to have regarded it as of no great importance, writing of it in passing to a friend in relation to a CIA sponsored coup in Guatemala.[550] Guevara Lynch, Che's father, later attempted to invent a pro-Perónist history for his son. .

On 25 May 1962 the Argentine community in Cuba gathered to celebrate their nation's independence day. Speaking before the Institute for Cuban-Argentine Friendship, he addressed the

546 Jorge Castaneda, Companero: *The Life and Death of Che Guevara* (London: Bloomsbury, 1998), 33

547 Ibid., 49.

548 Ibid., 32.

549 Ibid., 24.

550 Ibid., 34.

Ernesto "Che" Guevara - Argentine medical student in 1950

Argentine community in Cuba, including Perónists (although John William Cooke, had increasingly distanced himself in favour of Marxism) and several hundred representatives of the Argentine Communist Party, the latter actually being at odds with Cuban revolutionary doctrine. Guevara, as one would expect, however, spoke in favour of armed struggle. As for Cooke, who had been a Perónist senator during the first Justicialist administration, already in 1961 he 'no longer spoke as a Perónist… but as a Communist'.[551] Cooke backed Guevara's call for Latin American revolution; a position endorsed by Perón. Guevara's call for unity with Perónists enraged the Communist party functionaries.[552] It will be recalled that the Communist Party had always opposed Perón. A letter written by several Argentine Communists in Cuba, to party leader Alcira de la Pena, living in Moscow, noted Cuba was training

551 Ernesto Goldar, '*John William Cooke de Perón al Che Guevara*', Todo es historia (Buenos Aires), vol. 25, no. 288, 26, 27, cited by Companero, ibid., 238, n. 3.

552 Companero, ibid., 239.

Argentine guerrillas, centred around John Cooke, and funded by Guevara. Among these 'were a group of Trotskyists'.[553] It is evident that Trotskyists had already subverted the Argentine guerrilla movement of what must have been predominantly of a Perónist nature. Indeed, as we have seen, genuinely 'third positionist' Justicialists, including Perón, recognised Trotskyites as among the vanguard of those who subverted Perónism, leading to the groups that eventually opposed Perón while being funded by oligarchs.

Guevara in any event failed with the Argentine guerrilla movement, and he and Cooke failed to persuade Perón to leave Spain for Cuba[554] to more directly patronise a guerrilla movement that was often using Perónism as a façade for the followers of Mao and Trotsky. Ciro Bustos had been assigned by Guevara to prepare for his return to Argentina by organising dissident Communists, Perónists and Trotskyites.[555] Guevara did not make it back to his native land. He had by then fallen afoul of the USSR and the Communist parties loyal to it throughout Latin America.[556]

While the extreme Left of the Perónist movement was to prove catastrophic, and among the most effective at destroying Perónism, and while Che was upheld as an icon of these subversives along with Mao and Trotsky, Guevara himself had fought for a revolution that was both national and social, despite the Marxist rhetoric, and one moreover that was – like Perónism – opposed by Communists, oligarchs, and plutocrats alike.

Perón, perhaps overly charitable towards an individual whose attitude towards Perónism was far from clear, eulogised him on hearing of his death in the Bolivian jungle:

553 Cited by Companero, ibid., 239.

554 Ibid., 246.

555 Ibid., 364.

556 Ibid., 382-383.

Comrades!

I have received with deep sorrow the news of an irreparable loss to the cause of our people struggling for their liberation.

We are united with those who have embraced this ideal, anywhere in the world and under any flag, who fight against injustice, misery and exploitation. We are united with all the courage and determination of those that face the insatiable greed of imperialism, with the complicity of the military oligarchy and puppet states propped up by the Pentagon to keep the people oppressed.

Today in this struggle, a hero fell, the most extraordinary young man to give his life to the revolution in Latin America, Comandante Ernesto Che Guevara.

His death breaks my heart because he was one of us, perhaps better than us all, an example of selfless behaviour, the spirit of sacrifice and renunciation. The strong belief in the righteousness of the cause he embraced, gave him the strength and courage, courage that today elevated him to the status of hero and martyr.

I have read that some seek to portray him as an enemy of Perónism. Nothing is more absurd. Supposing it were true that in 1951 he had been linked to an attempted coup, how old were you then? I myself, being a young officer, participated in the coup that overthrew the popular government of Hipolito Irigoyen. I also at that time was used by the oligarchy.

The important thing is to recognise those mistakes and correct them. And Che fixed them!

In 1954, when Guatemala struggled to defend the government of Jacobo Arbenz against the arrogant armed intervention of the Yankees, I personally gave instructions to the Foreign Ministry to help solve the difficult situation facing this brave young Argentine and this is how he left for Mexico.

His life, his epic – is the clearest example to our young people, young people throughout Latin America.

There will always be those who will attempt to tarnish his name. Imperialism has a huge fear of charisma, and he managed to win the hearts of the masses of our subjugated people. Already I have received news that the Argentine Communist Party, has begun a hypocritical smear campaign to discredit him. This is not surprising, because it was always known that they act contrary to the historical national interest. They were always against the national and popular movements. We Perónists can attest to that.

The Hour of the people's national revolution in Latin America has struck, and this is an irreversible process. The current balance will be broken! It is childish to think that no revolution can overcome the resistance of the oligarchy and it's imperialist investor monopolies.

The socialist revolution must be carried out, no matter under what flag the revolution is fought. We should stand united for the sake of all our national movements. Solidarity among ourselves and in the face of the privileged exploiters. Most Latin American governments are not going to solve national problems simply because they do not care about the national interests.

To carry out the socialist revolution, revolutionary speeches are not enough. We need organized revolutionary action, strategy and tactics, to make the revolutionary victory possible.

At the forefront of this should be those who embrace the struggle! This fight will be tough, but the final victory will be won for our people. Our enemies have a significant financial advantage over us, but we have an extraordinary moral force that gives us confidence in the justice of our struggle and the historical justification of our actions.

Perónism, in accordance with the traditions of our struggle and, as a national, popular revolutionary movement, give our tribute to the idealist and the revolutionary Comandante Che Guevara – Argentine guerrilla, who was killed in combat, fighting for the national revolutionary victory in Latin America.

Juan Domingo Perón

Madrid, October 24, 1967

The Third Perónist Period

The return of Perón from 18 years of exile had been irredeemably marred by the attempts of crypto-Marxist youth groups to gain ascendancy. Perón was to die one year later of heart failure, or perhaps more precisely of a broken heart caused by the killing of his heir Rucci by the Montoneros. Within that short time, Perón, with his wife Isabel as Vice President, enacted the 'Programme of Reconstruction and National Liberation'.

The new regime aimed to increase the home market by equating consumption with production. Foreign trade was again placed under State control, and earnings were given back to the industrial sector, while also maintaining income for agriculture. The State sought land reform, including the expropriation of uncultivated land, but this caused conflict. Exports were aimed at new markets such as Cuba and the USSR. State owned companies were advanced state credit, and purchased materials from Argentine producers. The Corporation of National Companies was formed, in keeping with the Perónist aim of a corporatist state. Generous subsidies were given to large industrial projects in the 'national interest'.[557] The State resumed control over credit and instituted price controls. Public works were again a factor, and new state companies were established. A wage and price freeze for two years was agreed between the CGT and the CGE, although a general wage order of 20% was granted. Results were rapid, with inflation curtailed and a favourable balance of payments achieved with a large surplus. However, by December 1973 Argentina was hit by the world oil price crisis, undermining trade relations and increasing production costs. Additionally, the European Common Market shut off Argentine meat exports.[558]

The CGE, representing private business, failed to take measures to restrain their members from undermining the Social Pact between business and labour, resulting in stockpiling, price markups, black marketing, and exporting that bypassed the

557 Luis Alberto Romero, op. cit., 205.

558 Ibid., 206.

State apparatus. This in turn resulted in union action outside of the CGT, at factory level, by the union rank-and-file, causing industrial chaos.[559] Added to this was the ever-present state of civil war that had been launched by the Montoneros against their own movement in tandem with the Trotksyite-turned-Maoist terrorists of the *Ejército Revolucionario del Pueblo* (ERP), the People's Revolutionary Army.

While Perón had urged a unification of the Perónist factions on his return, the Montoneros made it clear that their revolution would continue, as they sought to eliminate rival leaders. The Montoneros brought about their own repression by the assassination of CGT leader José Ignacio Rucci, on 25 September 1973, two days after Perón's election, shooting Rucci 23 times. Rucci had been close to Perón, and was being prepared as his successor. The Montoneros had thereby killed the best credible chance for a successor to Perón, who would be dead the following year. In early 1974 several Montoneros were arrested and charged with planning to kill Perón.[560]

After the May Day mass Leftist walk-out, and the increasing intransigence of both unions and employers to adhere to the 'social pact', Perón offered his resignation in June 1974. The CGT responded by a mass rally on 12 June, to reassure Perón of their support. Perón appeared on the historic balcony overlooking the Plaza del Mayo, on a 'freezing cold' winter day, despite having been bedridden by a cold. Perón did not recover his health, and died on 1 July.[561] He had declared to the people gathered at Plaza del Mayo

> I carry in my ears what is for me the most wonderful music: the word of the Argentine people. My spirit is present among those who have the responsibility to defend

559 Ibid., 207.

560 'Montoneros', National Consortium for the Study of Terrorism and Responses to Terrorism', University of Maryland, http://www.start.umd.edu/start/data_collections/tops/terrorist_organization_profile.asp?id=236

561 Anotnius C. G. M. Robben, op. cit., p. 79.

the country. I also believe that it is time that we put the record straight…

We know we have enemies that have begun to show their nails. But also we know we have the people on our side, and when they decide to fight, they are usually unbeatable. Today is the visible sign of our struggle, that we have the people on our side, and we do not advocate or defend any other cause than the cause of the people. I know there are many who want to deviate in one or another direction, but we know perfectly well our objectives and we will go directly to them, without being influenced or pulled from the right or from the left.

The Government of the People is meek and tolerant, but our enemies should know that we are not fools. While we do not rest to accomplish the mission that the people have placed on our shoulders, there are many who seek to manage us with deception and violence. When the people know our aims, there is nothing to fear. Neither the truth, nor deception, or violence, or any other circumstance, may influence the people in a negative sense, nor can it influence us to change our direction for the country. We know that in this action we will have to face maliciousness. Neither those who seek to divert us, nor speculators, and profiteers of all kinds, may, in these circumstances, thrive on the misery of the people. We know that in the progress that we have undertaken many bandits try to make us stumble and stop, but with the help of the people no one can stop us. I therefore wish to take this opportunity to ask each one of you to become a vigilant observer of the events that are provoked and to act according to the circumstances.

Each one of us must be a director, but must be also a preacher and an agent to perform our task, and to neutralise the negative sectors. Comrades, this popular gathering gives me the support and the answer to what I said this morning.

> So I want to thank you for the trouble you have taken to get to this plaza. Burned into my eyes, I take in this wonderful demonstration, in which the working people of the city and province of Buenos Aires bring the message that I need. I want to extend my thanks to all the people of the Republic and state my desire to continue working to build and liberate our country. These slogans, which more than mine are those of Argentine people, I will defend to the last breath. To conclude, I wish that God bestows upon you all fortune and happiness. I thank you deeply for having come to this historic Plaza del Mayo. [562]

Multitudes passed by his body as he lay in state, with the Perónist Youth and the Montoneros having the audacity to respectfully pass by giving the 'V' for victory salute.

Perón's widow, Isabel, who had been elected as vice president, assumed the presidential office. She seems to have been accorded few praises, yet she inherited an impossible situation, with a civil war between the Right and the Left, and the military waiting in the wings. Lopez Rega, whom Isabel had met in Argentina in 1965 when acting as Perón's envoy, returned to Spain and became the Peróns' closest confidante during the years of exile. He assumed the position of Minister of Social Welfare on Perón's return. When La Tendencia launched its war on the Perón regime Rega organised the paramilitary organization, Triple A (Argentine Anticommunist Alliance) to meet the insurrection with counter-force.

On 6 September 1974 'the Montoneros declared that the second period of Perónist Resistance had begun'.

That was the state of Argentina when Perón died in mid-1974, wracked by conflict, subversion, and economic problems arising from external factors. The vision had been still-born, not least

562 Perón, Message delivered on 12 June 1974, from the balcony of the State House, to workers gathered in the Plaza del Mayo.

CGT leader José Ignacio Rucci

because Perón's heir, Rucci, had been gunned down by extreme Leftists proclaiming themselves Perónists, while being funded and assisted by agents of the 'international synarchy', some of whom also posed as allies of Perón.

Isabel assumed office during the international oil crisis, 'causing high inflation, a decrease in capital investments, and external debt growth'.[563] When she assumed the presidency she called for collective labour negotiations, but the new economics minister, Celestino Rodrigo, devalued the *peso* by 100% and decreed huge price increases for fuel and public services. Labour was demanding wage increases ranging from 40% to 200%. Isabel Perón refused, creating more antagonism, and a 48-hour general strike was called. It was the first CGT general strike against a Perónist government. Isabel surrendered to the wage demands, and Rodrigo and Rega resigned.[564] The Montoneros, Perón Youth and ERP Maoists escalated their violence. Rega's 'Triple A' counter-terrorists launched a bloody offensive against the extreme Left, that continued into the post- Perónist years.

563 Celina Andreassi, '*History of Perónism*', (Part II), 17 October 2011, http://www.argentinaindependent.com/currentaffairs/analysis/the-history-of-Perónism-part-ii-/

564 Luis Alberto Romero, op. cit., 209.

Having failed to take over Perón's funeral ceremony, and founding an 'Authentic Perónist Party', despite Perón's unequivocal denunciation of them, the Montoneros resumed their terrorist activities.[565]

ERP had been founded in 1969 as a wing of a Trotskyite communist party, but moved over to Castroism and Maoism. ERP specialised in kidnapping businessmen and in killing hostages. They continued their terrorism with the assumption of Perón to the presidency. During 1975 ERP terrorists attacked soldiers and policemen and raided barracks. When Perón assumed the presidency ERP focused on rural actions designed to secure a land base from which to hit at the State. By December 1974 they had gained control over one-third of Tucumán province, and organised a base there of 2,500 supporters.[566]

Isabel Perón ordered a military offensive against the ERP controlled Tucumán in February 1975; *Operacion Independencia*, while their urban supporters were also rooted out. ERP had been crushed by October 1975, although there were isolated pockets of resistance in the Tucumán Mountains. However, the Montoneros continued their attacks in alliance with remnants of ERP. In October the Destroyer A.R.A. Santisima Trinidad was severely damaged with explosives. On 30 December a bomb killed six soldiers as the headquarters of the Army base at Buenos Aires. The Leftist terrorists had seriously undermined the Government, despite the success of *Operacion Independencia*. In the last months of Isabel's administration there was an average of one political killing every five hours and one bomb explosion every three. Production went to a virtual stand-still and inflation reached 1000%.

To avoid a military coup, Isabel called an election for 1976, but this was pre-empted. The lack of confidence from the Army

565 Ibid., 213.

566 Paul H. Lewis, *Guerrillas and Generals: The Dirty War in Argentina* (Greenwood Publishing Group, 2002), 105.

prompted General Videla to oust Isabel in March 1976. From then until 1983 the military regimes were involved in a counter-insurgency war that killed around 12,000 Leftists and Perónists in the 'Dirty War', while approximately 13,000 had been killed by Leftists.[567] A combination of external forces, with the extreme Left ever-ready to serve its historic function as the lackeys of plutocracy, had brought down the Perónist State.

Appeal For Unity And Discipline

Addressing the Justicialist movement in 1973, prior to his return to Argentina, Perón had appealed for unity against the common enemy, among the bitterly opposed rival factions that had arisen during his exile. Returning to the wider implications of Justicialism, Perón called for a 'third position' continental revolt against capitalism and Marxism, while also alluding to a world struggle:

> All peoples of the continent are engaged in a struggle for liberation. A vast network is enveloping the world, consisting of peoples who do not want to enter the deceptive game of imperialism in simulated battle, who do not want to submit to the dominant imperialists east or west of the Iron Curtain.[568]

Perón explained that this was an 'international synarchy' which he here termed 'this satanic sacrificial pooling of interests', for which peoples across the world pay with 'misery, injustice and pain'. The answer was the 'third position' that Justicialism had been 'launched almost twenty years ago', but which 'apparently fell on deaf ears'. 'But time has passed, and in the current circumstances we show that a large majority of nations have been placed in that position, that people begin to take action'.

---

567 *Wall Street Journal*, 3 January 2011. Estimates vary widely, with some going up to 30,000 killed by the military.

568 Juan Perón, '*The Politics of the Antipueblo*', Buenos Aires, 1973.

Perón counselled the Argentine people that they were not alone in their fight, 'which is just beginning'.

> In our country, we have witnessed decline caused by the worst of our colonial reactionary periods, but the Argentine people is with a burning faith, inculcated with a doctrine and a mystique that will enable them to reconquer what was lost, because their core values have not been destroyed. Fortunately, to face the struggle for our liberation, we are not alone. Many other people are fighting for the same. They are united with us and work in their areas of influence for the same freedom.
>
> It is necessary that the Argentine people know that the sacred cause of their release must be the work of their own efforts and their own perseverance, and arranged accordingly to remain firm with the resolve to overcome. We have been pioneers in the world, and we have suffered the blow of the reaction. But that reaction has been defeated. We must organise and present a united front in solidarity to confront the bloody or the bloodless fight of the future. [569]

Perón urged unity among Perónist factions whose rivalry was threatening civil war:

> I hope that each of the leaders, each of the Perónists of the masses, regardless of their current position, understand the reality of the country and the people of Argentina and placed in their position, to work faithfully for compliance with the principles of our movement, forgetting personal interests or factions, that in the salvation of the nation and the liberation of our people these cannot have any importance.[570]

Alluding to a quite unique situation where it was the State that

569 Ibid.

570 Ibid.

developed a revolutionary doctrine, it was now time for the doctrine to be institutionalised.

> All revolutionary liberation movements inevitably meet four stages. The doctrine, the coup, the dogma, and the institutionalisation. If we take the example of Marxist revolution in Russia, Lenin represents the doctrinal stage, Trotsky the revolutionary stage, Stalin the dogmatic stage, and Khrushchev, the institutionalization.
>
> Our Movement cannot escape this same scheme. Our generation has had the doctrinal stage. Special circumstances made this stage come from the government. What matters now is the fulfillment of the rest. So Perónism, during the ten years of my government, gave much importance to training schools in the movement and the unions that were formed, and of training the Perónist youth to fulfil its mission.[571]

This was an appeal to the factions claiming to be Perónist, who wanted to 'continue the revolution' in some type of Trotskyite style, enamoured with revolution as an end in itself. Perónism, however, had triumphed after a long struggle, and it was now time to resume the building of the Perónist State. In particular the Perónist youth had to recognise it now had responsibilities towards the State, not against it. It was the time for youth to fulfil its mission as the next generation of Perónist leaders, in implementing the doctrine of the State:

> We and the generations that preceded us, accomplished the mission we had in the first half of the twentieth century. Now we turn to the next generation to finish the job in the second half. Maybe we will not witness the moment of triumph, but we feel we have prepared for it. For this to happen it is necessary that the youth take leadership

571 Ibid.

> and responsibility. We are left wishing they exceed us in the effort. The experience gained by us we used to advise and guide our youth… Many young people have come to me, with the just concerns of their aspirations, and no one can argue the necessity and appropriateness of new blood, because if you miss the youth there is no future.[572]

However, the responsibilities of the new generation of political leaders must be earned by those who have proven themselves 'in every day political work'. 'It is essential to hold political virtues, because within these virtues of honesty, loyalty, fidelity to the cause they have served and been selflessness ... This is fundamental'.[573]

Perón reminded the Justicialists of all factions that the movement had a command authority, and that discipline is required in following its directives. Perón was a military man, albeit one of remarkable peace and reconciliation. Reconciliation and national unity, after all is one of the fundamental premises of Justicialism. The message was aimed at the extreme Left that had in effect declared war on Perónism while claiming the mantle of Perón. The radical Left that had been revising Justicialism in Perón's absence, and had then sought to literally capture him as their own when he was about to land at Ezeiza airport, had then resorted even to killing Perón's personal and political heir, José Ignacio Rucci. After Perón's death they continued a guerrilla war against the Perónist State that justified the military coup against Isabel Perón and the return of the suppression of the Justicialist movement. Perón continued, warning:

> The governing bodies of the Movement have the broadest authority to conduct and direct. Their resolutions, inspired … by the wisdom in the choice of means to fulfil its mission, cannot be discussed outside its scope. No Perónist may be entitled to criticise the Command or its members outside the body itself, and although it has an absolute

572 Ibid.

573 Ibid.

> right to do so against its members, must think that doing so is to be exposed to the consequences. Without a fair and proportionate respect for the driving Command, all steering becomes impossible and leads to anarchy. The institutionalisation of the Movement imposed rules to which all must be subordinate if we are to maintain its organic function. When a command is given it is because the time has passed for discussion. The unity of action, key to success, has its original demands. Nobody has the right to break it by ideas, thoughts or personal interests.
>
> Nothing can justify a Perónist leader who is subordinate to the demands and voices of our enemies… In such cases, the authority of the Movement is obliged to proceed with his immediate replacement to prevent uncertainty or distrust.[574]

The mission of fulfilling the Justicialist doctrine must motivate the Perónist. This requires avid educators and propagators of that doctrine. Perónism is more than political; it is also spiritual: 'Each Perónist leader must be a tireless preacher of our doctrine, because his mission is not only to direct training, but also to form spiritually'. Educational centers for Perónism were required throughout the country.

Perón addressed factionalism within the movement stating that 'the use of falsehood and rumour is one of the main actions of provocation. The Perónist who naively falls for this is not ready for the fight'. However, the greatest evil is done by those 'scoundrels who, feigning credulity, dishonestly take advantage of rumours to attack their own comrades, for the benefit of hidden intentions or plans'.[575]

Perón, having addressed the problem of *agents provocateur* and rumour-mongers claiming to be Justicialists, next addressed what

574 Ibid.

575 Ibid.

he said was a common problem: individuals claiming authority on behalf of the Movement, without having the authorisation of the Justicialist High Command. Only those properly authorised can speak for the High Command. The Perónist leader should have the knowledge and discipline to know how to act in the interests of the Movement, and not to have dealings with non-Perónists in matters pertaining to the Movement. What Perón is asking for is a military type of discipline and discretion of Perónists and particularly those in leadership positions. There is a chain of command, and a Justicialist ethos:

> A leader without the spirit of sacrifice will always be a threat to the cause he serves. The Justicialist ethos establishes a principle of immovable hierarchy: first the country, then the movement and then men, because politics cannot be seen as an end but as a means to serve the community in its core values.[576]

Perón warned of the development of factions within the Movement that were self-serving rather than having the interests of Argentina above all else. Perón saw factions developing that claimed to be fighting in the interests of the nation, but were serving other interests with dishonourable means, while invoking dogmas for their own ends. The Perónist acts according to Justicialist honour, and does not descend to the level of his enemies, who are debased by their actions: 'The sectarian serving of a group or party, but not of the country, will use dogma as a pretext, but the real solutions the country needs are and will always be above political interests'. Perón warned of those who serve their own or factional interests 'when invoking the homeland' as being a 'fraud or scam', 'as when in the name of peace in the country they resort to the most unworthy or arbitrary procedures, serving shameful interests, but never the cause of the country or Argentines'.[577]

The Movement is obliged to sacrifice everything for the

576 Ibid.

577 Ibid.

> country and decide for the best of the people's aspirations and interests of the nation. The political struggle is justified only if we undertake to win with firm resolve, whatever the sacrifice we must make.[578]

The Perónist movement is an organism, and like any organism requires unity among its cells. The disunity of an organism is a pathogen, a cancer. The organic character of the Movement reflects the Justicialist aim of creating the organic state, or what Perónists call the 'organised community'.

> A broad spirit of unity and solidarity is imposed in the leadership and in the mass. For a Perónist there should be nothing better than another Perónist. Just give us a spirit of cohesion such that the struggle has imposed, and give us the unity of action needed to overcome… Our enemies will work tirelessly to divide us and influence Perónist leaders by enemy slander, or be encouraged consciously or unconsciously to be traitors to their cause.[579]

Nothing could be done without unity. Those who cannot understand this would serve 'anarchy'. 'Individual values are positive for the Movement, when added to the overall momentum, and negative when they serve personal interests'. 'Any damage caused to one Perónist will eventually fall on another Perónist…'

> Disagreements must be aired within the Movement, but never outside Perónism. If the criticism is appropriate, it will be against evils that can be remedied, and not used by those who can destroy us. The Perónist movement has an obligation to defend itself against enemies within and without. Institutional bodies like physiological bodies succumb when they lack self-defence mechanisms, but these self-defences are developed and act against pathogens. So even the defector is often useful to political

578 Ibid.

579 Ibid.

> institutions, if his action causes self-defence, but for this to be positive it is necessary that the organic body is healthy and robust. [580]

Perón stated that the robustness of the movement depends upon 'stronger unity and solidarity'. 'Perónist Discipline must be of substance and not form', so it is the responsibility of the movement to replace leaders whenever necessary, should they fail through errors or treason. However, discipline is best when it comes from within 'free men', and is 'not transformed into subservience', becoming an 'indignity' rather than a 'virtue'.

The Ezeiza Massacre

On 20th June Perón returned to Argentina, and three and a half million Argentines[581] waited to welcome him after he was to land at Ezeiza international airport. However, factions of Justicialism contended for primacy as they awaited Perón, and shots were fired in a gunfight between trade unionists and Montoneros and others of La Tendencia. At least 13 people were killed and 350 wounded. Perón's plane was diverted, and the spectacular welcome was wrecked.

The responsibility for the 'Ezeiza Massacre' is generally ascribed to 'Rightist' Perónists aiming to eliminate their 'Leftist' rivals by mercilessly gunning down the young idealists who had come to welcome Perón. This is incorrect. The Montoneros were heavily armed. As the crowd awaited Perón, armed Leftists 'were positioning themselves behind the trees while others were climbing up into them'.[582] A few minutes after Oscar Bidegain, the Leftist Governor of Buenos Aires, arrived with two buses loaded with weapons, along with several ambulances. A shot was fired. Those on the overpass podium, from where Perón was to address the crowd, were fired on with volleys of bullets by the extreme

580 Ibid.

581 Antonius C.G.M. Robben, op. cit., 69.

582 Paul H. Lewis, *Guerrillas and Generals: The 'Dirty War' in Argentina* (Westport, Ct.: Praeger Publishers, 2002), 88.

Montoneros and Trotskyist La Tendencia supporters at Ezeiza Airport

Left positioned in the trees.[583] Security guards returned fire. Panic and a stampede among the crowd ensued. A grenade blew up one of the two buses that had brought Governor Bidegain's men.

> Around 3pm. there was a lull in the fighting. Each side secured its positions. Then, about half an hour later, the Montoneros moved in from the trees and, behind an intense barrage of fire, made an assault on the bridge. It was a frenzied and nearly successful attempt to break the Perónist Right once and for all and to establish the Left's supremacy, but the defenders held their ground. [584]

According to *La Prensa*, 500 Montoneros stormed the podium, were stopped by security, and ran back towards the trees, then resumed firing. Later there was a further exchange of fire between security and snipers still positioned in trees near the podium. Shooting did not stop until 7pm.[585]

The Montoneros were routed and pursued by Perónist security. Many were caught, held at the International Hotel at Ezeiza airport, and interrogated to find out who had ordered the attack. Perón's aeroplane had been diverted to an air force base and he

583 Robben, op. cit., 69.

584 Paul H. Lewis, op. cit.

585 Robben, op. cit., 70.

went to his home under heavy guard. Perón did not refer to the chaos at Ezeiza during his address to the nation that night on radio and television. However, he later met with army commander General Jorge Carcagno, who stated that he believed the Left were preparing riots.[586]

On 21 July, the Perónist Youth, having become convinced that Perón was being kept from them by a sinister Rightist cabal, marched on Perón's residence, although he was not at home. He invited four representatives to meet with him. His response to their position was to appoint Lopez Rega intermediary between the Perónist Youth and himself, thereby making it unequivocal – again – that he was not suddenly going to embark on a Marxist course, thereby repudiating the 'third position' in favour of what seems to have become a stereotypical youthful idolisation of Che Guevara, Fidel Castro and Mao Zedong.

Appeal After Ezeiza

The day after the disaster at Ezeiza Airport, Perón issued an appeal for unity in the work of reconstruction.

Perón stated that there must be a starting point on 'a long march' to rebuilding the Perónist State even if it is apparently 'vague and indecisive'. However, Argentina had been reduced to dire circumstances with 'a debt that exceeds six billion *pesos* and a deficit of close to three billion *pesos*'. In this reconstruction the Justicialist Movement aimed to join with 'all political, social, economic and military' sectors in 'this crusade of liberation and reconstruction'. The ethos would be 'first the country, then the movement and then the people, in a large national and popular movement that can support it'. What was required was a 'revolution', but one that was to be 'built peacefully… without costing the life of one Argentine'. Work alone might serve to rectify past errors. The new leaders of State would be drawn from the most intelligent, having 'genuine

586 Paul H. Lewis, op. cit., p. 89.

values', subordinating personal interests. The Armed Forces must defend 'national sovereignty and the constitutional order', but must do so as brothers of the people, under a 'constructive peace'. 'We must return to legal and constitutional order as the only guarantee of freedom and justice', as 'every Argentine has the inalienable right to live in security and peacefully'.[587]

In a warning to those who sought to destroy the state, including those who had sought to hijack Perón at Ezeiza , Perón stated that the Government had the obligation to maintain security and called on all sides to coexist, and to fight anarchy. Perón identified the international synarchy as profiting from the anarchic forces, which, after his death, were able to retake Argentina.

> I know exactly what is happening in the country. Those who believe otherwise are wrong. We are living the consequences of a post-Civil War… To this are added the evil intentions of the hidden factions that, in the shadows, work ceaselessly behind shameful designs that are no less real.[588]

Perón warned that all had the duty to fight the forces of anarchy and subversion lest they perish, which indeed was the fate of the Perónist State. Shortly after Perón's death a year later, Isabel Perón's regime succumbed to the axis between the extreme Left and international synarchy. Now, however, Perón stated that 'none can pretend that the conflict between factions can end overnight', 'but we all have the inescapable duty to actively confront those enemies, lest we perish in misfortune, desperation or our negligence'.[589] Perón called for the joining of 'our compatriots in La Hora del Pueblo, the Civic Liberation Front and Justicialist Liberation Front', 'pooling our ideals and our efforts … Justicialism, which has never been sectarian or exclusionary, calls today to all Argentines, irrespective of

587 Juan Perón, 'Call for National Reconstruction', radio address, Buenos Aires, 21 June 1973.

588 Ibid.

589 Ibid.

factions, so that severally we join in the urgent task of national reconstruction, without which we are all lost'. [590]

What was required was the creation of 'a single class of Argentines, fighting for the salvation of the country'. However the aim was 'severely compromised by enemies outside and inside'. Those who were trying to 'deform' the Justicialist Movement, 'whether from above or below' had to be 'neutralised'. He reminded Argentines that the movement still stood for the Twenty Justicialist Principles, and that Justicialism would not be achieved by 'screaming Perón', 'but by keeping the creed for which we struggle'. The youth, with 'misleading shouts', and 'insisting on the wildest fights … cannot fool anyone'. 'Those who do not agree can subject their aims to the electorate'.[591]

> Those who naively think they can surround our Movement or take the power that has been regained are wrong. No pretense or concealment, however ingenious, may mislead a people that has suffered as has ours and that is animated by a strong will to win. So, I warn those who try to infiltrate the State or use bribery. I advise all of them to take the only road that is genuinely national: our duty as Argentines. We will order the State. That will be the main task of the government. The rest will be done by the people of Argentina, which in past years has shown a maturity and a capacity greater than any adversity. I want to offer my last years of life in an achievement that is all my ambition. I just need Argentines to believe and help me fulfil it. The ineffectiveness by which at times we have to live, is a crime against the Patria.

Perón then appealed for those Argentines who had left the country to return and help in national reconstruction, and to former adversaries and factions, while also warning those who continue to work against the Patria:

590 Ibid.

591 Ibid.

> We have a duty to produce, at least, what we consume. This is no time to be vague or irrelevant. Scientists, technicians, artisans and workers who are out of the country must return to it in order to help in the reconstruction we are planning and aiming to implement in the shortest time. Finally, I urge all my fellow Perónists to throw back the bad memories and engage in thinking about the future greatness of the country, which may well be right now in our own hands and our own effort. To those who were our adversaries, to accept the sovereignty of the People… when you want to banish the specter of foreign allegiances.[592]

> The enemies, cloaked, concealed or hidden, I advise you to cease you intentions because when people run out of patience thunder often makes a lesson. God helps us if we are able to help God. The opportunity usually happens very quietly. A big, warm hug to all my colleagues, and affection and respect to the rest of the Argentines.[593]

Perón swiftly moved against the Left after the Ezeiza shoot-out. Representatives of Perónist Youth, a faction of the Left, were removed from the Supreme Council of the Justicialist Party. Rucci was instructed to purge the labour movement of Marxists. The Left's crowd mobilisations were replaced by a return to guerrilla tactics, this time against rivals in the Perónist Government, and by infiltrating unions and other grass roots organisations. On 10 January 1974 Perón stated that the 'social pact' would be imposed if necessary; a determination that Perónism was not based on the 'class war' of the Montoneros and other crypto-Marxists.

On 19 January the Marxist People's Liberation Army (ERP) attacked the Azul army base. Perón believed there had been collusion with the Governor of Buenos Aires, Oscar Bidegain, a supporter of La Tendencia Revolucionaria, who had shown up at Ezeiza with busloads of arms. Perón also obtained the

592 Ibid.

593 Ibid.

resignations of eight Leftist congressmen. The Right retaliated against Leftist insurrection by bombing a dozen chapter offices of the Perónist Youth.[594] As was Perón's habit, he invited youth leaders to a meeting to discuss differences. The Perónist youth refused to enter discussions that included the Perónist Right. This was a personal affront to Perón. The Left had shown they were committed to a type of Trotskyist permanent revolution, rather than the rebuilding of the state.

The Leftist Governor of Cordoba was removed, and the magazine *El Descamisado* was closed.[595]

The Perónist Left now factionalised into three groups: those who remained loyal to Perón, those who aimed at grass roots mobilisation, and those who wanted to violently confront the Right.

The final break came on 1 May 1974. Perón had promised that on every 'May Day' he would present himself before the masses to ask their approval to continue as leader. This May Day the Left was organised for a confrontation. Gathering outside La Casa Rosada, on the Plaza del Mayo, where the Perónist movement had been born from the working masses three decades previously, the Partido Justicialista and Montoneros supporters began rival chanting, and there were intermittent skirmishes as factions positioned themselves in the square. There had been an agreement that only Argentine flags would be displayed. However, the Left lowered its flags, and spray-painted 'Montoneros' on them.[596] After respects are paid to Perónist martyrs, Perón was met by chants from the Left. Perón retorted that 'youngsters' were dishonouring the founders of the movement, the workers and their unions; 'brats who expect to have more merits than those who have been fighting for the last twenty years'. Thousands of Leftists left the Plaza del Mayo *en masse.*[597] Although this breach delineated the rival

594 Antonius C. G. M. Robben,op. cit., 75.

595 Ibid.

596 Ibid., 76.

597 Ibid.

factions of Justicialism and crypto-Marxism, the strain on Perón was likely to have directly contributed to his death soon after.

Perón had assumed the presidency from the caretaker President, the Justicialist Hector Campora, who resigned the presidency within several days to allow Perón to run for the Office. Perón ran with his third wife Isabel Martínez de Perón as vice president. This Perón/Perón team won 62% of the vote.

Frigerio's MID endorsed Perón. However, the movement exercised little influence. Perón died of heart failure on 1 July 1974. The military ousted Isabel Perón in 1976. Frigerio supported the coup, but soon found that the new military regime embarked on a totally new course that froze wages, deregulated financial markets, and encumbered Argentina with massive foreign debt, undoing the achievements of both Perón and himself. The new Minister of Finance, José Alfredo Martínez de Hoz, had served as a provincial minister of economics following the 1955 coup. A personal friend of American global wire-puller David Rockefeller, Martínez de Hoz obtained loans from the International Monetary Fund and Rockefeller's Chase Manhattan Bank for $1 billion immediately following his appointment. It is therefore evident whose interests were served with the overthrow of the embattled Isabel Perón.

Juan Perón was not buried until 2½ years after his death, an indication as to the seemingly superstitious dread that his enemies have of his spirit. His body was transported to a local cemetery in an ambulance, accompanied by four vehicles filled with security agents. Evita's body, lying next to his at the presidential residence, had been removed to the family mausoleum shortly before. General Jorge Videla, head of the junta that ousted Isabel Perón the previous March, lived at an army barracks, 'Government sources' saying that he had avoided the presidential residence because of the two bodies.[598]

598 Juan Perón Finally Buried', *The Morning Record*, Connecticut, 20 December 1976, 11.

After Perón

José Alfredo Martínez de Hoz, economics minister under the Videla regime, was a wealthy estate owner and former president of Argentina's largest private steel company. He had close connections with the oligarchy. He embarked on a free trade economy, lowering tariffs, privatising state companies, and denationalising banks.[599] 'Martínez de Hoz initially counted on the support, almost of a personal nature, of the international financial organisations and foreign banks – which allowed him to circumvent several difficult situations – and of the most concentrated sector of the local economic establishment'.[600] The Perónist corporatist organisations were dismantled and income declined.[601] The CGT was purged, factories occupied by the Army, collective bargaining was eliminated, strikes prohibited, wages frozen, interest rates deregulated, State subsidies ended, and new private lending institutions proliferated. The most significant features of Argentina's new liberal economy were the flood of cheap imports, and the speculative nature of investments, driving up interest rates. Foreign currency flooded in, currency speculation ran rampant, and debt escalated. Financial speculation, rather than the great productive programmes of the Perón years, was the basis of the economy. Investments were mostly made short-term and there were no restrictions on currency leaving the country. Private industry was sunk in debt. Bankruptcies were common.

Perónism had an ally within the Videla regime, Admiral Emilio Massera, who had opposed the liberal economics of Martínez de Hoz. Massera had served as navy minister in Isabel's Cabinet, and was a former business partner with Lorezno Miguel, head of the metal workers' union. Admiral Massera and General Carlos Suárez Masón, commander of the Campo de Mayo calvary base, had been members of Pro-Patria until 1983, a secret

599 Paul Lewis, 'The Right and Military Rule 1955-1983', in *The Argentine Right*, op. cit., 173.

600 Luis Alberto Romero, op. cit., 222.

601 Ibid.

lodge organised by Lopez Rega.[602] General Masón attempted an abortive coup against General Videla in 1979, incensed that Jacobo Timerman, the Zionist-Socialist media luminary, had been released from jail.[603]

General Roberto Marcelo Viola assumed the presidency in March 1981, amidst economic chaos, speculation, and debt.[604] Martínez de Hoz resigned and a new economics team was installed. The *peso* was devalued by 400%, and inflation ran at 100%. The state had to take over private commercial debts. In 1981 the CGT called a general strike, calling for 'bread, peace and work'.

In March 1982 the CGT called for a demonstration in the Plaza de Mayo. This was violently suppressed.[605] Other factions that had previously been antagonistic towards Perónism, such as the Church, which had supported the military regime's anti-Leftist offensive, distanced themselves from the regime, with anti-Perónist political parties such as the Radicals and the Christian Democrats aligning with Justicialists to form the *Multipartidario.*[606]

General Leopoldo Fortunato Galtieri, who had gained support from the American Government during his stay in the USA, replaced Viola within a year. His minister of economics, Roberto Alemann, drew his team mainly from those who had worked with Martínez de Hoz, and returned to the liberal economics of 'disinflation, deregulation, and destatization', while economic conditions worsened and labour and business grew more restless.[607] Galtieri's solution was to direct attention towards the invasion of the Malvina Islands (Falklands). Galtieri's loss of the war meant his removal. The recourse was again to parliamentary

602 Paul Lewis,op. cit., 174.

603 Ibid., 173. .

604 Luis Alberto Romero, op. cit., 224-225.

605 Ibid., 237.

606 Ibid., 239.

607 Ibid., 241.

democracy, with the ban on political parties lifted in 1983. One third of those eligible to vote joined a party.[608] The Justicialist Party was still under the nominal leadership of Isabel. For the first time in the history of the party, the Justicialists lost the 1983 presidential election. Raúl Alfonsín of the Radical party became president.

The Radicals inherited an economic mess, which they were unable to overcome. Alfonsín also came into conflict with the Church, for broadly the same reasons as Perón, when divorce was legalised in 1987.[609] The Radical's economic programme in the first year had some similarities to Perónism, and included state control of credit, exchange rates and prices; and social aid programmes.[610] The success was short-lived, with escalating inflation and debt. 'Austerity measures', the panacea of the International Monetary Fund, were introduced. The IMF 'demanded policies designed principally to institute immediate payment of the interest in return for loans'.[611] Again the recourse was to privatisation and deregulation.[612] Between 1984 and 1988 the CGT responded with thirteen general strikes.[613]

The September 1987 elections saw major gains for the Justicialists, taking most of the provincial governments. In keeping with the new spirit of demoliberalism, which Perón had always dismissed as a façade for oligarchy, Carlos Menem of the Justicialist party drew to him big business and labour, conservatives, Churchmen, and 1970s militant Leftists. In typical demoliberal party political manner, he was all things to all people. His contacts with business included the Bugne y Born conglomerate[614] that epitomised the oligarchy. Matters culminated in 1989 when the World Bank and the IMF withdrew support from the Alfonsín

608 Ibid., 251.

609 Ibid., 258-259.

610 Ibid., 269.

611 Ibid., 268.

612 Ibid., 272.

613 Ibid., 266.

614 Ibid., 281.

Government.[615] This resulted in presidential elections in May 1989, with Menem gaining the presidency after a resounding victory for the Justicialist party.

Romero cogently states:

> [To deal with the economic crisis] a general recipe had become common among economists and politicians throughout the world during the 1980s: Facilitate the opening up of the national economy to make possible an appropriate insertion into the global economy, and dismantle the powers of the welfare state, labelled as costly and inefficient. In Argentina's case and that of Latin America in general, these ideas had been distilled in the so-called Washington Consensus. U.S. government agencies and the great international financial organisations such as the IMF and World Bank transformed these prescriptions into recommendations or requirements whenever they came to the aid of governments to solve their immediate problems with foreign debt. Economists, financial advisers, and journalists tirelessly devoted themselves to disseminating the new dogma and gradually managed to turn these simple principles into common wisdom.[616]

It is this 'general recipe of privatisation', 'austerity' and globalisation that remains the common practice over much of the world today. It is a 'recipe' that Menem followed, reversing the premises of Justicialism. Romero states in a manner even suggestive of Perón's references to the 'international synarchy' that Menem's 'prescription was also pleasing to the international financial institutions and to the select group of financial gurus who advised them, that is to say, the powers capable of stirring up or calming the waters of the economic crisis'.[617] Since his time as governor of La Rioja province Menem had been surrounded

615 Ibid., 282.

616 Ibid., 286.

617 Ibid., 287.

by 'a shady group of opportunists and social climbers'.[618] Menem announced that he was a devotee of a 'popular market economy', and ridiculed those who 'had remained in 1945',[619] that is, those who remained committed to Justicialism. His friends from Bunje y Born headed the ministry of economics, but later pulled out of the chaos.[620] Menem was to state that 'had I said what I was going to do, no one would have voted for me'.[621]

Andreassi states:

> During his ten years in government, Menem finished off—in economic terms—what the last dictatorship had started: the establishment of a neoliberal model to replace the Perónist-era import substitution industrialisation, putting finance at the centre of the economy. The pillars of the new paradigm were the mass privatisation of public utilities—including strategic assets such as the energy network— the pegging of the *peso* to the US dollar to curb inflation, a strong market liberalisation and a reform of the State which, in theory, would make it smaller and more efficient.[622]

While state asset sales provided the revenue to keep the state afloat for about ten years, after 1994 the economy collapsed. The overvaluation of the *peso* made industry uncompetitive and local manufacturers were undermined by a flood of imports; import controls being anathema to neoliberal economics. Menem followed the neoliberal formula of reducing labour costs and slackening labour laws. Industry constituted 16% of the Gross Domestic Product in 2001, down from 35% in the 1970s. Foreign debt and unemployment rose sharply.

Menem also repudiated the role of Perónism as a 'third position' in foreign affairs, withdrawing Argentina from the Movement

618 Ibid.

619 Ibid., 288.

620 Ibid.

621 Quoted by Andreassi, op. cit.

622 Celina Andreassi, '*History of Perónism*', (Part II), op. cit.

of Non-Aligned Countries, and drawing particularly closely to U.S. presidents George Bush and Bill Clinton. Argentine troops were sent to Serbia, a war fought to impose globalisation over Serbia's economy and mineral resources behind the façade of 'democracy'.[623] It was a moral travesty that saw Argentine soldiers fight for the 'international synarchy' against a beleaguered state, at the command of a supposedly 'Perónist' regime.

After ten years of Menem, Fernando de la Rúa of the Radical party assumed the presidency on in December 1999, although his platform on privatisation and economic liberalism was the same as Menem's.[624] What the Radical party inherited from the IMF/World Bank imposed panacea of privatisation was a government deficit of $15,000,000,000, unemployment running at 13%, and 40% of the population below the poverty line, while little remained of Argentina's assets and utilities. Menem, in the name of 'social justice', had embraced the ideology of oligarchs and plutocrats, no less than the 'socialists' of the Labour and Social Democratic parties around the world. This is precisely why Perón developed Justicialism as a 'third position', seeing in orthodox socialism, including communism, a confidence trick for plutocracy to dupe the working masses. Menem had betrayed Justicialism by following the same path.

Nonetheless, the Justicialist party remained powerful, retaining control of many provinces, a large representation in the Chamber of Deputies, and a majority in the Senate[625]

Andreassi states that the CGT, the backbone of Perónism, had become corrupt; most of the veteran leaders were gone, and the so-called 'fat cats' oversaw the deconstruction of the economy for the sake of foreign capital. New Perónist groupings emerged. Among these was the Frente Grande, led by Carlos 'Chacho' Alvarez, who

623 For the economic reasons for the war against Serbia see K. R. Bolton, *Babel Inc.* (London: Black House Publishing, 2013), 161-173.

624 Luis Alberto Romero, op. cit., 334.

625 Ibid., 337.

joined an alliance with the UCR (Unión Cívica Radical)[626] between 1999 and 2001. Congresswoman Cristina Fernández de Kirchner also led an anti-Menem faction. Several major factions broke with the CGT and formed their own labour confederations, including the Central de Trabajadores Argentino in 1991, and unions led by Hugo Moyano; who opposed the Menem government.

By December 2001 the Central Bank only had $5,000,000,000 in reserves, down from $30,000,000,000 when Fernando de la Rúa had assumed Office. Fernando de la Rúa's regime was one of turmoil, with increasing social protest. He resorted to calling back Domingo Cavallo, Menem's former economics minister. Cavallo now undertook several measures that were of a more Perónist character than the policies he had pursued under Menem: tariffs were increased to stimulate the home economy, and a tax on bank transactions was introduced. [627]

In the October 2001 elections Perónists achieved majorities in both houses of Congress. On 20 December a mass of middle class demonstrators, the Radical's support base, converged on the Plaza de Mayo, in protest at the freezing of deposits and savings. They were joined by youths who had rioted through the streets. Cavallo resigned the following day. The army moved against the crowds. Fernando de la Rúa resigned and fled the presidential palace in a helicopter.[628]

Between 21st December and 2nd January 2002 there were five presidents. Perónist Alberto Rordíguez Sáa assumed the interim presidency and promptly announced Argentina's default on the foreign debt. However, there were many Menem supporters

626 The UCR was founded in 1891 to represent middle class interests. The UCR at first sought support from U.S. Ambassador Spruille Braden when Perón assumed office. However there was a faction, the UCR Junta Renovadora that supported Perón, and aligned with the Labour Party to back his presidency, thereafter merging into the Partido Perónista. After Perón's ouster in 1955, there were disagreements within the original UCRT over the extent to which Perónism should be opposed. See Celian Andreassi, 'The History of the UCR' (Part I), 20 September 2011, http://www.argentinaindependent.com/currentaffairs/analysis/the-history-of-the-ucr-part-i/

627 Luis Alberto Romero, op. cit., 342.

628 Ibid., 348.

in his Cabinet, rioting continued and he resigned within two months. Eduardo Duhalde, Menem's rival for the leadership of the Justicialist party, assumed Office, with the backing of Alfonsín and the Radical party.[629] Duhalde had briefly been vice president in the Menem Government (1989-1991). Appointed by the Legislative Assembly for a term of two months, he stayed in office for one year. Duhalde upheld the debt default and freed the *peso* from the U.S. dollar. Despite an increase in inflation, the economic situation stabilised and home industry revived. Determined to keep Menem from running for the presidency in 2003, Duhalde backed Néstor Kirchner, governor of Santa Cruz Province, who assumed the presidency in May 2003.

Duhalde established his own faction, *Perónismo disidente,* in 2005 with a caucus of 25 Congressmen. He backed Alberto Rodríguez Saá for the presidential candidacy in 2007, but Saá was defeated by Cristina Fernández de Kirchner. *Perónismo Federal*, which includes Eduardo Duhalde, gained 45 Congressmen and 10 Senators in the mid-term 2009 elections. However, *Perónismo Federal* is divided between Duhalde's Popular Front, with a working class base, and Saá's Federal Commitment.

While Menem resorted to the market economy, the Kirchners have pursued a 'left-wing' course. How close this is to the 'third position' is debatable. Nonetheless Néstor Kirchner's four year regime (2003-2007) included a 70% increase in real wage levels, 9% economic growth; unemployment fell from 20% in 2002 to 9% by 2007, the poverty rate from 50% to 27%, and home market consumption increased by 52%. Public works increased fivefold, increasing public housing and infrastructure, and there were large increased expenditures on scientific research and education. By 2007 public expenditure had increased by 30%.[630] Kirchner retained Roberto Lavagna, economics minister under

629 Ibid., 349.

630 Steven Levitsky and María Victoria Murillo, 'Argentina: From Kirchner to Kirchner', Journal of Democracy, 17, Vol. 19, No. 2, April 2008.

Duhalde. The Menem packed Supreme Court was purged.[631] Kirchner governed in significant part by executive decree.[632]

Alberto Rordíguez Sáa's 2002 default on the debt to the IMF placed Argentina in a good position to renegotiate, and Kirchner rescheduled $84,000,000,000 in debt for three years, and in 2005 restructured $81,000,000,000 in public debt. In December 2005 Kirchner cancelled the IMF debt in full and offered a single repayment. Kirchner also returned to the 'third position' in foreign affairs, opposing the Free Trade Area of the Americas,[633] rejecting the 'War on Terrorism', and aiming to enhance Mercosur, the Latin American economic agreement.

Kirchner, a veteran Justicialist during the years of military repression, having joined the Perónist student union at National University at La Plata in 1969, died in 2010. His wife Cristina Fernández won with 45% of the vote during the 2007 election, well ahead of opposition candidates, with the mainline Justicialist party controlling both the Chamber of Deputies and Senate. Many dissidents of the Radical party, the 'K Radicals', supported both Kirchners.[634]

Cristina Fernández's assumption to the presidency was marked immediately by allegations from the USA that she had received funds from Venezuela. This she and Hugo Chávez called a 'garbage operation' designed by the USA to divide Latin America. Cristina Fernández responded by limiting the contact of the U.S. Ambassador to her Ministers; an action normally reserved towards hostile nations. *The Economist* commented on the friendship between Argentina and Venezuela:

> Mr. Kirchner's government forged an alliance of convenience with Mr. Chávez. Since 2005 Venezuela has

631 Ibid.

632 Ibid., 19.

633 Intended as part of the NAFTA set up.

634 Levitsky and Murillo,op. cit., 18.

> bought $5 billion of Argentine bonds, most of which it has passed on to friendly local banks at a steep discount; it has sold Argentina diesel fuel under special arrangements that include the purchase of Argentine products from providers selected by the governments without competitive tenders.[635]

This is the type of Latin co-operation that was Perón's vision, and the mantle of a united Bolivarian bloc largely fell to Chávez.

'American officials have long been searching for evidence to back up their claims that Mr. Chávez is using Venezuelan oil wealth to fund political allies across Latin America'.[636] If this is the case it is certainly laudable, and one can but hope that the post-Chávez Bolivarian regime has continued to assist other national-revolutionaries across Latin America. Another feature of the U.S. reaction is the rank hypocrisy: The U.S. State Department in conjunction with private think tanks and foundations, have planned, organised and funded civil disorder and revolts that have toppled regimes – 'regime change', as it is called by the USA – across the world, all behind the façade of 'spontaneous protests'.Soon after the U.S. Government backed off, and the U.S. Ambassador, Earl Wayne, said that the allegations were 'never made by the U.S. Government', but by its independent judiciary;[637] a moot point at best.

While there has been much criticism of the Kirchners by Justicialist traditionalists, Cristina's regime has also retained certain major aspects of Justicialism, and has not only met criticism from the USA, but also from Perón's old opponents among Organised Jewry. It should be kept in mind that the slightest deviation from Zionist expectations will provoke a frenetic outcry,

635 'Slush and Garbage', *The Economist*, 3 January 2008.

636 'Sluch and Garbage', ibid.

637 U.S. Embassy, Buenos Aires, Argentina, 'Statement by U.S. Ambassador Earl Anthony Wayne', 31 January 2008, http://spanish.argentina.usembassy.gov/rel244.html

on this occasion, concerning Argentina's relations with Iran.[638] At the U.N. General Assembly in September 2012, Cristina Fernández, in the tradition of Perón, gave ample reason for the 'international synarchy' to worry. She called for a Palestinian State, and lambasted the IMF for 'threatening Argentina,' 'as if issuing a red card in a game of football. My country is a sovereign nation and is not subject to any threat from outside'.[639] Of particular importance is the role of the Central Bank, which, under Perón, had issued state credit. In 2012 a Bill was introduced to ensure that the Central Bank resumed its function of implementing state policy, on the basis of 'social equity'. Government minister Eric Calcagno, in describing the Bill to amend the Central Bank Charter repudiated the 'neoliberal' economic policies with the aim of returning to the Central Bank

> its full role in the national credit system. An important part of that role is as lender of last resort. Next to that role designed to prevent or manage crises, is the one in normal times, which is to monitor the distribution of credit, propel and steer it towards development needs. This role as director and as lender of last resort was severely restricted during the period of neoliberalism, not only through the Central Bank Act which proposed reform, but also with the Convertibility Law, which are now deleted... Because in practice, monetary decisions are essentially political, and that affect the distribution of credit, setting interest rates and therefore the exchange rate, and therefore determine gains or losses. Nothing less.[640]

Calcagno, in repudiating the neoliberal doctrines that have obsessed states throughout much of the world for several decades,

638 Jaime Rosemberg, 'The Jewish Community redefines it relationship with the Government over Iran', Lanacion.com, 30 October 2012, http://www.lanacion.com.ar/1521910-la-comunidad-judia-redefine-su-vinculo-con-el-gobierno-por-la-apertura-con-teheran

639 H.E. Ms.Cristina Fernández, President, Summary of Statement to the U.N. General Assembly, 67th Session, 25 September 2012.

640 Eric Calcagno, 'The institutional nature of the new Central Bank', Miradas al sur, No. 198. 4 March 2012.

referred to the matter as one of 'sovereignty', and of pursuing state objectives. The bank still appears to act within the confines of orthodox banking and lending. However, Calcagno at least affirms a heretical view that 'foreign capital investment' is not a panacea but a curse that serves none but predatory international finance. In a recent article Calcagno questioned the efficacy of 'foreign capital as a solution, writing that

> the real contribution that FDI [Foreign Direct Investment] brought to the country in 2010 meant only 3.8% of gross domestic fixed investment. At the same time, the overall FDI in 2010 distributed profits of 6.002 million dollars, or nearly double. In the Argentine case, the axis of national funding and equity given trends in international capital flows is unlikely to constitute a significant contribution to finance development.[641]

Perhaps one of the most significant aspects of traditional Perónism to endure is that of syndicalism. The Constitution, in the Perónist spirit, institutionalises the rights and duties of labour and unions, including profit-sharing and co-management.[642] Labour representation in an enterprise is undertaken by workers' delegates, or by internal committees. All the workers in the enterprise elect workers' delegates and members of internal committees. They must be union members, and to have worked in the enterprise for at least one year. Office is held for two years, but delegates can be re-elected.[643] Another syndical principle is the formation of 'consumer and user associations', represented in state bodies, ensuring 'consumers and users of goods and services have the right to the protection of their health, safety, and economic interests; to adequate and truthful information; to

---

641 Alfredo Eric Calcagno and Congressman Eric Calcagno, 'The Argentine Course', Marisada al sur, No. 260, 12 May 2013.

642 Constitution of the Republic of Argentina, Section I: 14b.

643 Arturo Bronstein, 'National Labour Law Profile: Republic of Argentina', 'Workers' representation in the enterprise', International Labour Organisation, http://www.ilo.org/ifpdial/information-resources/national-labour-law-profiles/WCMS_158890/lang--en/index.htm

freedom of choice and equitable and reliable treatment'.[644]

Another interesting aspect of the Constitution is that 'the Federal Government shall foster European immigration'.[645] While racial discrimination is unlawful, and the Amerindians are especially recognised,[646] Argentina is possibly the only nation left in the world to codify a preference for European immigrants.

While Kirchnerism has declined in popularity in recent years, there is no reason to believe that Perónism will remain anything other than the most popular doctrine among Argentines. There are extra-parliamentary organisations that represent the Perónist tradition politically and metapolitically, while there are also dissident Perónists in the Chamber and Senate.

For example the Movemento Perónista Autentico[647] maintains an avid street presence. The MPA declared at its first national convention in 2002 that the official Justicialist party was an obstacle and no more than an expression of liberalism, 'without any substantive difference with the other political parties in the system'.[648] The party leadership is a prisoner of the liberal ideas of oligarchy. The MPA outlined its programme for rebuilding an 'authentic Perónist party:

1. Assume a project of revolutionary transformation of our country as a strategic approach based on the liberating experience of Perónism.

2. Build a real participatory democracy with full popular control including, among others, recall of those who deviate from the mandate of the people who elected them as their representatives.

644 Constitution of the Republic of Argentina, II : 42.

645 Ibid., I : 25.

646 Ibid., IV : 17.

647 Movemento Perónista Autentico, http://www.mpa.org.ar/

648 Atilio Lopez, 'National Meeting of the Movemento Perónista Autentico', 7-8 September 2002, http://www.mpa.org.ar/encuentrosmpa.php

3. Clearly identify the historic enemies of the Argentine people: imperialism, oligarchy and economic groups.

4. Characterise the current political leadership as a parasitic political class, and the current institutional and political representation system as a neo-authoritarian electoral system unable completely to channel popular interests and needs.

5. Reform the organisation as essential for the development of a strategy of power, claiming the historical experience of the working class struggle.

6. Organise on comprehensive and participatory structures, summoning all social sectors, employed and unemployed; protest organizations of Indigenous Nations, students, neighbourhood and cultural expressions, small and medium entrepreneurs, traders and producers, NGOs, cooperatives, mutual societies, neighbourhood centers and all the organisations or individuals who identify with the national and popular project of the Movemento Perónista Autentico.

7. Return the political-ideological debate and confront ideas resulting therefrom with our own practice.

8. Encourage by all means popular mobilisation and organisation, in its broadest sense as a method of struggle for the reconquest of our social and political demands.

9. Recognise the employed and unemployed, the excluded and neglected, and youth, as the recipients and main activists of our proposals and policy actions, in order to restore political and social power of the workers as a natural backbone of Perónist Movement AUTHENTIC, the national movement, and restore work as essential for the realisation and transcendence of man as an individual and as a social being.

10. Recognise that electoral bodies are an opportunity to access the formal power, so we must consider having a tool when our political development requires that channel.

11. Recognise the Patriotic Front of National Liberation as a

manifestation of the National Movement, and as a strategic political organisation of the Argentine people.

12. Assume that the possibility of advancing the process of National Liberation in our country is inseparable from a process of political, economic, military, social and cultural integration on the Latin American level.[649]

Another, very different movement, has formed around Dr. Carlos Alejandro Biondini, director of the radio programme Alerta Nacional, and president of the Neighbourhood Flag Party, Partido Bandera Vecinal (PBV).[650] Biondini was raised by his maternal uncle and godfather Américo Ott, who had served as liaison between Perón in Spain and the Perónista underground, and had organised the flight that returned Evita's body to Argentina from Italy. Biondini has been a Perónista activist since his student days, and was a founder-member of the Union of Secondary Students in 1972. The attempted takeover by the Montoneros of the welcoming proceedings for Perón at Ezeiza Airport, during which Biondini was involved in their expulsion from the square, was a defining moment in his life. In 1981 he became head of Juventad Perónista for Buenos Aires; in 1982 served as a volunteer in the Falklands War.

In 1983 Biondini founded a newspaper, *Alerta Nacional*, which ran until 1989. He was also involved in other Perónist organisations, such as the National Front of Perónista Loyalty, and established the National Institute of Indoctrination, to impart Justicialist doctrine to leaders and ideologues. In 1984 the Agrupación Justicialista Alert Nacional was established, which was militantly involved in fighting the Alfonsín Government. In 1990 Biondini broke with the Justicialist party and formed the Partido Nacionalista de los Trabajadores (Nationalist Workers Party), renamed the Partido Nuevo Triunfo, and the newspaper *El Nacionalista*. In June 1991 President Menem demanded that a

649 Ibid.

650 Alerta Nacional, Partido Bandera Vecinal, http://www.alertanacional.com/modules/wordpress/

proposed Congress called by Biondini be suppressed at any cost, although 22 Congressmen opposed the ban. Terence Todman, U.S. Ambassador, congratulated Menem. While Biondini was arrested, the party's co-founder, René Tulián, was killed.[651] Between 1992 and 1997 Biondini was extremely restricted by various charges brought against him, but most of these were overturned. In 1997 he founded the online magazine *Libertad de Opinión.* In 1999 he launched a radio programme, Ciudad Libre Opinión. In 2009 he was a co-founder of CADEPA (Autoconvocados Citizens in Defence of the Fatherland), campaigning for the resignation of President Fernando De la Rua.

On 14 December 2005 President Nestor Kirchner publicly condemned Biondini and stated that the Partido Nuevo Triunfo would be barred from the elections. In 2008 Biondini founded the radio programme Alerta Nacional, which is broadcasted nationally. In 2009 Biondini responded to the ban against the PNT by founding the Partido Alternativa Social, while the Partido Bandera Vecinal continues to campaign vigorously on civic issues.

Therefore there remain vigorous developments within Justicialism that will ensure its vibrancy and its relevance for the foreseeable future, while other movements, such as the Second Republic Project of Adrian Salbuchi, incorporate the primary elements of Justicialism within its programme.

651 René Tulián was hit by a truck, and died in hospital, the doctors on duty both being Zionists. The autopsy found that he had been injected in the neck with a drug.

MERCOSUR

The current Partido Justicialista states that Perón's vision of a Latin American bloc is being fulfilled in a regional economic alliance called MERCOSUR, established in 1991:

> In 1953 Perón explained at various public exhibitions his foreign policy concepts which he termed 'continentalism' and 'universalism'. He took the first concrete decisions aimed at boosting Latin American integration and proposed to Chile and Brazil the foundations of a union to be called ABC. This was the foundation of MERCOSUR, launched 30 years later.[652]

MERCOSUR comprises Argentina, the Federative Republic of Brazil, the Republic of Paraguay, the Oriental Republic of Uruguay, the Bolivarian Republic of Venezuela and the Plurinational State of Bolivia. Associate States include Chile, Colombia, Peru, Ecuador, Guyana and Suriname. The member states establish the free movement of trade, common customs, tariff and labour laws, and joint approaches to outside trade.[653]

To what extent MERCOSUR represents an *autarchic* bloc as envisioned by Perón is open to question. Certainly the European Common Market, from which the present European Union proceeded, did not, and its present form does not, represent the ideals of a United Europe envisioned by Mosley, Thiriart and others. Rather, Freemasons, globalists, bankers and U.S. interests hatched the present European Union as part of a regionalisation process towards a world economic order.[654] Other free trade regional arrangements such as that planned for the Pacific Rim, NAFTA, and the like, are part of this globalisation process. One should consider that Argentina entered the regional arrangement under the signature of President Carlos Menem, a

652 Juan Perón biography, *Partido Justicialista*, op. cit.

653 Mercosur, 'Who we are', http://www.mercosur.int/t_generic.jsp?contentid=3862&site=1&channel=secretaria&seccion=3

654 K. R. Bolton, Introduction to *Hilaire Belloc's Europe and the Faith* (London: Black House Publishing, 2012), 25-31.

nominal 'Perónist' who plunged his nation into privatisation and neoliberal economics.

On his return to Argentina in 1974 Perón continued his visionary advocacy of Latin American unity. Stating of 'the fundamental ideas that have inspired a new international politics in Argentina', he returned to the theme of the historical evolution towards ever widening integration from families, tribes, cities, nations, groups of nations and continents. He spoke of the increasing problems of overpopulation and 'super-industrialisation', problems not only of an economic and political character, but ecologically, sociologically, culturally and spiritually. The future of nations would depend on their stocks of food and raw materials. As a continent, Latin America is well endowed:

> Undoubtedly, our continent, especially South America, is the area of the world still, because of its lack of population and lack of extractive exploitation, with the largest reservoir of raw materials and food. This would indicate that the future is ours and that in the future struggle we are left with an extraordinary advantage over other areas of the world, who have exhausted their potential for food production and supply of raw materials, or that are unfit for the production of these two fundamental elements of life.[655]

However, it is because Latin America does have such resources and living space that the 'greatest danger lies'. One day the super-industrialised states, with declining resources and overcrowding, will look to taking those resources from Latin America. Perón stated that it is again Argentina that has taken up the standard of continental unity:

> It is this fact that has led our government to squarely face the possibility of a real and effective union of our countries, to face a life together and plan also a future common defence.

655 Juan Perón, Speech to National War School on Continentalism, Buenos Aires, 1973.

> If these circumstances are not sufficient, or that fact is not a decisive factor for our union then I do not think there are any other circumstances that are as important to achieve this. If what I said was not true, the union of this region of the world has no reason to be, unless it was a more or less abstract and idealistic matter.[656]

From 1810 to the present there have been many attempts at continental unity, first among newly independent Argentina, Chile, and Peru. These efforts all failed. If they had been a success they could have been extraordinary. San Martin and Simon Bolivar had tried. Perón believed that by the year 2000 Latin America would either be united or it would be dominated. He recounted how he began to address the question as early as 1946. The first efforts were at ministerial level, with speeches and banquets, according to 19th century diplomatic principles. These initiatives were unsuccessful. What Perón now advocated was that governments be bypassed for a direct appeal to the peoples of Latin America. Referring to the tactics of the Communist parties, he said: 'We have observed that success, perhaps the only extraordinary success of communism, is that they do not work with governments, but with the Peoples, because they are aimed at a permanent work and not an incidental work'.[657]

The basis of such unity was still Argentina, Brazil and Chile, comprising 'perhaps at present the most extraordinary economic unit in the world, especially for the future, because of all those vast reserves'. While other states are reaching the end of their resources, Latin America's has barely been tapped. Around these three states, the other Latin American states could unite. Perón recalled that when he started working for continental unity it was the leaders of Brazil and Chile who were the most responsive: 'Getulio Vargas totally and absolutely agreed with this idea, and undertook it as soon as he was in government. Ibanez made the same commitment'. Perón realised that 'for

656 Ibid.

657 Ibid.

personal and business interests' Vargas and Ibáñez would meet opposition in their nations. He knew that a myriad of petty interests would oppose union, and that unity must come from the peoples of these states, from below upward, and not from the state down. Since governments have failed it is time to try to reach the people. Argentina should even be willing to accept a subordinate status to that of Brazil for the sake of such a union.

What has emerged from Perón's vision has come not from Argentina, Chile or Brazil, but from Venezuela. It is the late Lt. Colonel Hugo Chávez who took up the flame for Latin American unity, in the name of the 'Bolivarian Revolution'. The 'Bolivarian Alliance for the People of Our America' (ALBA) was formed in 2004. In a 2008 meeting with Argentine President Cristina Fernandez de Kirchner, Chávez cited a speech by Juan Perón, and said: 'I am really a Perónist. I identify with this man and his thought, who asked that our countries are no longer factories of imperialism'.[658] Moreover, Perón's early adviser was the sociologist and political scientist Norberto Ceresole, who had served as an adviser to Juan and Isabel Perón during their exile in Madrid, and during the 1973-1976 era. Ceresole met Chávez in 1994. Chávez alluded to his ideological debt to Ceresole, writing in 1998 in *Habla el Comandante* that he 'was reconsidering the ideas of Norberto Ceresole, in his works and studies, where he planned a project of physical integration in Latin America. This will be a project which will integrate the Continent along Venezuela, Brazil and Argentina and their ramifications'. Chávez, despite claims to the contrary, never repudiated Ceresole, stating in 2006 that he was a 'great friend', and 'an intellectual deserving great respect'. He recalled their meeting in 1995 where geopolitical strategy was discussed.[659] Ceresole returned to Argentina in 2003 and established the Perónista Institute of Education and Training Policy.[660]

---

658 'Chávez: I am really a Perónist', lanacion.com, 6 March 2008, http://www.lanacion.com.ar/993340-chavez-yo-soy-Perónista-de-verdad

659 Chávez broadcast, Aló Presidente #255, May 2006.

660 http://ifcpjuanPerón.ar.tripod.com/institutoPerón/id42.html

Juan Domingo Perón: 1895-1974

Conclusion

Justicialism arose from the milieu that was fermenting in Europe from the late 19th century as a reaction against the liberalism, socialism, capitalism and democracy that had emerged and mutated like viral infections from the French Revolution. While this was a reaction from the Right to the destruction of the traditional social order, from the Left there was a realisation that Marxism and other economic interpretations of history and society were not only inadequate, but were in essence bourgeois.

Perón referred to Justicialism as the Argentine, and more broadly, the Latin American, variant of 'national socialism', this synthesis of national and social forces that had been brewing since the prior century. He always maintained that the Second World War was fought by international finance to destroy the new synthesis of 'national socialism'. He stated that Justicialism was part of a 'universal' movement, albeit nationally specific. He contrasted this 'universalism' with 'internationalism'. He stated that each nation must find its own path to 'national socialism', based on its own racial, national and cultural characteristics, and geopolitical circumstances. He rejected capitalism and Marxism equally, and described Justicialism as a 'third position'.

Justicialism has a heroic conception of life, it places the common interest before self-interest, aims to eliminate parasitism and fights 'international synarchy', which Perón stated includes international finance, communism, Judaism, and Freemasonry. The state took on the international banking system by implementing state credit and trade barter. Perón regarded political parties as a fraud, and aimed to establish a syndicalist state, which he also called the 'Corporatist Nation', and in particular the 'organised community'. Perón rejected all the 'modern' secularist, materialistic, liberal, democratic, 'enlightenment' dogmas that had dominated the intelligentsia since the 18th century, and regarded the Jacobin-democratic slogan of 'liberty, equality, fraternity', as a con to enslave the masses. He sought social and economic progress, but not at the expense of tradition, family and organic bonds.

Perón warned of the ecological consequences of overconsumption by capitalism. He was a father of the non-aligned 'Third World' resisting super-power hegemony, and a herald of the concept of geopolitical blocs to challenge globalisation.

The Perónist doctrine was developed by Perón's observations of Fascism in Italy, and National Socialism in Germany and refined by his experiences with syndicalism in Argentina. Perón was not only a military theorist, historian, and statesman, he was a philosopher, who readily drew from the depths of philosophy from the ancient Greeks onward, and from the insights of science while rejecting the worship of technology and insisting on the worship of God. His conception of man and society will have relevance long after *Das Kapital* lies under a mountain of dust. His name will be spoken and his ideas discussed when Lenin, Mao, Adam Smith and Rousseau are only recalled as interesting examples of long failed ideologues when considering the folly of the human mind.

It is therefore nonsense to contend, as do his detractors, that Perón was an opportunist who shaped his ideology to suit his career. His ideology has an unchanging predicate, solid and unmoveable, as can be seen from his speeches and writings, of which there is a vast corpus, from the days in the Secretariat of Labour in 1943, until his final speeches in 1974. While Perón readily admitted that he had made errors, or had failed in certain areas, as the spirit of the Age in which we live, demanded, he nonetheless achieved tasks of Herculean magnitude, making Argentina a modern state where before she had been a rural colony, while his name lives on among Argentines generation after generation until he has achieved mythic status. There have been few statesmen, leaders and philosophers like Perón.

What Justicialism offers continues to be valid, and not only for Argentina. It is a lesson in the success of the national-social synthesis, of how a nation divided along parties, classes, and other sectional and ego-driven interests can be united and mobilised in a great national effort to restore a national community based on social justice and sovereignty, against the malignant growth of international finance and super-power hegemony.

Index

A

B

D

G

H

I

J

K

L

M

N

O

P

Q

R

S

T

U

V

W

Y

Z

CPSIA information can be obtained
at www.ICGtesting.com
Printed in the USA
BVHW070434290421
606053BV00004B/128